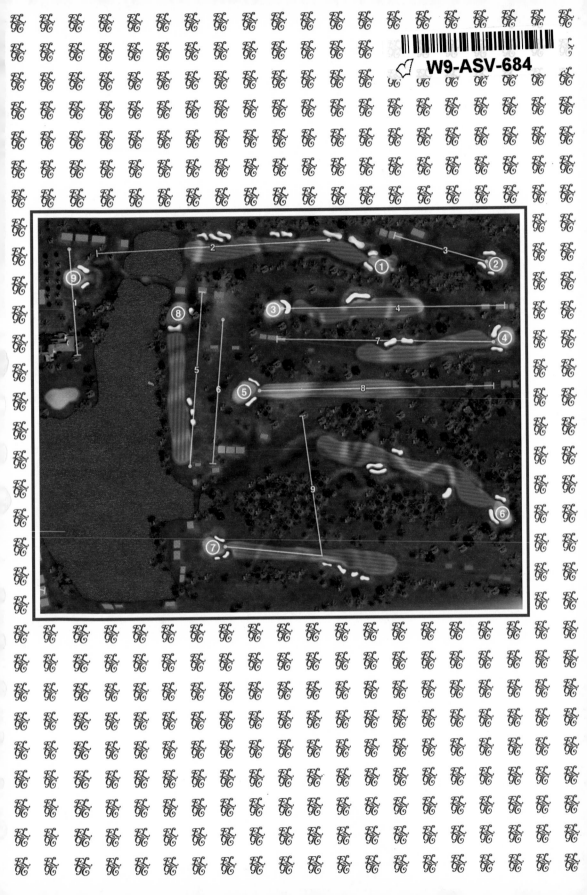

W9-ASV-684

EAST LAKE
WHERE BOBBY LEARNED TO PLAY

East Lake

Where Bobby Learned To Play

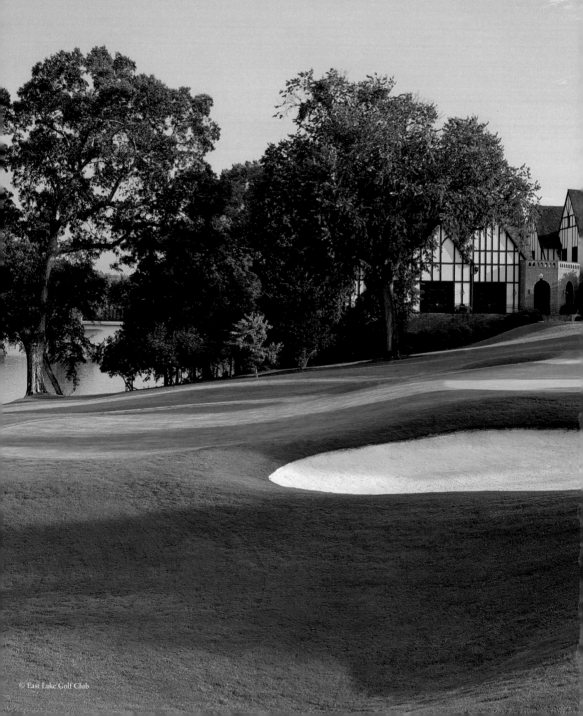

For Teed and Sadler, our
special treasures —
Priscilla & Lint
September 24,
2018

Linton C. Hopkins

Deodara Press LLC
Atlanta

For
Laura Priscilla Holeman Hopkins
and the rest of our favorite foursome,
Linton and Laura

PERMISSIONS

The author and publisher wish to thank the following for the use of copyrighted material: Marty Elgison and Robert T. Jones, IV for excerpts from *Down the Fairway*; Sidney L. Matthew for the photos of Bobby Jones on the cover, holding the U.S. Open and U.S. Amateur trophies, with King George VI, and for the sketch of Alexa Stirling; the *Atlanta Journal* for O.B. Keeler's article on the 63 and for "Alexa Stirling's Game;" W. Foulsham & Co., New York for portions of *The Bobby Jones Story*; Fred Russell and A. S. Barnes & Co. for excerpts from *Bury Me Under an Old Press Box*; the USGA and *Golf Journal* for photographs of Joyce Wethered, Tom Cousins, and Charlie Yates; Dave Sansom and Chet Burgess for their photographs of East Lake's course and clubhouse; Ted Ryan and the Coca-Cola Company for the photo of Bobby and his father; Meggan Gardner of Golf Canada and the Canadian Golf Hall of Fame for images of Alexa; PARS International Corp. for the *New York Times* obituary of Bobby Jones; the YGS Group for "Jones is Mourned at Scottish Links" (Associated Press); Trusted Media Brands for "The Most Unforgettable Character I've Met" in *The Reader's Digest*; Wright's Media for portions of "One of the Great Opens" by Herbert Warren Wind published in *The New Yorker*, July 26, 1976; Simon and Schuster, Inc. for an excerpt from *Harvey Penick's Little Red Book*; Penguin Random House for parts of *Bobby Jones on Golf, Bobby Jones On the Basic Golf Swing*, and *Golf is My Game*, all by Bobby Jones, and for portions of *Jungle Rules*, by John P. Imlay, Jr.; HarperCollins Publishers for an excerpt from *The Legend Of Bagger Vance*; the Georgia State Golf Association and Kim Crisp for the biographies and photos of East Lake golfers in their collection; Shannon Baller and *Golf Georgia* for a photograph of Charlie Yates; *Georgia Trend* for the photograph of Bobby Jones and Robert Woodruff; Johnny Vardeman and Anne Thomas for use of his article in the *Gainesville Times* featuring her memories of Bobby Jones; *Smoke Signals* at Big Canoe for use of the essays by Jack Schroder and John Lambert in "The Final Years;" *Georgia Outdoor News* and Daryl Gay for an excerpt from "The Legend of Charlie Elliott;" and Charlie Elliott and Cherokee Publishers for excerpts from *The East Lake Country Club History*.

Published by
Deodara Press LLC
95 Wakefield Drive
Atlanta, Georgia
30309

Copyright © 2018 by Linton C. Hopkins

Printed in the United States of America by Fuse Graphics, Marietta, Georgia

ISBN 978-1-7323107-0-4
Library of Congress Control Number: 2018944528

FIRST EDITION FIRST PRINTING

CONTENTS

PART ONE
SIX GOLFERS

"The Most Unforgettable Character I've Met"
By Alexa Stirling Fraser

"My Love Affair with East Lake"

PART TWO
THE GOLF COURSE
A WALK THROUGH TIME AT EAST LAKE

PART THREE
LEGACY

"America's Greatest Untapped Resource"
By Thomas G. Cousins (2016)

"Bobby Jones, Golf Master, Dies; Only Player to Win Grand Slam"
By Frank Litsky (1971)

"Alexa Stirling Fraser – a Legend"
By Eddie MacCabe (1977)

The First Golf Course at East Lake

"What Golf Means to Me"
By Linton C. Hopkins, Sr. (1915)

"Bob Jones Lowers His Own Record at East Lake to 63"
By O. B. Keeler (1922)

More Hall of Fame Members from East Lake

The Friends of Bobby Jones

September Sunrise

TOM AND ANN COUSINS

One grew up as the child of the president of a large, southern public university, and the other became president of a publically-traded, southern real-estate investment trust. When they were a young married couple in Atlanta, they were mentored by Dr. Vernon S. Broyles, minister of North Avenue Presbyterian Church. Today, each of them enjoys the affection, loyalty, and support of friends from every part of society.

The qualities that are responsible for their still-growing success in life are their principles of integrity, loyalty, and the habit of thorough preparation. They never lie and do not tolerate being lied to. They keep their word and expect you to do the same. Neither one will repeat what you told them in private. There is no pretension in them, and they avoid pretentious people if they can. They both look you right in the eye and are disarmingly natural and approachable.

One of them enjoys bird hunting, fishing, flying jet planes, and playing golf more than the other, but they both love riding and simply being around horses and dogs of all types. They have traveled the west and learned its rich history together, but one looks more like an Indian chief and is a better poker player than the other. This is the one who identifies with young people who act impulsively and endanger themselves and their friends. One likes to read; the other prefers to write. One is a War Eagle who gets her way; the other is a tenacious Bulldog who never gives up. A golfer in the Georgia Golf Hall of Fame said the Bulldog has made more ten-foot putts on the last green than anyone else he had ever known. They both admire the mission, leadership, and the faculty of Columbia Theological Seminary in Decatur. They are sophisticated art patrons, and both appreciate folk art, American Indian art, and the glass figures of Dale Chihuly, but one likes pottery more than the other.

They have made close friends in New York. When their friend Eugene Black died, they invited his elderly sister to fly to the funeral with them. One of them constructed several buildings there in the 1970s that David Rockefeller's lawyer said saved Rockefeller University. In 1972, he built the Omni Arena, brought professional basketball and hockey to Atlanta, and developed Big Canoe in North Georgia. But a real-estate crisis hit him hard. After the recovery, in 1992, he built Nations Bank Plaza (now Bank of America) at Peachtree and North Avenue, still the tallest building in Atlanta. The next year, he bought the East Lake course and clubhouse and started the process that has brought the community back to life.

The renovation of the Donald Ross course
by Rees Jones in 1994

FOREWORD

In all my years as a golf course architect, the restoration of East Lake is probably the most rewarding and meaningful project I have ever worked on. It is a link between the past of the legendary golf course and a hopeful future for the East Lake neighborhood, generated by this restoration. The link to the past involves a man named Bobby Jones, golf's greatest amateur player, who grew up honing his game at East Lake, located in what was, in the first half of the 1900s, one of Atlanta's most charming suburban neighborhoods. The hope for the future involves a man named Tom Cousins, an Atlanta developer and philanthropist who bought the financially-struggling East Lake facility in 1993, the neighborhood being no longer charming but decidedly dangerous, basically in ruins, brought on by high unemployment, drugs, and crime. He formed the East Lake Foundation and started to invest enormous effort and money into not just the golf facility but the surrounding area.

I think Tom Cousins hired me to restore East Lake because he learned during my interview in 1994 that I had a strong connection to Bobby Jones through my father, Robert Trent Jones, who was also known as Bobby in his early career. In 1946, Bobby Jones called my father down to Atlanta to interview for the design of a course that became Peachtree Golf Club. After the meeting, they played nine holes at East Lake (Jones the architect shot 36; Jones the golfer shot 29) and their mutual admiration and friendship grew from there. During the building of Peachtree, my father began to use his middle name because, as he said to the great amateur, "There can only be one Bobby Jones in Atlanta, and that's you." The two men worked so well together that my father went on to make significant changes at Augusta National and they played many rounds of golf together at East Lake. Our family visited the Joneses every year at the Masters, and my mother and Mary Jones also became good friends. Tom

Cousins could be certain that I would give the restoration of East Lake my all, not only because I believed in Tom's vision, but also to honor a family friend.

During the early stages of the restoration work, Tom suggested I walk around the course with Charlie Yates, Charles Harrison, and Tommy Barnes, all members of the Georgia Golf Hall of Fame who played many a round at East Lake with Bobby Jones. The original design had been lost prior to the 1963 Ryder Cup matches, and I didn't have the great golfer around to hit shots to help me determine landing areas like my father had at Peachtree. I incorporated some of the design features of the past by listening to these men recount their experiences. They had watched Bobby Jones play the holes innumerable times and were able to tell me where just about every one of his shots landed. In fact, it was hard to stay focused on the course itself, they were so full of stories about his heroic drives and impossible putts. But it was clear to me that what was really important to them was not the golf itself, it was the friendships and the memories made during lively competitions.

Rees Jones touring the course with (L-R) Charlie Yates, Charlie Harrison, and Tommy Barnes

The importance of this restoration cannot be underestimated. Not only did the newly renovated clubhouse and golf course attract corporate memberships, but the course became the venue for the annual PGA Tour Championship, which generates additional funds for the East Lake Foundation. There are very few places in the golf world that have been held in the high esteem that East Lake had enjoyed for so many decades. Every year since the restoration, the regard for the course has continued to grow, enhanced by more people playing it and by having the best professional players confront its challenges. And across the street is the Charlie Yates course, where neighborhood kids take golf lessons, enroll in the caddy program, join the First Tee, and go on to excellent schools. Watching an East Lake youngster hit the ceremonial first shot at the beginning of the Tour Championship is a satisfying thing indeed. For me that moment symbolizes the link from past to future. It illustrates the intersection of golf on this great old course where Bobby learned to play and Tom Cousins' dream of using golf as a catalyst to change lives for the better.

East Lake — Where Bobby Learned to Play is not the usual club history book about an old institution and its golf course. It introduces the famous amateurs first, then it invites the reader onto the course and into the game. Stories from the past and present are told, and fresh new information is given on every hole. A favorite of mine from the earlier book, the mystery story, "One Down with One to Play" still fascinates me. This book has new reflections from Bobby's colleagues and touching stories written by former college students who kept him company in the evenings during his last few years.

Although he wrote *Where Bobby Learned to Play* over twenty years ago, since his retirement, Linton Hopkins has devoted much more time to the history of the great amateurs and to making a story out of every hole on the course. Finding the details of the best round by Bobby Jones at East Lake inspired him to write the first book, and his discovery of how Alexa Stirling played every hole was part of the reason for this new one. His accounts of shots played by other Hall-of-Fame golfers, members, and guests over the years are thorough, vivid, and often witty. It is a delightful read for anyone who has an interest in Jones or East Lake, or simply loves to read colorful stories about rounds of golf well played.

Would Bobby Jones have enjoyed this book? Most definitely. Would he have approved of the changes, detailed so thoughtfully in the book, that we made to the course he loved so dearly? I think he would have been extremely pleased to see what we accomplished. We recently reversed the nines at East Lake to have the Tour Championship end on a par five. My guess is Bobby Jones would have been very happy, as he did a similar thing at Augusta National for tournament play. At one time, he considered having a tournament at Peachtree, so having the Tour Championship at his home course would have suited him just fine.

Tom Cousins grew up playing golf at East Lake but never played with Bobby Jones. Had they been closer in age, that likely would have happened, and it would have been a match I would have loved to watch. To me, they are both heroes, in golf and in life. Tom had a broader vision for East Lake than just restoring the golf facility; he wanted to change lives. And he has. As Bobby Jones himself would say, Anything can happen.

Rees Jones

Building the 10th green — the extra soil came from the bottom of the lake.

INTRODUCTION

This book is about the oldest golf course in Atlanta and several golfers who learned to play on it. It tells the story of how it has evolved over 114 years from a successful, all-sports country club into a growing movement committed to changing the lives of families and children. Because of them, the influence of East Lake will reach far into the future. A review of that history is presented first.

Part One, "Six Golfers," includes profiles of Bobby Jones, Alexa Stirling, Charlie Yates, Tommy Barnes, and Charlie Harrison, and an essay by Bobby's friend, Charlie Elliott. Alexa (b. 1897), wrote the chapter about Bobby (b. 1902), "The Most Unforgettable Character I've Met" (Fraser 1960).

Mentoring, the theme of the book, is emphasized early. Bobby and Alexa met at East Lake and started to play golf the same year, but he was six, and she was eleven, a more significant difference when the boy is younger. Bobby needed more mentoring than the others. He lost control of his temper on the golf course and threw clubs during their informal rounds at age eight, and the episodes continued as he grew up, even in national championships, until the summer of 1921. Alexa was usually there with him, embarrassed at every outburst. He was aware of her disapproval and became angry when she intervened. In her chapter about him, she describes several minutes at the U.S. Open when he conquered his temper and put that behavior behind him. She believed it was the defining moment of his career.

The profiles will connect each of the six golfers to young people in the neighborhood today. All six played at East Lake when it was a safe, family-focused, and peaceful place. They were determined to succeed, and there were mentors there to advise them.

The Athletic Club has always been like a school teaching sports to all ages, and its golf program began with Bobby and Alexa. They were molded by George Adair and professionals Jimmy and Stewart Maiden. Charlie Yates, Tommy Barnes, and Charlie Harrison all learned from Bobby and watched his swing, but when Charlie Harrison was a teenager, Tommy was his closest model and mentor. Despite their sixteen-year age difference, they became friends and were partners and opponents on the course for over forty years. Storytelling was as hard-wired as golf, so facts and opinions on multiple subjects flowed freely in both directions.

Part Two, "The Golf Course — a Walk Through Time at East Lake" is a walk around the modern course, hole by hole in an imaginary foursome, two from the past and two from today. Because of articles in the *Atlanta Journal*, young Bobby and Alexa appear on every hole. She was interviewed on July 20, 1919 at age twenty-one and will give the details of how she played each hole and indicate those that were easier or more difficult for her ("Alexa Stirling's Game" 1919).

Bobby's shot details are from O.B. Keeler's article about his nine-under-par, course-record 63 on September 16, 1922. Although he was only twenty, it remained the lowest he would ever score.[1] The clubs he used from the fairway and putting information are given on every hole, and his driving distances are included on seven. These details allow golfers at East Lake to compare themselves to the greatest amateur to play the game and one of the best women amateurs (Keeler 1922).

After Bobby and Alexa play their shots, East Lake professionals Rick Burton and Chad Parker will tell stories about the course and describe illusions that might mislead golfers. Other amateurs from Part One will appear. Charlie Harrison will describe a shot hit by Arnold Palmer on the first hole and one by Jack Nicklaus on number six. Charlie Yates and Tommy Barnes will add their stories, and professionals from the Tour Championship and members and guests will occasionally join in.

There are diversions from golf in text and footnotes. The non-golf information includes history, geography, and how areas, distances, and elevations on the course compare to dimensions of familiar places, buildings, and ships. When the mood is right, storytelling and unusual comparisons can produce smiles and relieve the intrinsic frustrations and tensions of the game. The same is true of betting, which adds hope to every round. No matter how poorly someone is playing, even if the first bet is lost, a new bet can always be proposed.[2]

---

1   The round came as his life was changing rapidly. It was one week after the U.S. Amateur at Brookline in Boston, the worst defeat of his career, and nine months before his first national championship, the 1923 U.S. Open. A week after the round, he returned to Boston to study for a graduate degree in English Literature at Harvard.

O.B. Keeler was Bobby's Boswell; he wrote glowing articles about him and Alexa.

2   Tommy Barnes said Bobby Jones liked to play a golf-ball Nassau and encouraged buying new balls and other items inside to support the club.

The five chapters in Part Three, "Legacy," are memories of Bobby or stories by people he inspired. "Remembering Mr. Jones" is a series of essays by his law partners and other friends, and it continues the mentoring theme. For over thirty years, he was a senior partner in his firm and primarily a teacher and counselor. A young lawyer, Pegram Harrison, said one of his duties was to help Mr. Jones to his office. He met him at the elevator, rolled him in his wheelchair into the room, and lifted him into the chair behind his desk. Then he turned him over to his secretary, Jean Marshall. He described Bobby's special role:

He was available to help resolve anyone's knotty problems, which lawyers have in abundance. He could untangle most of them, but his enduring strength was his sense of ethics. Mr. Jones knew exactly what the right thing was, and he inspired us to do it.

"The Final Years," also in Legacy, was written by former college students recruited by Mrs. Jones to be Bobby's evening companions between 1968 and 1971, the last years of his life. By the time they met him, he was completely dependent on others, but his intelligence, personality, and sense of humor were unimpaired. They, and others in regular rotation, shared a few hours of private conversation, watched television with him, and were strong enough to provide the physical assistance he needed. Their last responsibility was to pick him up from his wheelchair and put him in bed for the night. His gracious champion's spirit prevailed to the end, and the experience changed their lives. Those young men saw him at his best.

In 1981, ten years after his death, "One Down with One to Play," a mystery story, was written by a golfer after one round at East Lake. He revered Bobby Jones and had studied his career but never met him. He felt his presence that day.

The last two chapters work together. In "Golf with a Purpose," Tom Cousins explains why and how the East Lake Foundation built a healthy neighborhood there. The model has now been adopted by other cities (Purpose Built Communities) and applied to troubled schools in Atlanta (Purpose Built Schools).

"East Lake Hospitality" is a tribute to everyone who works there. They are doing their parts, and they know about the larger mission. Their attitudes reflect it.

HISTORY

THE FIRST SIXTY YEARS

The farm land that became the first golf course at East Lake was bought in 1904 by the downtown Atlanta Athletic Club (AAC). Its name came from a lake east of Atlanta, and for over sixty years it was the country club of the AAC — the course, clubhouse, and parent club were all one entity.

Following in the footsteps of Asa Candler and Henry M. Atkinson, the owners of the land before 1904, the clubs at East Lake have been led with imagination and personal commitment that has allowed golf to be played there continuously for 111 years. Four different clubhouses have stood on the same spot surrounded by four different golf courses laid on top of each other. Although only the first course by Tom Bendelow had holes going in different directions from today, each of the others had different tees, fairways, bunkers, and greens.[1]

At the beginning of his manuscript, *The History of the Atlanta Athletic Club*, Charlie Elliott described a conversation in 1904 between George W. Adair and Henry M. Atkinson — Mr. Adair wanted to buy the property for the six-year-old club to build a golf course and clubhouse. Mr. Atkinson was the owner. His answer was brief and to the point:

You may have it at your own figure, and you may put me down for a cash subscription toward the building of the clubhouse.

I could at times visualize an American St. Andrews, but I never saw, even in the rosiest moments of the vision, an Alexa Stirling and a Bobby Jones, who were to carry East Lake to the top of the world of golf, a place in the sun shared only with St. Andrews (Elliott 1973).

Scotsman Tom Bendelow designed the golf course that young Bobby Jones and Alexa Stirling first played. It opened in 1908 when he was six and she was eleven but proved awkward to play.[2] In 1915, it was replaced by the Donald Ross course, a new design built in 1913 and 1914 that switched the finishing nine

---

1   Founders of the Coca-Cola and Georgia Power Companies.
    See Appendix, "The First Golf Course at East Lake," for the dates of courses and clubhouses.
2   The first nine ended beside the dam across the lake from the clubhouse, and many thought the remaining holes were too similar.

holes from west of the lake to the east. The downhill, par-five eighteenth hole became the ninth, and a new, long par three became the eighteenth. In 1928, the golf facilities doubled. Donald Ross designed and built a second eighteen-hole course across the street east of the 1915 course. It was known as East Lake No. 2.

Clubhouse fires in 1914 and 1925 destroyed all records and correspondence, but Donald Ross would have spoken to the leadership at East Lake about how to correct the deficiencies of the first course. The man who recruited the famous architect was the same George Adair who met with Henry Atkinson in 1904. He and Stewart Maiden had been playing the first course since it opened and had been thinking about how to improve it.

Adair lived at East Lake and was an important mentor to the young Jones.

Bobby: *George Adair did more than anyone, other than my father, to encourage my activity in competitive golf. Mr. Adair played many rounds with me when I was a youngster of twelve or thirteen years of age. He took me along with his son, Perry, to the first golf tournament I ever played in away from home, and was responsible for my first*

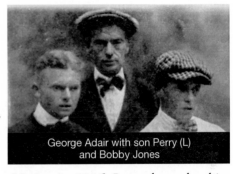

George Adair with son Perry (L) and Bobby Jones

appearance in a national championship at Merion in 1916. I was devoted to him in his lifetime and shall always revere him (Matthew 1999).

Alexa Stirling, Bobby Jones, and Charlie Yates grew up across the street from the course, learned to play there, and became international champions. The three of them, and Watts Gunn, Dan Yates, Tommy Barnes, and Charles Harrison, were part of a fifty-year period when the Athletic Club and East Lake were known throughout the golfing world.

National publicity began in 1916 when Alexa won her first U.S. Women's Amateur championship, and it accelerated after she returned from the two-year break for World War I still eager and able to win. Her next two championship years of 1919 and 1920 produced a spike in interest that rose steadily during Bobby's championship years, 1923–1930, and reached its peak with his Grand Slam in 1930, when he won the American and British amateur and open championships in the same year. Many still consider that the greatest individual achievement in the history of sport.

In 1938, the last summer before WWII, Charlie Yates won the British Amateur and brought East Lake back into the international spotlight.

During and after the war, the AAC continued to thrive as the number one all-sports family club in Atlanta. Fourteen-year-old Charlie Harrison was photographed receiving a trophy from Bobby Jones, but it was not for golf. It was for best all-round athlete in 1945, illustrating the breadth of the club's commitment to athletics.[3]

Another highlight was the roaring success of Arnold Palmer and his team in the Ryder Cup in October 1963. Palmer was the last playing captain and was praised for his leadership and play. He won four of his six matches in the new three-day format despite a sore shoulder.[4]

Five weeks and five days after the success of those international matches, President Kennedy was assassinated in Dallas. It was a tragedy that marked the beginning of a cycle of unrest and violence across America throughout the 1960s that affected every big city, including Atlanta and East Lake. The neighborhood became unsafe. The Athletic Club could not control or even modify events surrounding the golf course, so it had to move.

The move to the northern suburbs allowed the AAC to flourish a second time in a larger new property. Its clubhouse has rooms dedicated to the clubs and golf courses that hosted the Grand Slam in 1930 and honors the same champions from its years at East Lake. It has hosted the U.S. Open, three PGA Championships, and the U.S. Amateur.

In 1970, after the AAC moved, the No. 2 course became East Lake Meadows, a public housing project with an elementary school without windows. During the '70s and '80s, it evolved into a toxic combination that led to violence — unemployment, poverty, and drugs. The clubhouse and 1915 course survived only because a few members of the Athletic Club put up their own money and kept it open as the East Lake Country Club.

Because of the gritty determination of Paul Grigsby, Charles Yarn, Tommy Barnes, Bill Blalock, and many others, play continued, but there were hazards not experienced on other courses. Gun shots were frequent, and sirens were so

---

3   The club's facilities were extensive. Charlie said the trophy was for "inside sports" during the winter season. He had competed in swimming, badminton, racquetball, boxing, and gymnastics.

4   The tournament required major construction that closed the course for three years. Architect George Cobb removed all the winter/summer double greens and constructed larger, much faster bent grass greens. Large, shallow bunkers replaced the bunkers Donald Ross had designed.

common they inspired a grim humor.[5] To avoid personal injury, some members played without wallets, watches, or rings and carried enough cash to mollify robbers if they were held up. But in the late '80s, the club started to prosper. Members who joined during this period kept returning to play the challenging old course; but despite that, the neighborhood continued to suffer. No one in the club knew what would happen when the partnership expired.

BEFORE TOM STEPPED IN

By Chuck Palmer[6]

On April 9, 1968, the Atlanta Athletic Club sold the original East Lake golf course and clubhouse for $1,600,000 to East Lake Properties, Ltd., a limited partnership formed by several existing Athletic Club members committed to continuing the history and operation of East Lake. Georgia law at that time only allowed limited partnerships to have a life of twenty years, but the agreement was amended in 1972, and the twenty-year expiration was extended to December 31, 1992.

Over those twenty-four and a half years, East Lake Country Club went through a series of ups and downs, and the common interest of the partners to continue the club gradually disappeared. On February 3, 1993, the limited partners sued the general partners to dissolve the partnership and liquidate its assets. Boiled down to its essence, the lawsuit sought to force the sale of East Lake.

The limited partners moved to appoint a receiver, and a hearing was scheduled before Judge Isaac Jenrette of the Superior Court of Fulton County. Club manager Bill Blalock called me on June 16, 1993, the morning of the hearing, and I appeared as a friend of the court to oppose the appointment on behalf of the East Lake members.

---

5   A betting tradition known as "playing sirens" meant the value of winning a certain hole automatically doubled when a siren was heard.

6   Charles F. Palmer, Jr. was a young lawyer from Lindale, Ga. who became a member of East Lake at exactly the right time. Chuck had joined the East Lake Country Club in 1987, one year after graduating from Emory Law School. He had always admired Bobby Jones and loved East Lake, so he knew how lucky he was. He was aware of the approaching end of the partnership that owned East Lake, but didn't know what he could do until Bill Blalock, the General Manager and Chuck's golfing friend, called him into the fray. Luckily, Chuck had the perfect background for the new challenge. Before deciding on law, he had been both a golf course superintendent and an assistant pro.

Judge Jenrette denied the motion to appoint a receiver, but for the first time we all realized East Lake would probably be sold.

That led to a flurry of activity within the Board of Governors to consider ways to preserve East Lake and our memberships. The Board authorized the formation of East Lake Acquisition Corporation to serve as a vehicle through which the members could formally act and enter into contracts if needed. The Board and the new corporation realized that buying East Lake would cost much more than they could afford, so various funding options were considered. These included bank financing and a new relationship with either the Piedmont Driving Club or Ansley Golf Club, in-town clubs without eighteen-hole courses. Those options did not bear fruit.

I remembered that Tom Cousins had learned to play golf at East Lake and at one time expressed interest in buying the club, so I called his office to ask for a meeting. We met at the Cousins Properties headquarters building at Wildwood, looking down on the Chattahoochee River. In public and in person, Mr. Cousins has a presence that encourages getting right down to business, so after reviewing the status of the litigation and situation at the club, I decided to ask a straight-forward question. He had prepared, and I immediately received a decisive answer:

Mr. Cousins, would you be interested in financing the purchase of East Lake by the members?

No. But I would be interested in buying it myself and working out a membership plan so the members can stay.

Things continued to move forward in the courts, and on August 31, 1993, a hearing was held before Judge Frank Mays Hull. During the initial presentation, one of the lawyers launched into a detailed history of East Lake and Bobby Jones, but Judge Hull cut the history lesson short:

You don't need to tell me who Bobby Jones was. I grew up in Augusta.

At the close of the hearing, much to the delight of the members, Judge Hull entered an order to authorize the East Lake Acquisition Corporation to submit a contract to purchase East Lake from Mr. Paul Grigsby and Dr. Charles Yarn, East Lake's two general partners, and to establish a time schedule for the approval of that contract. The purchase price was to be $4,500,000, including earnest money of $150,000 which was promptly furnished by four members. On September 21, Judge Hull approved the sale to the East Lake Acquisition Corporation.

Tom Cousins and the Corporation began to work out a plan for the members to stay. Several meetings were held in what is now the Yates Room to negotiate the terms, and in many respects the final plan was what the membership itself would have done had it been able to raise the funds. Soon, on October 17, 1993, at a called meeting of the membership, the members voted 118–12 to approve assigning the purchase contract to East Lake Golf Club, Inc., an entity formed by Mr. Cousins. Three weeks later, on November 5, the purchase contract was formally assigned, and in December when the sale was closed, the new East Lake Golf Club came to life.

That meeting with Tom Cousins in December of 1993 was short and decisive, like the one between Henry Atkinson and George Adair in 1904. Scholars say the Renaissance period of European history began somewhere in the fifty-year period between 1350 and 1400; but for the 180 acres of the club and little neighborhood around it called East Lake, the time to mark is December 1993.

THE RENOVATION

When Tom Cousins bought the course and clubhouse, both had deteriorated, but their elegant design was obvious. He donated the properties to a local charitable foundation, and plans were developed to renovate the old clubhouse and golf course, restore the neighborhood, and revive the memory of Bobby Jones. It happened with as little publicity as possible.

The 1915 clubhouse was Tudor on the outside but had dark wood paneling inside. That so-called fireproof building was destroyed by fire in 1925, except for the porte cochère. It was rebuilt in 1927 by architect Philip Trammell Shutze, who changed the dark wood paneling of 1915 into his own lighter neo-classical style, but he did not keep the Tudor beams outside.

Today's 1995 building has the best of both versions — 1915 Tudor outside, and 1927 neo-classical inside. When a worker on a long ladder found a top-floor window on the west side to be in good shape, he called down to a supervisor on the ground, thinking it could be retained. The answer came back that it was not the 1915 style and had to come out. Shutze would have enjoyed being inside in 1995 when the rooms he designed were restored. Master plasterers in white uniforms re-created his molding around the ceilings and capitals on the columns. Ann Cousins picked interior designer Jacquelynne Lanham to decorate everything else, and when she finished, the clubhouse was ready to attract the members the project needed to be sustainable.

Bobby's friend, Charlie Elliott, and Charlie Yates, Tommy Barnes, Charlie Harrison, and others who had seen it when Bobby was there said the new version was better designed and more beautiful than it had ever been.

Tom Cousins and Charlie Yates

Re-creating the Shutze molding

Project Manager Walter Ashmore (L) with Tom Cousins

Rees Jones gave the Ryder Cup course the same treatment as the old building, right down to its bones. Major excavations lowered the elevation of the landing areas of the current fourteenth and eighteenth fairways by ten to fifteen feet, and huge boulders were removed. Every bunker and green was gobbled up by excavators the size of dinosaurs with buckets big enough for a small car. Only two greens were relocated, but every tee, bunker, and green was redesigned, redrained, and recontoured.[7] A modern irrigation system was added. Heat-resistant Zoysia was sodded in the fairways, and Bermuda was planted in the rough. The lower branches of trees were removed, eliminating

---

7   The twelfth green (now third) was relocated fifty yards south for protection from tee shots and the old seventeenth (today's eighth) was built down by the lake west of the old location.

time looking for balls underneath. On the greens, bent grass came first, but a new, heat-resistant Bermuda replaced it a few years later.

The transformation of the old golf course and clubhouse over the next two years was of personal interest to members itching to get back. Because the streets are close to the golf course, many found reasons to drive by to watch the construction through the fence. Every visible square inch of the clubhouse, inside and out, was replaced. They had walked away from a building falling down around them, but when they drove through the gate, it was a two-direction trip on a time machine — back to 1915 and into the future.

The plans for the neighborhood were taking shape. The 1970 housing project was replaced by new apartments, a school with big windows, and ample greenspace. Instead of all-subsidized housing, every other unit was market rate. Today, the houses around the course and the Charles R. Drew Charter School across from the thirteenth tee are the most visible signs of the transformation, but every neighborhood between East Lake and Decatur has felt the effects.

Before 1993, agronomist Ralph Kepple had kept the course alive with poor equipment, a small staff, and an ancient irrigation system, and he was asked to continue after Tom Cousins and Rees Jones changed everything. He has been innovative. Rees gives him credit for the success of Bermuda MiniVerde in this region.

When the club needed new leadership in the 1990s, Rick Burton was recruited to manage it and help attract corporate members to sustain it and make the neighborhood changes possible. Rick's leadership style was personal.

In an interview in 2016, he explained: *The success of East Lake has depended on people. When I came, my most important goal was to learn about everyone who worked at the club and their families. I even knew the names of their dogs.*

He and his family are tangible evidence of the changes in the neighborhood. They live across the street from the clubhouse.[8]

The design and construction project was finished before the 1996 Olympics, with time left over for the training of staff. Beginning caddies had to learn about the game of golf and the skill of caddying at the same time. They didn't know

---

8   Rees Jones already knew both Rick and Tom and thought they would work well together. He urged him to apply. Another friend Rick had in common with Tom also helped, and so did Rick's national reputation on the development and interpretation of the rules of golf. David Boyd, a member the Executive Committee of the United States Golf Association (USGA), had gotten to know him over the years. He took one of Rick's seminars on rules and became more impressed. David was from Atlanta and happened to be a close friend of Tom Cousins. When he first heard about the position, he picked up the phone, *Tom, I've known Rick Burton for years at the USGA – he'd be a great fit. You've got to at least talk to him.*

where they were supposed to be or whether to hurry to do something or stand still. They had to learn to think ahead on the course, avoid attracting attention, and be right at hand. They wanted to do everything perfectly but didn't know how. Members gave up their golf carts and became mentors. Patience was tested on both sides, and some dropped out, but in the end, senses of humor and mutual respect carried the day. Friendly relationships developed.

Jack Glenn, Jr. and Charles Steppes III (R) shared many adventures.

The quality of the club and the commitment of its supporting institutions gave East Lake such a boost that in 1998 it attracted its first championship since the Ryder Cup, the PGA Tour's season-ending Tour Championship. Three years later, in 2001, the USGA held the U.S. Amateur Championship at East Lake, enhancing the close connection of Bobby Jones to that tournament, which he won a record five times between 1924 and 1930. When the Amateur came to his home course, it seemed to complete a circle.

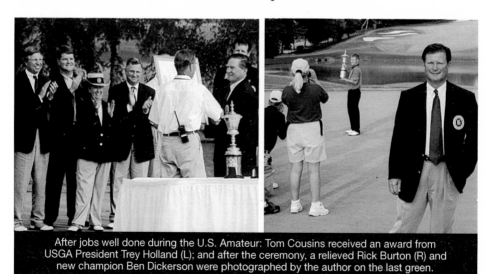

After jobs well done during the U.S. Amateur: Tom Cousins received an award from USGA President Trey Holland (L); and after the ceremony, a relieved Rick Burton (R) and new champion Ben Dickerson were photographed by the author on the last green.

A RESEMBLANCE TO BOBBY JONES

Like Tom Cousins before the transformation in 1993, Bobby Jones was quiet about his plans leading up to the Grand Slam. He wanted to start practicing law and support his family. He knew he would have to stop playing in national championships, but he did not want to quit abruptly. He needed to find his own way. He decided to try to win all four British and American championships in 1930.

After he won the British Amateur and Open, New York honored him with a second ticker-tape parade down Broadway.[9] This was the beginning of the Great Depression, and part of the explosion of positive feeling may have been in reaction to what had happened ten months earlier to the stock market. Or maybe the public appeal of Bobby Jones was greater than even O. B. Keeler could express.

His desire to be in the spotlight as briefly as possible seemed to fuel the excitement. After his last U.S. Open in 1930 at Interlachen, Minnesota, he spoke to several thousand spectators around the eighteenth green and many more listening around the country. He only had two things to say. He said he'd been lucky to win; then he turned the praise around and expressed his thanks to the spectators for their behavior and support of all the players. That was it.[10]

BACK TO THE PRESENT

The success of the foundation's comprehensive approach to the neighborhood led directly to the birth of Purpose Built Communities. Rick Burton attended the 2016 annual conference in Birmingham and was impressed with the energy and optimism he saw. People came from many other states to learn about the model.

For golfers, there were two other changes. In the fall of 2015, the first East Lake Cup was held. It is a national amateur tournament hosted by the Golf Channel. The top four men's and women's college teams from the previous season now compete there every fall in a match-play format.

---

9   The first was on July 2, 1926, after winning the British Open.

10   That U.S. Open has remained famous as the third leg of the Grand Slam, but sports broadcasting also set a milestone. The tournament was the first live, from-the-course, national radio broadcast (Price 2004).

SCENES FROM THE EAST LAKE CUP

Mascots in 2017: (L-R) Stanford Tree, Vanderbilt Commodore, Arizona State Red Devil, Oregon Duck, Northwestern Wildcat, U. of Oklahoma Sooner, and USC Trojan

Oregon golfer approaching the 5th

Scott Hansen with his grandson, Sam Ragland

The most recent change was the quietest but will affect everyone who plays the course and every match. After the 2015 Tour Championship, both the Tour and East Lake agreed to reverse the nines during the 2016 tournament. The idea of finishing the final tournament of the year and the Finals of the FedEx Cup Playoffs on a par five instead of a par three had become more and more appealing through the years, and 2016 was chosen to be the year.[11]

Rees Jones has been called on many times since he renovated the course in the early 1990s, and his most recent work was to prepare the new back nine, especially the eighteenth, for all the attention it would receive as the final hole of the tournament and playoffs. Two new bunkers were built to increase the chance of unexpected events and add drama at the end. They added an extra squeeze of pressure.

---

11 After the tournament, when members voted on whether the change should be made permanent, it was history vs. the present and future. The majority decided they wanted to play it like the PGA Tour professionals.

Average golfers will feel it, too. They all know how shaky they are, especially when leading on the last hole with five dollars at stake. At all levels of skill, the possibility of a three-shot swing on the last hole will make the leaders tighten up and give hope to everyone within reach.

East Lake is a walking course where each caddie carries two bags. The re-routing changed the number of the hole with the steepest hill from fifteen to six, making it nine holes earlier in the round and easier to climb — it was a strain so close to the end. The new back nine is now a walk in the park, and it's a treat to walk downhill on the eighteenth late in the day with sun on the clubhouse.

The eighteenth is appropriate to this story. It is the best connection back to Bobby and Alexa because it's on the same ground as the par five eighteenth of the original Tom Bendelow course, where they first began to play. When East Lake reversed the nines in August of 2016 and made this the last hole again, it made another full circle.

The club has been the permanent home of the Tour Championship since 2005, and the tournament has generated $26 million for the East Lake Foundation and the First Tee.[12] The TV coverage of the tournament by NBC has energized and challenged Ralph Kepple and his agronomy staff. Their morale resembles that of their counterparts at Augusta National.[13]

There's an unusual feeling at East Lake. The success of the foundation, First Tee, and Purpose Built Communities has reinforced the pride of experienced staff members and helped attract new young people. Whether they work inside or out on the course, each one is a host.

What does Tom Cousins say when asked to comment at the end of a program on the successes at East Lake? His speeches are short. He congratulates the students for taking advantage of the new education, and he challenges them to keep it up. Then he thanks the staff members who make it work and those who have supported the process.

Bobby Jones and Tom Cousins have a lot in common.

---

12 The first tournament was in 1998, and it has been the finals of the FedEx Playoffs since 2007. The First Tee is an international mentoring program for school children that blends golf instruction with character development.

13 Before play began on Saturday of the Masters a few years ago, a uniformed man was seen in the large fairway bunker on number one with only a small pair of scissors. He was trimming the grass in the face of the bunker closest to the green. When the visitor told him how impressed he was, and that he must be proud of how the course looked, he smiled and said, *Thank you. We all are.*

PART ONE

SIX GOLFERS

Bobby in 1928, age 26, with his fourth
U.S. Amateur trophy — Brae Burn CC, Boston

Alexa in 1919, age 22, with her second consecutive
U.S. Women's Amateur trophy — Shawnee CC, Pa.

Charlie Elliott at home in 1995 at age 89

Charlie Yates in his 20s

Tommy Barnes at age 77 in 1992

Charlie Harrison at 60

I

BOBBY JONES

Georgia Golf Hall of Fame Member
Inducted 1989

Robert Tyre Jones, Jr. was born in Atlanta, Ga., on March 17, 1902. He graduated from Georgia Tech and Harvard University. From 1923–30, he won 13 national golf titles: four U.S. Opens, five U.S. Amateurs, three British Opens and one British Amateur. In 1930, at age 28, he scored the Grand Slam of Golf by winning the U.S. Amateur, the U.S. Open, the British Amateur and the British Open. This master stylist's grace and ability brought publicity and honor to his state and his nation. He was made burgess of the town of St. Andrews, Scotland, sharing this title with only one other American: Benjamin Franklin. In 1933, Jones co-founded the Augusta National Golf Club, and established the prestigious Masters Tournament there in 1934. He was golf's greatest ambassador and is generally honored as its greatest competitor. Jones died in 1971 at the age of 69.

One might as well attempt to describe the smoothness of the wind as to paint a clear picture of his complete swing.

Grantland Rice

With his father three months before his first U.S. Open victory in 1923

Holding the trophy at Inwood, NY, age 21

With Watts Gunn (R) after the 1925 U.S. Amateur

Having a Coke with his father (L)

Robert Woodruff (R)

President Eisenhower (L)

19

The Most Unforgettable

Character I've Met®

Bobby Jones

BY ALEXA STIRLING FRASER

I WAS A FRAIL child, and that accounted for my meeting Bobby Jones—he was frail, too. Both our parents had moved out of the city of Atlanta, Ga., to live across the road from the East Lake Country Club in the hope that exposure to swimming, tennis and golf would improve our health. Bob was only five, and I was nine; we became playmates simply because there were few other children around.

We swam, experimentally. We tried tennis a little. Almost at once we settled upon golf. When it was clear that we were serious about the game, Bob's father cut down a set of clubs for him (clubs were wooden-shafted in those days), and for my next birthday I received a set of clubs to match my size. The club professional, a little Scotsman named Stewart Maiden—who had,

ALEXA STIRLING FRASER ranks among the great women golfers of all time. She was United States Women's Amateur Champion 1916-1920, and Canadian Women's Open Champion in 1920 and 1934. She is a member of golf's Hall of Fame.

55

20

I think, the most perfect swing in golf—gave us lessons, free of charge.

By the time Bob was eight he was obviously destined to become a remarkable player. Even then, adults watched his straight tee shots with envy, sighed over his crisp irons, applauded his deadly putting. However, he had one flaw—his temper. Let him make a poor shot and he'd turn livid with rage, throw his club after the ball, or break it over his knee, or kick at the ground and let out a stream of very adult oaths.

As I grew into my teens, Bob's temper tantrums began to embarrass me. It was perhaps amusing to see an eight-year-old break his club when he made a bad shot, but not so amusing when the boy was 12 or 13. People began to gossip about his conduct, and I wished my father could have a few words with him. My father, Dr. Alexander W. Stirling, a physician and for a number of years British consul in Atlanta, saw golf as a measurement of a man's character. He had sternly instilled in me the ethics of the game. When he gave me my own set of clubs, he said, "Alexa, play to win. But even more important than winning is your conduct on the course. Do not lose your temper at a poor shot. Do not sulk in defeat. Be gracious in victory."

Inevitably, Father did talk to Bob, but not in quite the way I would have desired. One afternoon Father and I were playing a round together and came upon Bob just as he topped a drive. He threw his club after the ball and swore loudly. Unfortunately, one expletive that he used was a most offensive word to the British. He shouted, "That bloody shot!"

Father, ordinarily a soft-voiced man, drew himself up and thundered, "Young man, don't you know better than to use language like that in front of a lady?" He took me by the hand and marched me off the course. That was the end of my games with Bob.

For the next two years I saw him at the country-club parties, but I wasn't allowed to play golf with him. He was a handsome boy, with a gentle, wry way of smiling, and, except for his bursts of temper on the course, his manners were impeccable.

Then a situation arose to which my father could not object. During World War I the Red Cross asked Bob and me to go on a fund-raising tour of exhibition matches. I agreed with some misgivings. By now I had played enough tournament golf to be steeped in the traditions of the game, and I didn't want to be humiliated by Bob's outbursts.

Sure enough, he lost control, and at the worst possible place—Boston's aristocratic Brae Burn Country Club. On the eighth hole he missed an easy shot. I saw the blood climb his neck and flood his face. Then he picked up his ball, took a full pitcher's windup and threw the ball into the woods. A gasp of surprise and shock went through the large crowd watching us. I wished only that the ground beneath me would open and let me sink from sight.

Later, when I berated him, Bob said, "I don't give a damn what anybody thinks about me." After a moment he added, "I only get mad at myself." Suddenly I saw him as a 15-year-old boy driven by the demand of perfection he made of himself. Whenever he fell short of it he went into a rage, not at the ball or the club or the course or the spectators or his opponent, but at himself. Worst of all, he knew that these temper outbursts released a psychological poison within him that upset his game.

In fact, Bob was just heading into what sportswriters came to call his "Seven Lean Years." During this period he entered a lot of the major tournaments and was frequently runner-up—but never champion. Always there would be one shot that would bring on the flood of rage; and always that one flaw would lick him.

One such unhappy event took place in the spring of 1921, when he and I were members of the U. S. group that invaded Great Britain to compete in their open and amateur tournaments. Only 18, charming, modest, thoughtful and, oh, so handsome, Bob was the center of attention wherever he went. He dressed gaily in fawn-colored knickers, a cashmere sweater and gleaming, handmade shoes. He was cheered as "Bonnie Bobbie," and the crowds fervently hoped he would take the British Open Championship at St. Andrews. But disaster awaited him there.

Bob made a creditable showing in the first three rounds. On the first nine of the fourth round, however, his game seemed to come apart, and he took a 43. Then, playing the 11th hole, he put an iron shot into the famous Strath bunker, which was terribly deep. Four times he chopped with his niblick, only to have his ball jump halfway up the precipitous cliff and roll back down. On his fifth try the ball flew out of the bunker, over the green and into the sea beyond. Bob tore his score card into tiny bits, threw the shreds into the sea and stormed off the course. The Scots and English were aghast. Withdrawing from a tournament is simply *not done*.

Back home, Bob's critics pulled no punches. They said he was a spoiled child, a sorehead. The return to East Lake must have been humiliating for him. He could not shut his ears to the attacks upon him, nor blind his eyes to the obvious fact that fewer admirers followed him around. He seemed a lonely figure as he strode through practice rounds, battling his game and himself.

Late that same summer he entered the U. S. Open at the Columbia Country Club in Washington, D. C. This was to be the turning point in his career. Until the last round he had a good chance of winning. Then, on the fifth hole, with every stroke a crucial one, he hooked his second shot out of bounds. He dropped another ball and, incredibly, hooked it to the same spot. The gallery stared apprehensively at Bob. He stood rigid, his hands gripping the club until his knuckles were white. But he made no move, no sound; his face was an expressionless mask.

The only thing he could not control was the wave of blood that poured up over his neck and face. Gradually it receded; then he relaxed his hands, gave the gallery a wry smile, dropped another ball and finished out the round. He posted a 77, his worst score in years, but it was the finest round of his life. He had at last mastered himself; he was ready to become the greatest champion in the history of the game.

In 1923 Bob won the U. S. Open; in 1924 the U. S. Amateur; in 1925 the U. S. Amateur again; in 1926 the U. S. Open and the British Open; in 1927 the U. S. Amateur and the British Open; in 1928 the U. S. Amateur for the fourth time; in 1929 the U. S. Open for the third time. Then, in 1930, he made the incredible "Grand Slam" of all four major championships: the U. S. Amateur and Open, the British Amateur and Open. This is a feat that has never been matched. It was the decade of Bobby Jones.

His fame rested not only on his phenomenal play but on his sporting conduct. He was the most modest of champions. He once said, "A fellow would be an idiot to get puffed up over a thing like playing golf." He was foursquare honest about the game. In a crucial match he penalized himself a stroke for accidentally moving his ball in the rough when he addressed it with his club. No one was near him or could possibly have noticed the slight movement of the ball, but he insisted on the penalty. When he was praised for this he said, "You might as well praise a man for not robbing a bank." Always generous to rival competitors, he once remarked, "I don't play against men, I play against par." It was still a battle with *himself* for perfection.

After winning his Grand Slam, Bob announced he was retiring from competition. There was nothing more to win, so he decided to make a few motion pictures about golf and then concentrate on his business interests and his law practice in Atlanta. He had made a brilliant scholastic record at Georgia Tech, Harvard and Emory; he had married a beautiful girl and was beginning to raise a family; he was surrounded by a host of admiring friends; he was 28 years old. All of us who knew Bob said to ourselves, "What a wonderful future is in store for him. And he deserves every bit of it."

What *really* was in the future was tragedy. In July 1948 Bob, now a successful businessman and a civic leader, played a benefit exhibition match to help raise money for a hospital in the little North Carolina town of Highlands. He found he was having some difficulty in coördinating, and he felt terribly tired.

But he finished the match. He put the experience down to general fatigue and decided he needed a rest. That was the last game of golf he was ever to play in public.

One evening a month later he had started to putt a few balls on the living-room rug when a leg suddenly gave way beneath him. He then submitted to a complete medical examination, and the grim truth was revealed. He had a disease of the spinal cord which caused a weakness of the muscles. The following year he had two operations, but they did not correct the trouble; he was likely to face pain-racked invalidism for the rest of his life.

I did not see Bob at this time. I had married a Canadian physician, moved to Ottawa and had a family of three children. But one day I received a letter from him saying that the United States Golf Association was going to have a celebration of the golden anniversary of the Women's Amateur Golf Championship, and he very much wanted me to come to Atlanta and participate.

Reporters and photographers met me at Atlanta's Peachtree Station and told me that Bob was waiting at the top of the stairs. This news came as a shock. He really couldn't walk downstairs! Until this moment I hadn't quite believed it. Halfway up the stairs I saw him, and I felt as if a steel band had suddenly clamped around my chest.

On the retina of my memory was impressed the picture of a handsome young man in knickers, swinging a golf club with tremendous power and grace. In tragic contrast there stood before me a man slumped on two canes, a brace on his right leg, his face gray.

We shook hands and then started toward his car. He didn't walk; he dragged his feet along without being able to lift them, his face set against the pain each movement cost him. When we reached the car he worked himself behind the wheel, and we started off for the Atlanta Athletic Club, where I was to stay. We talked of old times as he drove, and I found he was putting me completely at ease. Bob was not self-conscious about his problem; he simply ignored it.

During the following days I learned the truth about Bob's condition from his friends. He would not get better. He was in constant pain, but he went to his law office every day and to the East Lake golf club frequently. He had created the Masters' Tournament, which many of the country's leading players considered the most important of all, and he kept a proprietary eye on it.* He refused to use a wheel chair, although it would ease his pain considerably, and he succumbed to an electric golf cart only because he could not follow the matches otherwise. He doggedly maintained his interests and activities, fighting with all his strength against the slowly smothering paralysis. And he'd be *damned* if he

*This year's Masters' Tournament is being played April 7 through April 10.

was going to have any soupy sympathy. About this point he was profanely specific.

We were having lunch on the terrace at East Lake one afternoon when suddenly his face was bathed in perspiration. He reached into his pocket for two small pills which he popped into his mouth. Then he explained, apologetically, "The doctors said I should take them when the pain gets too bad."

That reference to his illness gave me the courage to discuss it with him, and to ask him how he managed to remain so cheerful. He laughed and replied, "One morning a few weeks ago I woke up without remembering my condition, and I stepped out of bed to walk to the bathroom. I fell flat on my face, of course. I lay on that floor and beat it with my fists and cursed at the top of my voice. For ten minutes nobody dared come near me. I would have bitten them."

He told the story with wry humor. I commented that if he could laugh at himself, it certainly showed he'd made an adjustment to his condition.

"Adjustment?" he said, squinting thoughtfully across the links now flooded with beautiful autumn sunlight. "If adjustment means acceptance, I'd say no. I still can't accept this thing; I fight it every day. When it first happened to me I was pretty bitter, and there were times when I didn't want to go on living. But I did go on living, so I had to face the problem of *how* I was to live. I decided that I'd just do the very best I could."

We fell silent, and my memory raced back to the day when he had won his first U. S. Amateur Championship and the reporters had pressed him to analyze his game, to explain in what way he was a better player than the others in the tournament. He had thought a moment, then said soberly that he didn't think he was a better player than some of the others; he thought he had won simply because he had tried harder. As I looked at my old friend now, I realized he hadn't changed.

And so Bob has gone on, tackling every problem he confronts with the same dogged perfectionism that he learned on the course. As long as I live, I shall never forget the morning during my Atlanta visit when we stopped off at a rehabilitation center where Bob was taking some physiotherapy. He climbed out of the car and started his torturous trip to the building entrance, dragging his legs one after the other. When, after what seemed an eternity, he reached the door, he turned to flash me a fleeting smile of triumph—the same expression he always wore when he made a good recovery from the rough, or blasted up to the pin from a sand trap.

From long ago I remembered his words, "I don't play against other men, I play against par." And his smile now, from the doorway of the hospital, said to me, "Well, I didn't take a bogey on *that* hole." ❦❦❦❦

II

ALEXA STIRLING FRASER

"GLORIOUS GOLFING GIRL,"[1]
RENAISSANCE WOMAN

Georgia Golf Hall of Fame Member
Inducted 1989

Alexa was born in Atlanta, Ga., on September 5, 1897. As Bobby Jones's childhood golfing partner, she was dubbed "The First Lady of East Lake" and "The Empress of Golf" to match Mr. Jones's "Emperor" nickname. Quiet and competitive, she won her first title at East Lake at the age of 12. In 1916, three days before her 19th birthday, she won the first of her three U.S. Women's Amateur Championships. When the tournament resumed after World War I, she successfully defended her crown in 1919 and 1920 and placed second in 1921, 1923, and 1925. She won the Canadian Women's Amateur Championship in 1920 and 1934 and finished second in 1922 and 1925. She became an honorary member of the Royal Ottawa Golf Club and maintained her interest in golf throughout her life. Her last visit to Atlanta was to open the museum at the Atlanta Athletic Club during the 1976 U.S. Open. She died on April 15, 1977, and was inducted into the Canadian Golf Hall of Fame in 1986 and the Georgia Golf Hall of Fame in 1989.

---

1   The title came from her competitors.

Alexa Stirling was not silver; she was a multi-faceted gemstone. Making little boxes led her to the violin at age six, which she took to the level of performing solo on stage at the Atlanta Municipal Auditorium with the symphony orchestra of her day. She was a good enough driver and mechanic to become a certified ambulance driver on the home front during WWI, responsible for maintaining the engine and brakes and responding to disasters, such as the Great Fire of Atlanta in 1917, when she transported the injured to hospitals. It took so much attention, she called her ambulance her War Baby. She was an expert carpenter throughout her life, and in 1921 she even worked in finance (Barclay 2001).

After becoming a golf champion, she described how her golf was enhanced by her other interests. In 1917, when she was the twenty-year-old U.S. Women's Amateur champion, she had also become a writer. The short autobiography requested by *Golf Illustrated* had an unusual opening.

The editor now comes insisting I write about myself — some sort of an autobiography. I was very much flattered. If others do not care for the subject, that is the editor's fault, and his magazine's misfortune ... He wants me to detail some of the things which influenced my golf ... As a manufacturer of boxes, fiddles, etc., I was productive if not profitable. My hands still bear the saw marks of bygone days. Out of the mechanical triumphs in my boyish days came something which was to influence all my life, even my golf. From a cigar box, a stick, and some string, I manufactured a fiddle, an instrument I had seen a little neighbor play ... My pleasing performances (they were inaudible) upon this cigar box attracted the attention of my fond parents, who were prevented from forgetting them by my continual demands for a real fiddle ... my parents thought one should be available for one dollar, but the clerk was a good salesman and prevailed upon them that I was no doubt a genius in the bud and seven dollars would be cheap for a first class little second-hand instrument. I made my debut when still only six years old. That fiddle got me accustomed to appearing before people, and at each performance I seemed to 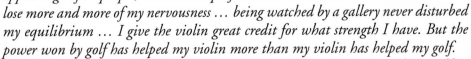 *lose more and more of my nervousness ... being watched by a gallery never disturbed my equilibrium ... I give the violin great credit for what strength I have. But the power won by golf has helped my violin more than my violin has helped my golf.*

And in 1920, in "Glorious Golfing Girl," an interview in *Canadian Golfer*:

I have never had any particular trouble with my iron shots, and this is due largely to the fact that even when I was a tiny tot I did not play with dolls as most girls do. I played instead with hammer and nails, and I still have scars on my hands where the hammer hit me instead of the nail. I like to do carpentry and plumbing jobs around the house. Of course I do not have to do this, but I do it because I like it and get a lot of fun out of it. I cut the lawn, tinker around my automobile, and do a lot of things that men usually do. I play the violin quite a bit, and all this has strengthened my wrists, my forearms and my fingers. My wrists are more like a man's than any other woman golfer I know ... the iron shots of women are not compact. They are weak. Women do not put what you call "stuff" into their shots.

The short biographic sketch has her born in Atlanta in 1897. Who were her parents, and where did they come from? Why did they come to Atlanta?

Her biographer, James Barclay, answered the first two questions:[2]

She was the second of three daughters of Dr. Alexander Williamson Stirling from Peebles, Scotland and Opera singer Nora Bromley of Yorkshire, England. Nora had been born in Bellevue House at the village of Goole, which stood on large grounds. Her father had a flourishing wine importing business. Alexa's mother had a fine voice and was offered a role in Gilbert and Sullivan's, 'The Gondoliers.' If she had accepted, she would have toured America with the D'Oyley Carte Company.

Dr. Stirling's specialty was eye, ear, nose and throat. While working as an eye surgeon at the Royal Westminster Ophthalmic Hospital in London, his studies took him to the University of Berlin and an eye clinic in Paris. To finance these continued studies, he became a ship's doctor for short periods, traveling as far as Buenos Aires. On a trip to the United States, he took the time to visit New York, Chicago, and Denver, with a mind to settling in North America. For by now, he had met his future wife and was determined to settle somewhere. He left England for New York in 1893 and spent two years there working as a lecturer at the New York Post Graduate College. They had planned to leave there for Chicago but changed their minds at the last moment and went to Atlanta (Barclay 2001).

In 2016, Alexa's daughter Sandra discovered the reason Atlanta won out. She found the answer in a history of their family written by Janet, her older sister:

After deciding to leave New York, Daddy planned to go to Chicago and had all the household goods shipped there, but some information caused him to consider Atlanta. He made the trip and stayed in the Aragon Hotel. On New Year's Day 1895, the sun was shining, the windows were open, and the Cotton States Exposition was in progress. He went back to New York, got Mother and me, and had all the

---

2   James A. Barclay wrote *Golf in Canada* and was inducted into the Canadian Golf Hall of Fame for leadership and for his careful research and writing. He was the author of the only biography of Alexa, *The Golfer and the Carpenter*, but died in 2011 before it was published.

stuff shipped to Atlanta from Chicago. Two years later, Alexa was born in a house on Piedmont Avenue between Sixth and Seventh Streets.[3]

James Barclay: *Dr. Stirling established his medical and surgical practice in the city, where he was also the British correspondent — a post described as nearly identical with consul.*

The parents of Alexa and Bobby would have referred to themselves as middle class, but both were well educated, successful, and descended from stable families in Britain and Georgia. In the rough and tumble, railroad town of Atlanta, they were definitely upper class.

The Jones family (1907) and Alexa's (1908) came to East Lake close to the same time for the same reasons. As children living in town, they were small and sickly, so their parents had them homeschooled to avoid exposing them to the common infections in every school. The moves worked out well. East Lake was healthier than town, and with golf, tennis, and swimming, it was more fun.

There is no evidence that Alexander and Nora intended to raise a golf champion when they moved to East Lake, but if they had, they picked the perfect place and exactly the right moment. In 1898, three years after their arrival in Atlanta, the Atlanta Athletic Club was founded, and in 1904 the new club bought land at East Lake for a golf course. It opened in 1906 with seven holes, and the Stirlings bought a lot that year across the street from the main entrance. They moved in two years later.[4]

Alexa wrote, *I was introduced to golf by my father when I was eleven.*

---

3   The Aragon Hotel was on the corner of Ellis and Peachtree Streets. Today, the spot includes an entrance to the Peachtree Center MARTA station and part of the Georgia Pacific headquarters property. It was, and still is, the highest point in the city limits of Atlanta, 1050 feet above sea level.

The Cotton States and International Exposition in Piedmont Park was Atlanta's first large multinational celebration and was held one hundred years before the 1996 Olympics. It attracted over 800,000 visitors from the U.S. and thirteen countries and was opened by President Grover Cleveland. John Philip Sousa composed the King Cotton March for the event. On the last night, the governors of Massachusetts and Georgia appeared on stage wearing hand-made, blue cotton suits and announced they had been made from cotton picked that morning.

Atlanta historian, Walter McElreath, described the scene Dr. Stirling dropped into:

The railroad yards were jammed every morning with trains that brought enormous crowds. The streets were crowded all day long. Every conceivable kind of fakir bartered his wares. Dime museums flourished on every street ... Vast stucco hotels stood on Fourteenth Street ... I spent a great deal of time on the streets looking at the strange crowds — American Indians, Circassions, Hindus, Japanese, and people from every corner of the globe — who had come as professional midway entertainers (McElreath, 1984).

4   James Barclay: *The address on the family note-paper was Cardrona, East Lake, Decatur, GA. ... In 1682 the Williamsons of Peebles had bought an estate called Cardrona and thereafter were known as the Williamsons of Cardrona. The Cardrona Tower in Peebles is still listed as one of Scotland's castles.*

She described Bobby in 1909:

My earliest recollection of Bob Jones was when, as a child of seven, he was lying asleep in his bed, recovering from the effects of an upset tummy. He was a rather spindly child, with a head too large for his small body, but he was even then the handsome person he turned out to be (Matthew 1999).

Back to her autobiography: *Perry Adair, Bob Jones, and I were all too insignificant for the honor of caddies, and the three of us would trudge round the course many a time playing thirty-six holes in the day, lugging our own bags and under a broiling sun. Sometimes we would wait at No. 1 tee for a couple of hours before we could get away … then we were off, nearly hidden by our bags, but as happy as could be.*

As I discarded a hat, my hair in places was bleached to a delicate straw, but the color of my nose made up for that. I grew in strength, if not in beauty, but Perry and Bob wore hats, and their good looks were not spoiled. At this period, it was the beginning of the fashion for boys to plaster their hair as close to their heads as possible. I thought it was very new, very stylish and consequently the proper thing to do … I nearly pulled out mine by the roots, applied water, and then held all that was left down tight by a 'slide.'

High tight collars were all the vogue amongst the ambitious youths, so I nearly choked myself. When looking down low for a golf ball, my eyes must have appeared as though they would

Miss Nora Stirling's Remembrance of Her Sister's Girlhood Days

leave their sockets altogether. Most people would have had heat stroke, but as far as I know, I never did.

As time progressed, we had many fun-filled days playing golf together. We had complete freedom to be on the course at any time with the exception of Sundays, at which time we would walk around and watch the better senior members. In this way, we hoped to improve our own games. All our attempts were under the watchful eye of Stewart Maiden, who was our guide and mentor for years to come.

It was with great gratification and admiration that I saw Bob grow to become the fine, broadminded, dignified gentleman he later proved to be.

She used "Jimmie" for Jimmy Maiden, her first teacher after her father:

Jimmie Maiden and I were good friends. I played my first match with Jimmie, who had also made my clubs. It was for a package of chewing gum, a secret treasure forbidden in the house, and it was one-hole long. He was to use one club with one hand, and I was to have all the clubs I wanted, and two hands. I think Jimmie won the match, but he was a thorough gentleman and the lady got the gum.

And about his brother Stewart Maiden, who followed Jimmy as club pro in 1908:

He and I soon became great friends, and he has never been above playing with me at any time that I might request. Like most speechless people (so I am told) he can chatter when he likes. I wonder if there is another professional in America who is on such terms of affection with his club members as is Stewart. He knows the evil golf habits into which I am to fall, and with certainty can put his finger on them and fix them.

She was more inclined to practice, and as they grew up she had a positive influence on Bobby. In her chapter about him, she described being embarrassed by his outbursts of temper on the course, but she did not mention his reaction when her father separated them. She also left out her positive effect on him.

When he heard that her father had decided to keep her away from him, Bobby blew up again:

A lot of good it does me to play golf with you @#$%&!!!^# girls. If I'm ever going to be a golfer, I've got to go and play with men. I'm just glad your old man stopped you (Matthew 1999).

He was aware of her disapproval of his behavior and eventually controlled himself, although it took a long time. In 1918, when she finally did confront and berate him at Brae Burn in Boston, she was twenty. She was the reigning U.S. Women's Amateur champion and known in golf circles throughout the country. She would turn twenty-one during the first week of September. Bobby had become sixteen in mid-March. He had won the Georgia Amateur at fourteen in 1916, also the year of his first appearance in a national championship, the U.S. Amateur. He did better than expected, losing in the third round. In 1917, he won the Southern Amateur. When he was a teenager, he probably could have beaten his older friend every time in golf, but when it came to behavior on the course, he was no match for Alexa.

After he conquered his temper on the course, he remembered her:

I read the pity in Alexa's soft brown eyes and finally settled down, but not before I had made a complete fool of myself. That experience had its proper effect. I resolved then that this sort of thing had to stop. It didn't overnight, but I managed it in the end, at least in tournaments (Jones 1960).

Alexa's game had developed quickly. She took up golf in 1908 and won her first U.S. Women's Amateur in 1916, one month after her nineteenth birthday. She had gone from beginner to national champion in eight years. The high point of her career came in 1920, when she won her third straight U.S. Woman's Amateur only one week after the first of her two Canadian titles. Her reputation soared.

Bobby would receive much more attention ten years later, but for now, the spotlight was all hers. The press was drawn to her because she was quiet and attractive with a natural, easy smile. When she spoke, she was eloquent. Her lofty status was illustrated by the tone taken in the *New York Times* in October 1920:

At least once each autumn there is a wanton waste of United States Golf Association funds, a leakage that should be plugged up. It seems that despite all advice to the contrary from the experts, the USGA moguls insist upon paying transportation costs, insurance fees and other expenses for safeguarding the huge silver trophy emblematic of the women's golf championship of the United States and moving it from Atlanta, Ga. to some temporary exhibition counter in a golf club. The point is that the valuable old cup always returns to Atlanta the following week. Why therefore disturb it? Miss Alexa Stirling, that happy, smiling, auburn-haired daughter of a Scotsman has once again proved that it is hopeless for her many rivals to try to pry loose the trophy ... No male amateur and no professional ever won an American golf title thrice in succession and only one woman ever accomplished this before now. But Miss Stirling's feat is considerably more than that of her illustrious predecessor, Miss Beatrix Hoyt, since she won her three championships over a period of five years, from 1916 to 1920 [There was no contest in 1917 and 1918 because of the war], *whereas Miss Hoyt won them in the successive years of 1896, 1897 and 1898* ("Golf" 1920).

More from "Glorious Golfing Girl" in 1920:

Miss Alexa Stirling of Atlanta, Ga. has not lost a golf match since the national Championship of 1915 ... There may be some question as to whether Francis Ouimet or Chick Evans is the best American amateur, and there is a considerable difference of opinion as to whether Jim Barnes, Walter Hagan or Jock Hutchinson is the best American professional player, but the women are all agreed there is no woman in this country who can beat the auburn-haired champion. The women players have called her the Glorious Golfing Girl, and her record bears this out.

Back to the *Atlanta Journal* in 1919: *I play all shots the same. I use the same stance for woods, irons, and even in putting. I understand Chick Evans does the same thing ... I crouch over the ball more than I formerly did. My right knee is bent and my left leg is kept straight. When I hit the ball, the left knee is bent and the right leg is straight. I find that I can pivot better this way and get my shots away much more smoothly and truly ... Jimmy Maiden ... is largely responsible for the new stance.*

And from Grantland Rice of the *New York Herald Tribune*, the most widely read sportswriter in America:

The race track has Man O' War, baseball has its Babe Ruth, and billiards has its Willie Hoppe. In the same way women's golf in America has its Alexa Stirling, who is just as predominant in her field as any male champion happens to be in his ... also, Miss Stirling would rather talk opera than golf, Scotia's ancient game running second to music in her scheme of things. Music first and golf second — but where is there finer music than the clear, clean ring of a truly hit iron?

After her peak in 1920, her golfing career was far from over. James Barclay described the reaction she evoked in the press when she visited England in 1921:

There was a heroic cast about Alexa. Her casual manner in championships showed no hint of nervousness, and that in itself unnerved those she played against. She was the absolute amateur. For her, life was more than striking a golf ball. That does not mean she had no will to win. She had an ability to probe deep down within herself and salvage victory from what often looked like certain defeat ... She crossed the Atlantic in 1921 to take British golf by storm, stealing golfers' hearts with her savoir vivre, and her grace and power on the course. She made the usually cautious British golf writer Bernard Darwin throw caution to the winds and write that she was the most stylish and dangerous woman golfer ever to breach British shores ... elegance, all elegance (Barclay 2001, Darwin 1944).

Alexa kept her eyes open for new opportunities and in 1921 diverted from golf into an entirely different world, the bond business. She worked in the New York office of S.W. Straus of Chicago and was only the twenty-eighth woman to sell bonds on Wall Street. The job may have come from contacts of friends in New York she had met in her travels. Because of her celebrity, her new position made the papers. An interview appeared in the *New York City Mail*:

33

Miss Stirling, of the red hair and brown eyes, looked up from her list of six percent mortgages:

'The successful businesswoman is today a person to be reckoned with. She manages her financial affairs like any man, often has a person or two to support, and must look to her future whether she marries or not, just as her brother does. The reason the place is so pretty (she waved her celebrated hand in the direction of a handsomely appointed reception room, reading room and dressing room with a neat little maid in it) is because women still love dainty things and tea and chintz and wicker, and always will, no matter how many bonds they sell or votes they cast or families they support with the work of their hands and brains' (Beckley 1921).

She had not won the American Amateur a fourth time the previous summer, or the Canadian when it was played at Rivermead Golf Club in Ottawa, but 1921 was an important year because she met her future husband at a dinner during the competition.

Her daughter Sandra remembered her father saying, *I first became smitten while watching this attractive, red-haired woman play from a bunker.*

Dr. Fraser was a Canadian doctor with the same specialty as Dr. Stirling, Alexa's father, so they had more than golf in common. They were married in 1925 in her house at East Lake and had the reception across the street at the club. They settled in Ottawa, and she devoted herself to her husband and to raising their three children, Sandra, Glen, and Richard.

Years later, when her children complained about her violin practice, she stopped playing, but she didn't quit golf. She and her husband enjoyed playing at the Royal Ottawa Golf Club, and she won the women's tournament there nine times. She won her second Canadian Amateur, her fifth national championship, in 1934 at age thirty-seven. She also never gave up her carpentry.

James Barclay: *Her children and grandchildren had watched her in her workshop in the basement of her home in Canada making furniture for their summer cottage. No nails — all tongue and groove.*

James would be pleased to know that in 2016, Sandra said her mother's twelve-seat dining room table was still in use at their cottage at Old Fort William, Quebec. The almost hundred-year-old, tongue-and-groove masterpiece has held up well.

He also described her last visit to Atlanta in 1976, a year before her death at age seventy-nine:

British golf writer Pat Ward-Thomas met Alexa Stirling Fraser in 1976 when he was reporting from the U.S. Open at the course of the Atlanta Athletic Club. She cut the ribbon at the opening of the Bob Jones room in the clubhouse:

'Meeting her was an unexpected delight. That morning in Atlanta it was easy to understand what an uncommonly appealing golfer Alexa must have been. A spry, charming little person, her lively talk belied her years. Her husband is dead, but she has seven grandchildren, all boys, and her spirit is ageless.'

Today, most American golfers have not heard of her despite her national championships.[5] She was a child of the nineteenth century, and her last major win in 1934 is ancient history to most young golfers. There was an Alexa Stirling clothing line for a time, but it has not continued, and no sets of golf clubs or golf courses are named for her.[6]

When the Georgetown University Women's golf team visited East Lake in 2016, one of the players introduced herself as Alexa but had never heard of the champion. She was impressed that the other Alexa had learned to play at East Lake with Bobby Jones and won national championships here and in Canada. She was told how to spell her last name and said she would look her up.

After the short visit at the water cooler by the fifth tee, she left to hit her drive, but after a few steps, she turned her head and smiled over her shoulder, still walking:

I've got it — last name not spelled like the silver.[7]

---

5   She is better known in Canada. Harry Kennedy in Toronto, a friend of East Lake, Tommy Barnes, and James Barclay, had this to say: *When Alexa was a girl, she was a determined, redheaded tomboy. As I read Jim Barclay's draft, this chapter and Mark Frost's references, during her competitive years she reminds me more and more of one of my all-time favourites, Marlene Stewart Streit. Alexa and Marlene were both of small stature and packed to overflowing with energy, confidence, determination, courage and tremendous strength of character.*

6   In 2018, the Athletic Club is hosting the Alexa Stirling Intercollegiate Invitational; and at East Lake, the Ladies Member-Guest tournament is known as the Stirling Cup. There is also an Alexa Stirling Putting Competition in the Bobby Jones Classic for CSF, a foundation dedicated to finding a cure for the disease that affected Bobby and improving the lives of those with paralysis. At the Royal Ottawa Golf Club, there is an Alexa Stirling Fraser Room, and she is recognized as their most renowned golfer.

7   Her first name is making a comeback. In April 2017, a couple was fixing breakfast for two friends. *I've been reading about Alexa Stirling,* a guest said. *She won three U.S. Women's Amateurs in a row.*
    I'm now playing songs by Frank Sinatra, a new voice replied.
    What was that? asked the guest.
    Oh, that's our new virtual assistant. It turns itself on and starts talking if anyone says its name — 'Alexa.'

Invitation from the Atlanta Athletic Club to celebrate
Alexa's first national championship at age 19 in 1916

Her favorite shot was hitting a mashie pitch close to the pin.

Total concentration

Invitation and photos courtesy of Golf Canada and the Canadian Golf Hall of Fame

III

MY LOVE AFFAIR
WITH EAST LAKE

by Charlie Elliott

Like Bobby and Alexa, Charlie Elliott (1906–2000) was multi-talented. He was Georgia's first great naturalist, the model for *Mark Trail*, the educational cartoon character, and a prolific author, especially on turkey hunting and fishing. He wrote Robert Woodruff's biography, *Mr. Anonymous*. A perfect replica of his living room with his books is a permanent feature at the Charlie Elliott Wildlife Center. The nature preserve has 6,400 acres and is located on Highway 11 between Covington and Monticello, about an hour east of East Lake. He was a frequent golfing partner of Bobby Jones and his favorite hunting and fishing companion. Longtime friend Daryl Gay wrote: *But if I dig deep enough for my favorite description of Charlie Elliott, two words come to mind — mentor and friend.*

I played my first game of golf on the East Lake course in 1935, and I played my last game there in 1994 shortly after it had been purchased by Tom Cousins. During those years, I became wedded to East Lake. I have followed a golf ball over many layouts across this country but never found another one with the charm, dignity, and challenge of the course at East Lake.

My golf was always a long drive from championship caliber, but I do remember a few special shots, such as the double eagle on number five when par there was five, and on number six, the island hole, where my tee shot bounced off the flagstick and stopped half an inch away, the nearest I ever came to a hole-in-one.[1]

The best score I ever shot at East Lake was when I played in a foursome with Bob Jones, Charlie Yates, and another golfer. I remember that a couple of pros were supposed to play, and they called at the last moment to cancel. I had no game, was not planning to play, and was on the club veranda having a beer when Bob asked me to join the match and make it a foursome.

You know I don't play that kind of golf, I told him.

You are not lousy enough to hold up the game too much, he said. *I'll take you as a partner and we'll try them.*

I am sure one reason I remember the game was that it was the best score I ever shot at East Lake. I can only guess I didn't want to show how much of a dub I really was and concentrated on looking at and hitting the ball. Also, they gave me quite a few putts I probably would have missed. I remember I shot a 68 but didn't figure in a hole. The other scores were as low or lower than mine, but Bob shot one of his best rounds and sank his last putt for a 64.

I played with Woodruff and Bob at both East Lake and the Peachtree course, but cannot remember the details of any of those matches, except that Woodruff always took Bob as a partner. No one objected, because we never played for more than a golf ball or a dollar, and Woodruff always picked up the tab for caddie fees and drinks.

Most of all, I remember the fellowship of the delightful companions who strode down the fairways with me through the years, when golf was a walking game with caddies and not dependent on vehicular transportation from shot to shot.

No matter how beautiful the golf course, or how well you strike the ball, unless you are a pro with an eye for a purse, the main pleasure and worth to be gotten from playing is the competitive fellowship of friends and associates who are special people in your life.

For years I played regularly with Bob Jones over the East Lake course. Because of his qualities of shot-making under pressure, the smooth, sweet

---

1   Today's fourteenth and fifteenth

poetry of his swing, his complete integrity, and his charm as an individual, many consider him the greatest golfer since the game began. Once he insisted on calling a shot on himself when he was the only person who saw his ball move as he addressed it. That added a stroke which cost him a major tournament.

If you didn't know of his celebrity, you'd never suspect it when you played with him. The quality of his shot making was still with him, but he was so down-to-earth, so considerate of those with him, so human in every way, that you would consider him only as a delightful member of your foursome all the way through the nineteenth hole.

In the nineteenth hole, I never failed to do my share when we sat around the locker-room table and held delightful post-mortems. Our little bailiwick was always the most fragrant corner of the locker-room. Bob's favorite drink was good corn whiskey, and one of my old-time mountain neighbors helped me keep him supplied with the pure corn, made only from meal and corn sprouts, with no other catalytic ingredients such as sugar or yeast.

I put a two-gallon oak keg in Bob's locker and kept it filled with corn. It had an insignificant leak that perfumed the area. Even Pierce Harris, the minister who had a locker among us infidels but was a complete teetotaler, admitted that he enjoyed the fragrance in that corner of the room.

Bob played golf all over the world in both competitive and friendly matches, but his favorite golfing layout at any and all times was the No. 1 course at East Lake. He started playing there when he was six years old, and his last few games, before he was stricken with a nerve disorder and forced to retire in his middle forties, were at East Lake.

Another golfer who was one of my longtime favorites as a partner, opponent and friend was Watts Gunn. Wattsy and I played in countless matches together. He was a brilliant shot-maker. I remember that about a third of the time when he made a good shot, the hat would fly off the back of his head. A bad shot would cause him to swear his favorite cuss word, *Jeepers!*, which was the most vulgar term I ever heard him use.

Watts and I played with many men who were famous or noted in their endeavors, though not necessarily in golf. One that I vividly recall was W.D. "Bo" Randall. Bo was the owner of several orange groves in Florida, but his chief claim to fame was his Randall-made knives. His cutlery was so much in demand that his factory in Orlando was never able to keep up with the orders.

The knife he made for the U.S. Marine Corps was said to be the finest military knife ever manufactured.

Bo had a fascinating weakness for lost golf balls — not those lost by him, but by other people. We played many rounds of golf at East Lake, but I'm sure he never set foot on one of the fairways there except to cross it from rough to green. He kept his shots down the middle, and his caddie was able to walk straight to them. Bo walked from the tee to his ball on the edge of the rough, and after his second shot, which usually landed on or near the green, he made his way to the ball through the rough again. His main pleasure in playing seemed to be finding lost golf balls. He was wealthy enough to buy any golf ball factory and give it away, but his day was highly successful only if he came back to the clubhouse with a pocketful of old balls. We often wondered what he did with them. I never saw him hit any ball but one that was new or had been played only a few holes.

A regular member of our Saturday morning foursome for many years was Charlie Yates. Charlie had won many tournaments, including the British amateur, and was one of the most noted of the amateur champions. For years we had a friendly game every Saturday morning at East Lake with Dr. Pierce Harris, a renowned Methodist minister, and Bill Murray, a very good golfer and prominent businessman. I was the heathen in that foursome. Every Sunday morning, while Yates and Murray were regular attendants at the church where Dr. Harris presided, I played golf in another foursome with Tommy Barnes, Billy Street, and Ernest Harrison. Dr. Harris was aware of this transgression and told me several times: *You are the worst member of my church, and if you knew some of the members you'd resent that.*

I well remember Colonel Bob Jones, who was Bob's father. The Colonel made up for his lack of skill with his colorful language. There was nothing vicious or ugly about it, but he knew all the words and seemed to find a lot of satisfaction in using them.

Tommy Barnes was the best golfer in our Sunday morning foursome, but the rare character in this group was Ernest Harrison. He was an excellent golfer with just enough information about the rules to start an argument after every wayward shot, especially those with untenable lies. Once he was just off the fairway where a dog had scratched to cover its leavings.

I can drop out of here, Ernest announced.

Why? he was asked.

The rule book says I can move out of a hole made by a burrowing animal.

That was made by a dog, Street said.

Everyone knows a dog is a burrowing animal, Harrison replied.

He continued to argue about it even after we had refused to allow him relief and he had lost the hole. This was written up in a national magazine and credited to someone else, but I was there and heard the original version.

Among the many topics we discussed during our games was the moon landing.

That's a lot of foolishness and a complete waste of our money, Ernest declared. *Pretty soon they'll have some guy landing on the sun.*

You dumb bastard, Barnes said. *Do you know how hot the sun is?*

Sure I do, our partner replied. *But they can always land up there at night.*

One of the unforgettable characters in the early days at East Lake was Stewart Maiden. I knew the old pro only for a brief time during his last years when he was pro at Peachtree Golf Club in North Atlanta, but I heard a lot about him from Bob Jones. When he was seven or eight years old and just starting golf, Bob copied Maiden's swing and went through his entire golfing career with the smoothest, easiest stroke that was almost poetry in its rhythm.

Bob told me many stories about the old pro's sense of humor. Once, when a member was taking lessons Stewart suddenly stopped him and caught his wrist in an iron grip.

Do you have to play golf? he asked.

Another time the pro, commenting to one of his clients during a play-practice round:

You're a damn fine golfer, he said, *but you have one failing. You can't get the ball in the hole.*

There's a well-known and much-repeated story that when Jones was in a major championship at Oakmont, he started trying to guide his shots and was missing them just enough to land in all sorts of trouble. Maiden listened to the radio reports and sent Bob a wire: *Hit the hell out of them. They'll go somewhere.* Bob said he followed this advice, and while many of his shots were still off line, he was hitting them over and beyond the trouble spots.

I played golf with Jones during the end of his club-throwing days and saw him a few times when he was so completely exasperated with a stroke that he tossed a club into the air. He was such a fierce competitor that it was frustration with himself, and we all understood it. He completely conquered this tendency in his final years.

Another member of the East Lake staff who came along in my time, and for whom I had a great deal of affection and respect, was Jimmy Brett. Jimmy was caddie master and official starter for twenty-eight years at East Lake. He later moved on to the Atlanta Athletic Club's new course at Riverview. Regardless of the weather, overflow of players and other adverse conditions, he never failed to keep play going smoothly over the course. For many reasons he was a member favorite. He treated everyone with the same pair of gloves. Jones told me that when he was President of the Athletic Club and in a hurry to get through a round and meet a business appointment, he asked Brett to move his starting time ahead of another foursome.

I'm sorry, Mr. Jones, Jimmy said, *but they came in and registered ahead of you, and you'll have to wait your turn.*

Dave Williams was another favorite. He kept the locker room and the clubhouse going for almost fifty years. He knew every member, and most of their families. His income included tips as well as his salary. I knew Dave for years before I discovered that his income was more impressive than I had realized. Often, when I wanted to discard a pair of shoes or an old suit, I took them out to Dave. Once when I came in with some shirts and worn trousers I thought he might use, I noticed his worried expression.

You look upset, I said. *Is anything wrong?*

Yes sir, he said. *I guess I am worried. The furnace in one of my apartment houses has gone on the blink, and I can't find anybody to fix it.*

I learned later that he had collected, saved, and invested enough money over the years to be as wealthy as many of the members he served in the locker room.

I remember that Bob was an opera fan and attended and contributed to the operas in Atlanta, but Bob and I never discussed music. He never indicated to me whether his contributions came from his love of music, or simply to support this fine art. He gave me a charming little book, *Opera Guyed,* by Newman Levy, published by Alfred Knopf in 1933. It was a burlesque and poetry on the opera stories. He indicated that two of his favorites in this book were *Thaïs* and *Carmen.*

If Bob loved anything more than his family or golf, it was fishing. He got so excited when he landed a fish that a time or two I thought I'd have to give him artificial respiration or some form of first aid.

© Daryl Gay

I have no record of the dates when Bob and I started fishing together, but I know he was still able to navigate on a golf course. We golfed and fished together for ten years or more, until he became unable to handle a golf club, and then we switched over to fishing completely. I'm sure we did some lakeside fishing for bream, but most of our fishing was from a boat. We wet our lures in many places in north Florida, on the Georgia coast, in the mountains, and in the large lakes closer to home. When he got to the point when he could no longer maneuver well in the ordinary fishing skiff, I built an eighteen-foot fishing boat to include a swivel bow seat with shelf and storage space within easy reach of his hands. We used this until his fingers became so crippled that he was unable to handle a fishing reel or rod.

Bob was interested in everything outdoors, and while we fished we watched and identified birds and other creatures. A few times we stopped casting to follow a deer swimming across one arm of a lake.

A big chunk of pleasure went out of my life when Bob and I had to give up fishing together.

I cherish these memories from my love affair of sixty years with the club and golf course at East Lake.

Addendum 2017

At Charlie's funeral in Covington in 2000 at the First Methodist Church, the young minister told the congregation about a visit soon after he'd arrived:

I'd been here a few months and didn't know many people in the Covington area. The office received a call that Mr. Elliott wanted to come see me, and my secretary told me how famous and accomplished he was. I was really looking forward to meeting him but was a little anxious, especially since I hadn't noticed him on Sunday mornings.

When he came in, he was carrying a big shotgun which seemed gigantic in my office, and I have to tell you it did not reduce the tension. But I relaxed when I took in his friendly smile and gentle expression, and that he'd made sure the gun was pointed where I wouldn't be hurt if it went off. After he had welcomed me to Covington and wished me every success, I asked why he was carrying the gun.

'I'm glad you asked,' he said. 'That's the reason I came to see you. I want you to bless this fine old shotgun.'

"Mr. Anonymous"

ROBERT W. WOODRUFF

of *Coca-Cola.*

by
Charles Elliott

Cherokee Publishing Company

ATLANTA
1982

IV

CHARLIE YATES

Georgia Golf Hall of Fame Member
Inducted 1989

Charlie Yates was born in Atlanta, Ga., on September 9, 1913. Boys High School of Atlanta, once the home of the South's finest athletic talent, probably never produced a finer golfer than Yates. During the 1930s, few golfing amateurs in the country were better known or more widely celebrated. He won the Georgia Amateur in 1931 and '32, the NCAA individual title in 1934, and the Western Amateur in 1935. This Georgia Tech star became an international name in golf in 1938 when he won the coveted British Amateur. In 1936 and '38, he played on the U.S. Walker Cup team and was captain of the team in 1953 and honorary captain in 1985. He was secretary of the Augusta National Golf Club and was the low scoring amateur in the Masters Tournament five times. In 1980, Yates was given the Bob Jones Award by the United States Golf Association. He was inducted into the Georgia Golf Hall of Fame on January 14, 1989, and the Atlanta Sports Hall of Fame on February 6, 2015. In 1998, East Lake's old No. 2 course was redesigned by Rees Jones and named the "Charlie Yates Golf Course."
Charlie Yates died on October 17, 2005, at the age of 92.

Charlie Yates learned to play at East Lake for the same two reasons as Bobby Jones — when he was a young boy, the golf course was directly across the street from his house, and his father liked playing. He cut down clubs for him, his sister Fran, and brothers Dan and Alan.

Fran wrote, *We played golf almost from the time we could walk.*

The three brothers were lifelong members of the Atlanta Athletic Club; and when Charlie won the British Amateur at Troon in 1938, he became the third golfer, after Alexa and Bobby, to learn to play at East Lake and go on to win national titles in two countries.[1] He joined the new East Lake Golf Club when it was founded in 1993 and remained a member of both clubs the rest of his life.

He briefly described his early years in an interview by Herbert Warren Wind:

You must remember that there was a gulf of eleven years between Bob and me. I knew him pretty well, though, I think. My family, beginning with my grandfather, had a summer place out at East Lake, so when I wasn't playing golf myself I'd follow Bob and watch him play. He was awfully nice to kids like me. From time to time, he'd give me a golf ball — not an old beat-up one but a nice, pretty ball.

Or when he saw you in the clubhouse he'd wave you over and buy you a Coke.[2] I can't tell you how much he meant to us all. I still remember hearing on the radio the special bulletin that he had won our 1930 Amateur, the last trick in the Grand Slam. I was so excited that I ran from our house to the clubhouse, yelling to everyone I saw on the course, Bobby's won! Bobby's won!

I have so many fond memories of East Lake. You know I love to sing — I have what is referred to as a locker-room tenor — and I particularly loved to sing in the showers with Bob's dad, the Colonel. He had a big, bellowing bass voice. Our specialties were 'Lonesome Road,' 'Ol Man River' and 'Home on the Range.' On that last one, we'd really shake the timbers (Wind 1976).

His grandfather's summer place was a brick and timber house at 307 Second Avenue, opposite today's thirteenth hole, where Charlie lived from age three in 1916 until he was sixteen. It was named Alanhurst, for Charlie's uncle Alan, his grandparent's fifth child and only son.

In 1929, the family had grown, and they moved, but they didn't leave East Lake. They bought a larger stone house a few lots north, 259 Second Avenue, where the Drew School is today.

---

1   The 1934 NCAA individual title and the 1938 British Amateur
2   Every time Charlie mentioned Coke in front of a group he called it, *the Elixir of Atlanta.*

Fran's three daughters, Fran, Julie, and Mary, have pleasant memories of that second house.

Julie: *The Athletic Club had two courses at East Lake in those days, and the house sat between them, with great views in both directions. As children up and about in the early morning, we usually played out back because of the road in front.*

There was a nice yard with a large hedge all around separating it from the new course, old East Lake No. 2, and there was a little path we used because we liked sneaking away through the hedge in the early morning before the golfers arrived. When we came out on the other side we saw a magical sight — a whole golf course at our feet, just for us.

Although the houses he lived in are gone, Charlie's name is permanently linked to East Lake. The short public course is named Charlie Yates Golf Course. Charlie's son Comer said his dad considered that one of the biggest honors in his life. It's the home of East Lake's First Tee, the international program for young people linked to performance in school.

The highlight of Charlie's golfing career came in 1938 when he won the British Amateur at Troon at age twenty-four. But for Comer and the family, an even more important moment came the next week at St. Andrews after a disappointing loss, the defeat of his U.S. team by the British in the Walker Cup. The British victory was an upset and a long time coming. The matches had been held every other year since 1922, and by 1938 there had been seven matches, all American victories.

By the time of the trophy ceremony, the celebration of Britain's first win was well under way and getting noisier. Charlie turned out to be a second stimulant because his victory in the Amateur the previous weekend had made him a national celebrity, and this was the first group of fans to see him.

As soon as he was spotted on the podium, the crowd began shouting, *Charlie, Charlie,* again and again, bringing the formal ceremony to a complete halt. All eyes were now on him, and what he did next saved the day for the men directing the event who wanted to proceed but could not. Charlie quickly took the arm of Gordon Peters, a friend on the winning British team, and they came forward to the microphone together, going with the mood of the crowd. They did not speak but smiled their thanks and both waved. Then, to everyone's surprise, Charlie broke all tradition. He raised his arms, and he and his happy opponent began singing the crowd's favorite drinking song, "A Wee Deoch and Doris," while gesturing for the crowd to join in. It is not known how many verses and choruses were sung, but the tension disappeared. The two golfers returned to their teams, and the program proceeded without further interruptions. In a few short minutes, the young American had restored order and won the hearts of the Scottish people. The moment also began Charlie's life-long friendships with the members of the Royal & Ancient Golf Club.

An eye witness, veteran sportswriter James "Scotty" Reston of the *New York Times*, said Charlie's mastery of that situation, *was one of the memorable moments of my sporting days.*

Many years later Charlie was asked why he didn't celebrate at Troon when he won. He quickly explained that singing at his own victory would have been boastful and made his opponents uncomfortable.

Over the years, he introduced his friends from both sides of the Atlantic to each other, and among them was John Imlay. He became an authority on the affection for Charlie in Scotland. As soon as they entered a golf club, the word spread quickly:

Charlie Yates is in the club … Charlie Yates is in the club. Frequently, that led to "He's a Jolly Good Fellow," and "A Wee Deoch and Doris."

Charlie's positive attitude and friendly demeanor encouraged people to work together when they didn't know each other. That was a key to his success when he led two Atlanta programs. From 1973 to 1983, he was president of the Atlanta Arts Alliance, now the Woodruff Arts Center, when it raised $20 million dollars to build the new High Museum. He was also responsible for bringing Robert Shaw to the city to lead the Atlanta Symphony Orchestra.[3] Less widely known are the ten years he was chairman of the Emory Committee for the Robert T. Jones Jr. Scholarship Program (1993–2003). He had helped raise money to fund it sixteen years earlier when it was started by Francis "Buster" Bird, Jimmy Sibley, and others.[4]

He was a storyteller who saw the humor in golf. In the afterword for Bobby's book, *The Basic Golf Swing,* he found room for the Colonel, Bobby's father:

The all-time best story about the Colonel took place one afternoon in the early days of the Masters when Cliff Roberts, finding himself short of a Rules

---

3   Atlanta sportswriter Furman Bisher wrote, *Look at almost any kind of uplifting committee in Atlanta and chances are you'll find Charlie Yates's name on it.*

4   Since 1977 Emory has exchanged over 150 newly graduated college students with St. Andrews University in Scotland for one year. Bobby's and Charlie's college, Georgia Tech, has now been added, and there is a longer Jones Fellowship that allows time to obtain a graduate degree.

Committeeman, asked the Colonel to go out to the most sensitive spot on the course, the twelfth hole. The Colonel was on the eleventh hole when he suddenly heard the call for a Rules Committeeman to come to the twelfth green.

The Colonel went there and saw a player standing on the bank wanting to know if he was outside the hazard and therefore entitled to a free lift. He asked the Colonel if the embedded ball rule was in effect, and the Colonel had not the slightest idea about this rule.

The Colonel countered, 'Let me ask you a question, son. How do you stand with par?'

The player replied, 'Well, sir, today I am seven over and, for the tournament, twenty-three over.'

The Colonel responded, 'Hell, son, I don't give a damn what you do with it – put the !!&@%^*# on the green for all I care!' (Jones 1969)

If the occasion had anything to do with Bobby Jones, and many did, Charlie specialized in illustrating the character of his older friend and poking fun at himself. After World War II, both General Eisenhower and Bobby asked him to become Southern Chairman of the USO, a job Bobby had to decline because of his poor health. One day he wanted his older friend's advice about an important letter to be sent to all the state chairmen. After reading it thoughtfully, Bobby looked up at Charlie and smiled:

Charlie, it's great, just about right for you, I'm sure. The only thing I can think to say is that it's a little bit flowery for me.

If he directed a group of twenty or so, he introduced each person to the others, and in the process, each person received a compliment and found out why the others were needed. His method was to take care of controversial business one-on-one behind the scenes. After the introductions, he reported something positive since the last meeting and reviewed the upcoming schedule. In a larger audience, he'd introduce a few of the ones he knew best, adding a sentence or two to relax the people he pointed out. Whenever a certain college friend from Tech was in the audience, the crowd heard something like:

There's ___ ____. He'll stand up so we can all get a good look. You can see he looks a lot like me. We both look like handsome hound dogs.

Bobby Jones was a master of the short, charming acceptance speech, but he was retiring in public and handed over the microphone as fast as possible. Charlie was happy to be up front, enjoying many people at once.

An example of a big meeting was one of his sold-out programs at the Atlanta History Center before the Masters. It was always well attended because of his reputation, but that night he shared the spotlight with a famous pro, Byron Nelson from Texas. Charlie was in his element. He didn't sing his favorite song, but his friends knew he would if he needed to. The lights dimmed, but nothing else worked. When he asked for the first slide, there was a "clunk" but no slide:

That's ok, run the video. Nothing. No light, no sound. Then he must have had a new thought because he broke into a smile.

Still ok, he said, *you can turn up the lights. We'll just visit with each other up here.*

Witnesses said what happened next was one of the greatest spontaneous conversations on golf and the Masters. It flowed back and forth between stage and audience and was capped off with a standing ovation. Everyone went home happy.

Comer remembers when and where he first heard his dad describe his career and talk about himself. It was at East Lake when Charlie and Tommy Barnes were invited to reminisce upstairs in the ruins of the Great Hall. Comer said it was late in 1993 and the last day of play in the old club before it was closed and transformed by Tom Cousins:

Charlie at the 1935 U.S. Open at Oakmont — age 21.

The old building was crumbling from neglect. Pieces of fallen plaster were all over the floor, and most of the lights didn't work. But someone kept refreshments coming, and the two old friends from East Lake opened up.

Charlie was admired for his behavior and personality as well as his accomplishments. Bernard Darwin wrote:

He hit the ball straight and far and was a sure and beautiful putter ... There has been no invading Champion more popular than Charlie Yates, whose cheerfulness and humour, of his own particular brand, made everybody like him (Darwin 1944).

In 1995, at the British Amateur at Hoylake, he was asked to sing again, and as usual he obliged his friends; they had not forgotten what he did when his side lost in 1938.

At St. Andrews in 1938 after Great Britain's first victory in the Walker Cup. Gordon Peters is smiling broadly to Charlie's right

Charlie with Arnold Palmer (L) in the 1960s. The best golfers enjoyed Charlie for more than his golf. He was chairman of the Press Committee at the Masters and responsible for the post-round interviews.

V

TOMMY BARNES

Georgia Golf Hall of Fame Member
Inducted 1989

Thomas William Barnes was born in Monroe, Ga., on November 9, 1915. A lifelong amateur golfer, Barnes qualified for the U.S. Amateur 16 consecutive times. He won the 1935 and '37 Atlanta City Amateur and the Bobby Jones Four-Ball and Dogwood Tournament five times each. During his college years, he captained the 1937 and '38 Georgia Tech teams. In 1941, he captured the Georgia Amateur title. He took the Pan-Am title in 1944, while serving in the U.S. Navy. Other titles include the 1938 and '46 Southeastern Amateur, 1946 Southeastern PGA Open, and 1947 and '49 Southern Amateur. Barnes played in the 1950 Masters Tournament. In 1988, at age 73, he shot a 62 at East Lake Country Club, breaking Bobby Jones's 1922 record of 63. He also served as a GSGA Director for 18 years, was the USGA Southeastern Sectional Committee Director for 14 years, directed the Southern Golf Association, and served as president of the Atlanta City Golf Association. Barnes was inducted into the Georgia Tech Athletic Hall of Fame in 1981, the Southern Golf Hall of Fame in 1987, and Atlanta Athletic Club Hall of Fame in 1995. He died on September 20, 2007.

Tommy Barnes was a legend at the Atlanta Athletic Club and East Lake.[1] Bobby Jones recommended him for junior membership at age fifteen after noticing the quality of his play in the City Amateur. Bobby was looking at a

---

1   He liked to say, *I'm a legend in my own mind.*

copy of his own swing. He committed himself to golf after watching Bobby hit one shot, and he said he needed help to see it:

It was a bright, sunny morning, and a crowd had formed around the first tee of the James L. Key Golf Course in 1923, when I was eight. I was so small I had to stand on a running board to see him, but I remember every detail like it was yesterday. Bob had on an outfit that had already been made famous in the newspapers and short films — tan plus fours, Argyle socks, and a collared shirt. His face was tanned, and he had a wide smile. He looked like he was honored that so many had come out to see him.

The first hole was a short par four, and when he hit his tee shot over the green, the crowd went wild. I was hooked and thought, 'I want to learn to do that just the way he did.'

When Tommy decided to get serious about copying Bobby's swing, he found a movie clip, played it again and again and built his own version. At East Lake, Bobby and Watts Gunn were his role models and mentors, but Watts was three years younger than Bobby and slightly closer to Tommy in age. They went out together more frequently.

Tommy: *I remember once when I had Watts down two or three holes in a match, and I was full of confidence, really hitting the ball. He was struggling, but he never stopped thinking. While walking off the tee after hitting our balls on number six [fifteen], he turned to me, 'Tommy, I didn't know you had changed your grip.' That made me wonder about my grip which, of course, I hadn't changed at all. After that I got to thinking that maybe I had, so I must have done something different from then on in. I got beat. At another time, Watts said, late in the day, 'Well, I see we're in the shank of the evening,' just to get the awful word in my head.*

After WWII, Tommy became Charlie Harrison's friend and mentor. Charlie was sixteen years younger, and they enjoyed each other. Although no formal lesson was given, Tommy shared his knowledge and experience during their frequent matches.

When the Athletic Club moved away a few years after the 1963 Ryder Cup, Tommy became a minority owner of East Lake, something beyond his wildest dreams in the 1930s. During the twenty-five-year period before Tom Cousins stepped in, all members and guests at East Lake Country Club who had never laid eyes on Bobby Jones knew that watching Tommy was as close as they could get.

He lived close by in Avondale and owned service stations that didn't take up much time. He would have come to play at East Lake every day anyway, but during those twenty-five years, he had two more serious missions in life. He was everyone's host and, since he was well known and proud of his home course, he was determined to keep it in shape. He was the oldest top golfer and felt responsible for its maintenance. He studied soils, grasses, drainage, effects of weather, and countless other parts of the game he had not thought much about when the Athletic Club's professional agronomists were there.

He called the U.S. Amateur the National Amateur, and although he qualified and competed again and again he never made it beyond the quarterfinals. When asked about Bobby's career he said, *The most impressive thing Bob Jones ever did was winning the National Amateur five times.*

A round of golf with Tommy Barnes was unforgettable. He was in constant motion, except when someone else was standing over a shot. When an older visitor was faced with an uneven or wet teeing area, he'd grab the tee markers and move them to a better spot:

Mr. _____, tee it up over here.

He was a natural teacher. When paired with a struggling, mediocre golfer, he knew what to say. He did not say to stop leaning toward the target when hitting, but suggested something positive.

Keep your head behind the ball.

On the green, since he was usually closer, he held the flag for everyone else. He read everyone's putts and conceded short ones, but usually putted his own, studying the line with a quick cock of the head before settling down to business.

"Think positive" was his mantra. A favorite story involved Pete Brown, a former Georgia Tech football player. When paired with Tommy in a club championship, Pete had no confidence in his swing and thought fate was against him.

Pete, Tommy said, *no one can be successful in this game with negative thoughts. You've got to have a positive attitude.*

That seemed to help, but in a few more holes, Pete fell back into negative language and became upset. This went on throughout the round. On the eighteenth tee, Pete's confidence collapsed again, and he started cussing himself, the game, and anything else he could think of. For about the tenth time, Tommy said, *Pete, you've got to stop all that negative talk.*

Finally, a smile crossed Pete's face.

Don't worry Tommy, he said, *I know I'm talking negative, but I'm thinking positive.*

Tommy had weathered so many personal storms in his life he was determined to enjoy every moment, but once in a while he came upon someone in a different mood: frustrated, sullen, and hostile. After being snarled at one day, he rode back to his group saying, *That guy needs to go to charm school.*

Allan Levey was a visitor who learned the game in Wisconsin. He played East Lake with Tommy before the renovation:[2]

It was magical to play with him and feel the presence of a Georgia golf legend. He changed my grip and swing during the round, and my game immediately fell apart. I tried to do it his way for several months, but finally gave up. I went back to my Yankee ways and was relieved I could hit the ball again.

In 1994, at age seventy-eight, Tommy visited Rosedale Golf Club in Toronto. He was hosted by Harry Kennedy and was the toast of the club. Members had been told in advance he'd played golf with Bobby Jones, and that was why they wanted to meet him. But when they heard his old-fashioned Southern accent, saw his animated face and eyes, and heard him tell a story, they stayed close. Although he was on his longest trip in many years and in a city and golf club he'd never seen, their hospitality made him feel at home.

There was a meeting of the Historical Society that night, and the member in charge of the program was ready to start, but very few members had appeared. The mystery was solved when they checked the bar. There was Tommy with a big grin, surrounded by about ten members and their wives. Everyone was in stitches from something he'd just said. Canadian-American relations took a big step forward that night.

The next morning, Tommy played Rosedale with Harry and Professional John Porter. John had come to Canada from South Herts Golf Club, the club in England where Harry Vardon had been the professional before John's time. Out on the course, while watching Tommy's swing at age seventy-eight, he smiled and shook his head. It seemed like the pro was checking off a list in his head, whispering to himself. Tommy's turn and swing weren't as full as they had been, but his new friends at Rosedale also knew where it had come from.

---

2   Chairman of Neurology at Emory

When Tommy was sitting or standing still, he looked his age, but on the golf course, he moved and played like a man in his fifties. He played so fast you had to keep watching or you'd miss the shot. There was no practice swing. As soon as he chose the club he wanted, he picked his target from a step or two behind the ball. Then he quickly stepped to the ball, took one last look, and settled down. He waggled two or three times, and then it started, slow and graceful and still working perfectly, as predictable and lazy as an old oil well, slowly rocking as it pumps. The shoulder turn was full, and the weight shifted smoothly back and forth as he came through the ball. The left knee came in, the right moved out, and everything was in fluid motion, except the head and eyes. They were fixed, rigid, and stable while surrounded by motion until they turned to follow the shot. He stayed behind the ball. The result was a slight draw at medium height.

A Canadian Eagle

On Saturday, October 21, 1995, during the only World Series won by the Atlanta Braves, Tommy helped host those same friends from Rosedale and Harry's son, John Kennedy. The three visitors had just started their long-awaited round at East Lake with him when John hit the shot of his life:

It was a two iron slightly uphill to the green of number one from 210 yards.[3] I could see it carry the bunker from where I was, but Tommy, who was much closer on the left up the hill, started yelling, 'It's in the hole!' and waving his arms. When we reached the green, I saw the pin was about twenty feet in on

(L-R) Tommy (in yellow), John Kennedy, John Porter, and Harry Kennedy, flanked by caddies in winter whites.

---

3   Now the tenth

my line from the front edge. Tommy, still celebrating, told us it hit and skipped right into the hole.

John stayed hot, for a while:

My score on the front nine was a bright light — 33, but the light was not so bright coming back in — 43, I think. I try not to think about that.

He ended his story with what may be the best short description of Tommy's swing ever written:

Tommy had a smooth, liquid swing that repeated itself effortlessly, over and over again.

A Visit with Rachel Barnes in 2017[4]

Tommy had typhoid fever in the first grade and almost died. He lost a lot of weight but fully recovered and gradually got his strength back. He first hit golf balls at the James L. Key course, but he frequently visited Doc Tumlin, who was a member of the Athletic Club and played at East Lake. That was really where he learned to play.

At age eight he worked as a caddy at the Key golf course and had to get there early for one special group of three young doctors who were interns at Grady Hospital. They paid him fifty cents to caddie nine holes before they went to work. Then Tommy went home from the course to get ready for school. He gave his mother the money, and she gave him a nickel, an apple, and a peanut butter sandwich.

He was given a five-dollar gold piece when he won his first tournament, which was for juniors at Druid Hills. He arrived with his clubs but without a golf bag, so a member loaned him his. I don't know how old Tommy was, but he was still small. I've seen a picture of him standing behind that bag, and it looked like a golf bag with a head on it.

He volunteered for the Navy on December 8, 1941, one day after Pearl Harbor, and was sent to Charleston for training in 1942. I was there working in Navy Public Relations in the Fort Sumter Hotel on The Battery. Our office published a newspaper featuring the young officers assigned there, so I saw pictures of all the young officers as they arrived. I picked out Tommy from a group that included John F. Kennedy. All the other girls were talking about Kennedy, but Tommy was the one I was interested in. Sportswriter Ed Miles was there in public relations and knew Tommy, so I asked him to introduce us.

Tommy patrolled for submarines along the South Carolina coast in 1942, but the Navy didn't have enough boats, so they had to use refitted shrimp boats. I have a picture

---

4   Tommy's wife for sixty-four years.

of him in his Ensign's dress whites standing on the bow. He looks like he's the captain of a battleship.[5] After Charleston, he was assigned to Radar School in Miami. He could not leave for three months, so I decided to go there. We were married in Miami on June 10, 1944. Charlie Yates was his best man.

After the war, we settled in Atlanta in 1945 near East Lake. Our first house was on Tilson Street off East Lake Drive, but the next year we moved to Alston Drive across from the golf course. That second house was on the lot where Rick Burton lives.

The passage of time makes it difficult to remember how many tournaments an accomplished golfer won, but certain honors will last. The Georgia State Golf Association (GSGA), a force for golf since 1916, describes its award process:

The GSGA recognizes Players of the Year for men, women, senior men, senior women, junior boys, and junior girls during a luncheon following its annual meeting. The overall Player of the Year receives the Tommy Barnes Award.

Kid Stars Warm Pals

Tommy (L) with Charlie Yates

Tommy could reach the green of the par five 16th (now the par four 7th) in two shots

---

5   There are men and women alive today who were babies on the beach at Pawley's Island in 1942 when Tommy was patrolling for German submarines off shore.

VI

CHARLIE HARRISON

Georgia Golf Hall of Fame Member
Inducted 1989

Charles Harrison was born in Atlanta, Ga., on June 25, 1931. He won the 1947 Atlanta City Junior Championship and then went on to letter in golf for four years at Georgia Tech. A lifelong amateur, Harrison won the Atlanta Amateur a record 10 times, captured the Atlanta Athletic Club Championship nine times, and the Atlanta Country Club Championship six times during his illustrious career. He also claimed victories in the 1955 Southern Amateur and the 1959 Georgia Amateur. In 1966, Harrison was ranked 13th-best amateur in the country, and in 1967, he was an alternate for the U.S. Walker Cup team. He qualified for the U.S. Amateur 16 times, placing as a quarterfinalist in 1959 and finishing fifth in 1972. He was also a quarterfinalist in the 1980 British Amateur and twice played in the Masters Tournament. Harrison served as a director of the Southern Golf Association and was president of the Atlanta Golf Association from 1971–85. He was elected to the Georgia Tech Hall of Fame in 1978 and Georgia Sports Hall of Fame in 1991. The East Lake Golf Club has honored him by establishing the Harrison Scholarship for its employees.

This Georgia Golf and Sports Hall-of-Fame member also grew up at East Lake and learned the game there. His father joined the Athletic Club during WWII, and Charlie's first swings were taken while following his dad around the course. He was a natural athlete and found himself in the perfect place. The AAC had all the sports he wanted, inside and out, and golf champions were there every day.

Charlie: *When I was fifteen, Assistant Professional Henry Lindner told me about a junior tournament at Bobby Jones Golf Course in Buckhead and said I should enter. I shot 118 that first try, but the next year in the same tournament had an 82 at Druid Hills. Several things happened during that year to explain the thirty-six shot difference. I became taller and stronger and also became a better putter, mainly for one reason. Juniors couldn't play on weekends without a regular member to take them out, so I spent a lot of time on the practice green waiting to be paired up.*

Although I continued to play golf and other sports, I had not had any lessons. I had forgotten about that tournament until Henry reminded me a few days beforehand. He said if I would meet him in the practice area the next morning, he would give me a lesson that would help. He asked to see me hit my eight iron a few times, then asked me to hit it 'like Charlie Yates.' He explained, then showed me what he meant by taking the club back on the outside and bringing it down inside without stopping at the top, making a loop at the top. When I tried it, I saw a little hook for the first time. Later, I learned it was called the figure-eight swing. Jim Furyk is the best example of it today on the PGA Tour, but Lee Trevino also has that loop, so I'm in good company. I had attended a Harold Sergeant junior clinic with eight others at fourteen, but that thirty-minute lesson at sixteen from Henry Lindner was the only personal lesson I had.

I really learned to play by watching Tommy Barnes. I adopted his stance and his waggle on the course, but I didn't follow him in one way. Even on the practice tee, Tommy would put the next ball down and go through his complete pre-shot routine, first taking his stance a step or two behind the ball, set up there, then set up again over the ball. I was too impatient for all that.

Like Bobby, Charlie Yates, and Tommy, Charlie went to Tech and joined the golf team, but unlike the others, he was competitive in other sports. He and his swimming teammates set the 1951 Southeastern Conference record in the 400-yard freestyle relay.

As a young boy he lived a few miles north in Decatur, so he didn't live across from the golf course when he began, like Bobby, Charlie Yates, and Alexa, but eventually, he came full circle. He and his wife, Sylvia, live across Alston Drive from the course.[1]

---

1   Charlie lives in the most historic house at East Lake and one of the earliest still standing in Atlanta, the Robert Alston House, located opposite the landing area of the twelfth hole. Rick Burton lives across from the tee of the same hole, just a strong drive east of Charlie. For them, home course has a double meaning.

Because of ROTC military training at Tech, when he graduated he joined the Army as a 2nd Lieutenant but didn't have to give up golf. The high point of his two-year commitment came when he was captain of the Fourth Army team that won the 1953 All-Army Championship at Pebble Beach.

I was the only officer so was automatically made captain, but I was a clear number three in golf. The best was Private Billy Maxwell, who came to East Lake ten years later as a member of Arnold Palmer's Ryder Cup team. Our number two was another future pro, Private 'Buster' Reed.

After the service, Charlie joined the insurance firm of fellow East Lake golfer and World War II hero, Bill Leide.[2] It was a perfect job for him. Bill was more experienced and became another friend and mentor. And since the careers of golf and insurance complemented each other, he was able to play golf and compete in tournaments when he was at his physical and mental peak.

Bobby Jones and Charlie Yates were well known for their gentlemanly behavior when they lost, so Charlie was asked how Tommy behaved when he was beaten. His first answer was, *I don't know, I never saw him lose,* but after a few minutes, he remembered he had beaten Tommy once in a club championship. After the match, Tommy came up to him smiling and said exactly the right thing: *Charlie, I knew you were going to win. You always play your best in tournaments.*

He was greatly complimented. After that day, when he fell behind in competition he thought, *Tommy said you were at your best in tournaments, so get your act together and win this thing.* His competitive career flourished.

Like his role model, Charlie thinks positive, and respect for others is built-in, especially people he meets and likes on the golf course. During the U.S. Open qualifying rounds at East Lake in 1965, he was paired with George Johnson, a fine black golfer whose company he enjoyed on the course. In between the morning and afternoon rounds, all players typically had lunch in the clubhouse, and Charlie invited George to join him inside. The reaction of some members took him by surprise.

Mandatory separation of the races seems strange today, but in Atlanta in the mid-1960s, it was the rule. Some members Charlie considered his friends

---

2   After D-Day, Lieutenant Commander William Leide received a citation from Admiral R. Stark for conspicuous bravery as commander of a landing craft tank (LCT) task force. He was also director of naval operations under General George Patton during the crossing of the Rhine. Later, he shook the hand of King George VI and received medals from Britain, France, and Belgium. He grew up in Atlanta and graduated from Boys High School at age fifteen and Yale at twenty.

didn't like what he had done. There was talk of trying to get him suspended or even removed from the club. But later, after being told to back off by more level-headed members, especially Tommy Barnes, they thought better of it. No effort was made against him.

Charlie had a conversation with Bobby Jones about the issue of clubs hosting national tournaments in those days. During their conversation, Bobby told him he had written Augusta National about their position on racial matters. He said his letter was on file there clearly stating that anyone who qualified for the Masters would be invited to play. Their race would not be considered.

These experiences brought Charlie closer to the black community. When the chance came for him to join the board of a bank serving the minority population, he followed his instincts and joined. That took his education to a different level, and he made good friends in the process.

Since he was such a successful golfer, it is possible to dwell on the tournaments he won and how he hit certain shots, but this is not primarily about his golf game. Instead, it will focus on what he did with those skills off the course and how he helped advance the new mission of neighborhood revival. Golf became the best way for him to teach and encourage children living in the neighborhood, and he didn't have to commute from another place. He lived there.

At first, his role was to help recruit corporate members to support the mission of East Lake and attract minority members. A phone call gave him a new role.

In 1994, the club president, Walter Ashmore, asked me to put on a golf clinic for about forty kids in the summer. But since our golf facilities weren't ready, he agreed to let me start a motivational clinic instead. I went to work setting it up.

Scarlet Pressley came to Atlanta to join the newly formed East Lake Foundation as its first Director of Community affairs. She was the liaison between the foundation and families living there.[3] She and Charlie taught and mentored children from the housing project and neighborhood, and they reached out to the wider community for new role models and experiences.

---

3   Scarlet Pressley-Brown was at East Lake for the important first six years, but she didn't retire from good works. She remains a positive force in Atlanta. She serves as Vice President of Marketing at the National Center for Civil & Human Rights and was awarded the Outstanding Georgia Citizen Award by the Secretary of State. In 2006, the Atlanta Business League named her one of Atlanta's Top Black Women of Influence.

He called the bank president, who responded quickly and offered more than Charlie had asked for — his daughter and her boyfriend would come mentor the young people. She was a state record-holder in track, and he was Donnie Davis, the Georgia Tech quarterback that year.

The summer mentoring program was designed to broaden the horizons of the children and be fun. After breakfast at the club, they either stayed there to interact with successful people who came to them, or they went on field trips.

We took them to interesting places, including the Naval Air Station in Marietta during the first Gulf War, where they met soldiers, including helicopter pilots, and to the Falcons' training camp in Suwanee to watch practice, thanks to John Imlay, one of the team's owners. They met coach June Jones and star Billy 'White Shoes' Johnson.

Charlie called another friend who was head of personnel at Church's Fried Chicken, and he brought his son, a high school soccer star. Also, an Equifax executive invited them to the home office to look over the computers.

That two-week clinic was a good beginning, and Walter, Scarlet, and Charlie were encouraged. The next year, Walter asked them to bring twelve youngsters to the club every day after school, six from the housing project and six from the neighborhood. Scarlet identified the twelve and received their parents' permissions. Charlie recruited two black golf professionals, Ruel Martin and Billy Clark. He and Scarlet shared the job of taking the children home. He delivered six to their front doors inside the project after dark. There were no incidents. She took the neighborhood children home.

Two students from East Lake Meadows illustrate the difference between teaching and mentoring. The first stands out in his memory because of the striking difference between his ability to drive and putt. He could hit the ball a long way, but almost every putt he tried was hit so hard the ball went off the green. He kept saying he hated to putt, hated to putt, again and again. He stayed negative until a famous man became involved. One day, Charlie happened to tell the students that Jack Nicklaus always said putting was important and a big reason he won so many tournaments. The student came to the next session with a library book on Jack Nicklaus, and Charlie decided to write Jack. Soon, the student received a carefully written, three-paragraph letter from Jack himself on his Golden Bear stationery. It began, *A mutual friend, Charles Harrison, told me …*

The letter encouraged him and let him know it was important to learn to putt well. It also emphasized hard work and persistence, and it changed the young man's attitude. Charlie had the letter framed and gave it to him on his birthday.

The effect of focusing on the individual is also illustrated by a second student. Since children naturally want to hit a ball with a stick and run around, even a small group can get out of hand. Leon and Charles quickly found out that the way to impose discipline was to make them earn the privilege to play. Access to golf depended on listening and on their behavior in class and after school. The young man loved golf and ran to the tee as soon as he could, but his behavior became a problem. When he balled up his fist at a teacher, punishment was swift. He was allowed to come to the tee but could not touch a club. He had to sit and watch his friends, who all knew what had happened. Soon, the messages from the school were positive.

A teacher asked, *What happened to cause your grades to go from Fs and Ds to Cs and Bs?*

She got a simple answer: *I want to play golf.*

He took advantage of his second chance and was eventually selected by the foundation to introduce Tiger Woods before the opening tee shot at the Charlie Yates Golf Course, the home course of the academy.

Charlie had discovered his new mission, a late-life career that let him use his golfing talents and friendliness to contribute to what he already knew was an important program committed to the success of children. Personal experience had taught him that self-study and practice required time-management skills, turn-taking, and listening — all fundamental in golf. The charge to him was to use his experience in the game to reach common ground with the children and teach them life lessons. When asked for a specific example, he quickly described the importance of paying attention:

I loved asking the students, 'What sport does Michael Jordan play?' Every hand always went up, 'Basketball, basketball!' 'No, I didn't ask what he did play. I asked what does he play? The correct answer is golf. He plays every day.'

The tiny program received a grown-up name, The East Lake Junior Golf Academy, and Leon

Leon's successor, Sam Puryear, on May 12, 1998, teaching the new generation how to play – (Golf With A Purpose)

Gilmore, a graduate of Hamilton College, was hired to run it. His father had grown up in public housing and become an engineer. When Leon arrived and asked Charlie to help him, the East Lake program flourished.

Charlie and his wife, Sylvia, unexpectedly became joint landlords. Soon after he arrived, Sylvia asked Leon where he planned to live.

I'll stay with friends in Vinings, he answered.

Sylvia said Atlanta traffic and living so far away would make it hard to arrive on time and get home when he wanted to. She showed him a house they had just finished renovating to sell, a four-bedroom red brick house nearby on Tilson Street. When Leon saw it, he said he couldn't afford it.

How much can you afford? she asked.

$500, he replied.

You just rented it.

Leon was happy there and had a positive effect on the kids. He also got an education. When he visited apartments in the East Lake Meadows housing project, he was stunned to see so many children at home instead of in school, alone or with a parent on drugs. The TV was blaring away all day; kids were eating cereal with only water, on and on. After his first visit, Leon came to Charlie and Sylvia with tears in his eyes.

Charlie: *He was always welcome at our dinner table. We became close — he called us his white parents.*

Today, the annual Charlie Yates Memorial Golf Tournament pairs young people from the First Tee and Drew Charter School with community supporters of East Lake.[4] Yates family members host the event.

Charlie's leadership with children at the beginning of the East Lake Foundation and his ongoing commitment to the staff at East Lake led to an honor that will preserve his name, The Harrison Scholarship. Since its founding in 1998, more than eighty educational scholarships have been awarded to employees of East Lake Golf Club and the Charlie Yates Golf Course.

A final memory connects Sylvia to his other loves, golf and storytelling. His favorite year was 1980 because it was the year they got married and took a

---

4   The First Tee of East Lake is the new name of the East Lake Junior Golf Academy that Charlie began and nurtured with Scarlet, Leon, and Sam. Sessions include a fun, group setting for youth ages seven through eighteen regardless of background or previous experience. It is now part of the World Golf Federation's First Tee program that has over a thousand chapters in the U.S., including five in Hawaii. Canada and Japan also have chapters. Its Founding Partners are the LPGA, Augusta National Golf Club, the PGA, the PGA Tour, and the USGA. The First Tee is growing and is here to stay.

dream honeymoon trip to Paris, but it wasn't a typical first trip by a bride and groom. First stop was Porthcawl, South Wales, for him to play in the British Amateur. When he learned his first-round opponent would be the current Mid-England champion, he told Sylvia, *We'll be in Paris sooner than we thought.*

They made it to Paris, but not right away. He won his first four matches and at age fifty found himself in the quarter-finals, the only American still playing. When he lost his last match on the first extra hole, off to Paris they went, as happy as two clams at high tide.

The 1980 British Amateur, he said, *had really been a win.*

Walking together down the fairways during that tournament on their honeymoon stands out as one of the fondest memories of their lives.

Charles Harrison receiving an Atlanta Athletic Club trophy from Bobby Jones in 1945

Charlie with the platter for winning the 1953 Atlanta Amateur and (L-R) his brother Jim, with his first-flight trophy, their father Jim, and mother Louise Wickliffe Wurm Harrison

Charlie and Sylvia walking up his favorite fairway in 2017, as happy as two clams…

PART TWO

THE GOLF COURSE

A WALK THROUGH TIME
AT EAST LAKE

VII

THE START
ONE THROUGH SIX

Before golfers start to play, they typically hit practice balls and putt, and at East Lake both places are unusual. In the 1990s when Jack Nicklaus gave a demonstration, he first said a few words to the audience, then turned to hit some shots with his sand wedge. He smiled and shook his head:

This is the only practice range I've ever seen over water.

There are two putting greens — a large one down by the lake and a smaller one close to the entrance.[1] But a hundred years ago, when Alexa and Bobby started their rounds, the larger green down by

Before he turned to his left to hit

the lake did not exist; there was only a smaller one between the first and tenth tees. This is where young Bobby liked to practice putting in the moonlight:

I remember back in my high school days, I was living within the range of a good iron shot from the East Lake course, and on nights when the moon was out, I used to go over to the club and putt, with a friend and neighbor, on the practice green near the tenth tee [today's first]. The moonlight, of course, revealed the hole, and it also made visible the more prominent slopes and irregularities — worm casts and the like. In this half-revealing light, it was a source of wonderment to my friend and

---

1   Three of Bobby's most famous putts are easy to re-create on the big green. End to end, there is room for the longest putt he made in competition, the 120-foot eagle putt in the 1927 British Open; and there's enough elevation change to try the other two. Next in his career was the twelve-foot, downhill left-to-right putt he made for par on the eighteenth to reach the playoff in the 1929 U.S. Open at Winged Foot. The third is best visualized by standing on the part of the green closest to the lake. He made a double-breaking, uphill birdie from forty feet on eighteen to win the U.S. Open at Interlachen in 1930. It was the third leg of the Grand Slam.

me that we invariably putted better than in broad daylight, especially when it came to holing out from distances up to eight or ten feet.

There must be something to be learned from that moonlight putting. I believe it to be this — the men who putt well on greens good and bad must have schooled themselves to see a putting green as we used to see it in the moonlight (Jones 1966).

He quoted Alex Smith's response to why he never removed worm casts from the path of the ball since the little obstructions might deflect the ball away from the hole:

Aye, and they might bounce it into the cup, too.[2]

HISTORY ACROSS THE FENCE

Alexa's house and her parents

The first tee is in the middle of the historic side of the property. If not playing a match and there's time to linger on the tee, it's interesting to imagine it's early summer in 1913. Close to 2 p.m., golfers would have heard the Suburban Express pulling up at the end of the streetcar line close to the entrance of the club. The regular streetcar ride from Atlanta to East Lake took thirty minutes and made many stops, but for packages and small freight, there was one nonstop car every day called the Suburban Express, which left downtown at the corner of Alabama and Pryor Streets. It brought medicine

---

2   Alex Smith, from Carnoustie, was the first head professional at East Lake; he became a two-time U.S. Open champion (1906 and 1910). As club pro, he preceded his brother-in-law, Jimmy Maiden, Stewart Maiden (the model of the Jones swing), 1909 U.S. Open Champion George Sargent, and his son Harold Sargent, who became President of the PGA.

or other supplies to the village of East Lake that had been put on the car by husbands working downtown.

Most of the houses across the fence on Alston Drive would be filled with families who have just arrived by moving van from Atlanta for the summer. A man with a beard might be standing with his family in front of the stucco bungalow next to the corner lot on East Lake Drive. That would be Dr. Stirling, the specialist from Scotland, with Nora, his English wife, and their three daughters — Janet, Alexa, and Nora.

East of the Stirling house, the ground sloped down to the frog pond at the bottom of the hill.[3] During the summer, the Goldsmith family lived in a brown shingled house, which stood facing east on Daniel Avenue at the corner of Alston Drive. In 1913, their nine-year-old daughter, Mariana, might be watching the tee from outside the fence. She would be dressed for swimming and waiting for golfers to hit their drives. As soon as they finished, she would sneak under the fence, dash across the fairway, and dive into the lake to *start my perfect summer.* In 1917, Mariana was one of the young women photographed raising the flag in front of the two-year-old clubhouse.[4]

After crossing the lake, an old-fashioned one-story brick house, now painted gray, is visible in the middle of the block on Daniel Avenue, facing the

Mariana, checking her story in 1996

1917 TEEN-AGERS AT EAST LAKE DEDICATION
Letf to right, Mrs. John S. Knox (the former Mariana Goldsmith), Virginia Ashe, Mrs. Paine Saffarans (Douglass Paine) and Mrs. Fleming Law (Margaret Rogers).

---

3 The brick house east of the Stirlings, the park, and the playground were not present.
4 The flag-raising photograph is displayed in one of the tall kiosks in the Great Hall.

park. A white wooden structure is behind it. The brick house was Mary Bell Meador's boarding house. Mariana said the wooden structure (then located on the street beside the boarding house and also owned by Mrs. Meador) was where Colonel Jones first brought his wife and five-year-old son to escape the heat in the city in 1907. Bobby took his first swing at a golf ball in the front yard of the boarding house. He had been given an adult cleek [one iron] by Fulton Colville, a family friend, who noticed the end of the long club *poked him woefully in the stomach so that he missed the ball altogether.* Mr. Colville quickly sawed it off, and the young boy took to it (Keeler and Rice 1953).

The old boarding house is a hundred yards from the ditch along the golf course, the distance of Bobby's first golf hole. Daniel Avenue and the ditch became a makeshift course he played with Frank, Mrs. Meador's son (Jones and Keeler 1927).

Mariana remembered that everyone planning to eat with Mrs. Meador responded to the announcement of mealtime. Wiley, Mrs. Meador's butler, used a megaphone to call across the golf course, *Supper is all ready.*

Painting in the clubhouse of the 1st hole

ONE

Photo © 2015-2017, Dave Sansom

Today, members play the first as a 493-yard uphill par five that begins with a drive over water, so golfers who take time to hit practice balls over the lake will be glad they did. In professional tournaments, it has been a par four — 411 yards in the 1963 Ryder Cup and 469 in the 2016 Tour Championship.

Alexa commented on this hole in 1919 when it was a 408-yard par four: *This is a drive, a brassie, then a mashie or niblick.*[5] *I can average a five.*

In 1922, Bobby played it as a 425-yard par four. O.B. Keeler wrote: *Drive far up the hill. Mashie to ten feet from the cup. Missed putt, ball hitting cup. Took a four.*

In the 1920s, after Bobby won the U.S. Open in 1923, his friends used to kid him because he'd never had a hole-in-one. He took them over to the fence to look down on Daniel Avenue and the ditch along the road and announced,

I had several one-shot holes in that ditch before I was six years old.

---

5   Names of clubs in 1919 and 1922: Driver–Driver; Brassie–two wood; Spoon–three, four or five wood; Baffy–approach wood; Cleek or Driving iron–one iron; Mid-iron–two iron; Mid mashie–three iron; Mashie iron–four iron; Mashie–five iron; Spade mashie–six iron; Mashie niblick–seven iron; Pitching niblick or Lofting iron–eight iron; Niblick–nine iron; putter–putter; Jigger–an iron with a thin blade frequently used for chipping with an angle of loft similar to a five iron. The pitching wedge and sand wedge did not exist.

Alexa's and Bobby's clubs had hickory shafts. Their woods were all wood, except for leather grips and lead weights. Bobby called his driver Jeanie Deans, after Sir Walter Scott's heroine in *The Heart of Midlothian*. His named his putter Calamity Jane.

Arnold Palmer came to East Lake for an exhibition match in 1958 after winning his first Masters, and Charlie Harrison remembers a shot he hit on this hole. When he reached his drive, he asked his caddie for the distance to the green and was told 180 yards. Arnold seemed uncertain and looked at Charlie, who said it was 140. Arnold nodded and selected the club that put him on the green.

The 2016 Tour Championship was the first to play with the new routing, and after the tournament, Rick Burton and Chad Parker rode out on new number one, which had been the tenth for 101 years.

Rick: *Rees moved this fairway to the right and built those mounds on the left side to keep balls from going into Alston Drive. The green was moved to the right to make more room for the new back tee on number two.*

Chad: *On the green, Rees added a pin position back right by flattening an area to make it more suitable. It's difficult to see unless you're on top of it. The new pin position created an uphill putt and a challenging chip from over the green on that side. The hardest putt for me here is from back left to a pin down front or left of center. A little short of the green is a good chipping and putting position on this and most others. Many holes at East Lake have a little apron in front.*

Rees Jones gave his greens elevations and depressions, and some are obvious, but many are not. This is one reason caddies are so important. They play the course themselves and understand the greens. When golfers don't know the greens and are surprised by unseen breaks, time is wasted and frustration builds. A caddie is an important companion out there on any round but especially when guests or family members are there. Praise of good shots by an East Lake caddie helps everyone relax.

Over the years, the course has been used many times as a qualifying site for major tournaments, especially the National Amateur, and one day in the late fifties, Charlie Harrison and Tommy Barnes tried to qualify together.

Charlie remembers Tommy had an excellent first twenty-seven holes:

He'd been playing so well he probably could have bogied every hole on the back nine that day and still qualified.

Nonetheless. like every other golfer, a good performance only whetted his appetite for more.

Charlie: *Years ago, there was a large oak tree on the right side of this fairway. Since there were no bunkers on the left and the fairway tilted that way from the center, a player would risk OB with a drive to the center of the fairway out of the way of the tree. Almost always top players went a little to the right and had to deal with the big tree. Well, on his second shot, Tommy hit a hard, low fade, just like he wanted to, but as so often happens, it hit the last branch and dropped straight down. Tommy took his iron, walked angrily up to that branch, and swung like he was going to chop it off. Instead, he lost his balance and cracked himself hard on the right ankle with the blade. He could hardly walk the rest of the back nine, he had hurt himself so badly.*

Many years later, Tommy got his revenge. He was in exactly the same situation behind the same tree. A playing partner laughed and challenged him by saying to the others in the group, *Well, let's see what the great Tommy Barnes does now.*

A few seconds later, Tommy sliced his iron around the tree, and the ball bounded up onto the green and jumped into the hole for eagle two … Tommy winked at his friends and said, *There's nothing to that shot.*

The beginning of the back nine (U.S. Amateur final, 2001)

The former house of another famous East Lake golfer, Watts Gunn, is across the street. The two-story frame house still sits just off the first green, surrounded by huge magnolias. Bobby and Watts were opponents in the final of the U.S. Amateur at Oakmont in 1925. It was, and still is, the only time two members of the same club have faced each other in the final of that tournament. On the first tee at Oakmont, Watts turned to Bobby and asked, *Are you going to give me my usual four strokes?*

He said later that Bobby smiled and said, *I'm going to give you hell today.*

He wasn't kidding, Watts said. *That's exactly what he did.*

Actually, Watts was a sensation at Oakmont. He electrified the large gallery all week with his excellent play. The final match turned on the famous Ghost Hole, the twelfth.

Bobby: *And my third shot (the hole is of 600 yards) was bunkered at the green, and Watts' was well on, for a sure par five. When I went down into that bunker I was morally certain of one thing. If Watts took that hole from me I'd never catch him. He was playing the most ferocious brand of inspirational golf I had ever seen; he was 2 under par now, and he was about to take another hole from me* (Jones and Keeler 1927).

Bobby got up and down with a ten-foot putt for a half, reeled off a *hot run,* and finally *settled matters* in the afternoon round.

Watts was also famous for his golfing advice: *Keep your head down and your tail up,* and his favorite exclamation: *Jeepers-Creepers!*

In 1993, before the renovation, Watts was taken on a ride around East Lake, which he hadn't seen for years. Cart paths and golf carts were all over the place.

He said, *East Lake, I can't believe it; where are all the caddies?*

Photo © 2015-2017, Dave Sansom

The entrance to the 1st green

TWO

© Chet Burgess

For the PGA Tour this is a 197-yard par three, but it ordinarily plays 181. It's slightly uphill, and when the pin is on the left, the bold shot risks being discarded down a steep hill.

The bronze plaque by the tee describes Bobby's first hole in one and is fixed to a boulder that has been at East Lake for eons. When Rees Jones rebuilt the course in 1994, a goal was to open up the view of the lake on what are now the fourteenth and eighteenth holes. The stone was unearthed during those excavations and placed with a few others on the hill overlooking the eighteenth fairway. It was brought here in 2016 to display this Bobby Jones story where it happened. It has been above ground only twenty-four years.

Bobby's shot was in 1927, and he used a hickory-shafted mashie iron (four iron). The ball traveled exactly 173 yards. His second ace, also with a four iron, was at Augusta Country Club in 1932. Bobby's friend Eugene Black is quoted: *No man has mastered golf until he has realized that his good shots are accidents and his bad shots good exercise.* The plaque ends with statistics. For amateurs the chance of making an ace is 1 in 13,600. For professionals it's 1 in 2,500.

Alexa: *175 Yards, Par three — I play this with a spoon. I can't quite make it with an iron; I quite often get a three.*

Bobby played the same distance in 1922: *Jigger to twenty feet from pin. Two putts.*

Rick: *I like this hole — it's one of the best out here. If you're putting from anywhere above the pin, you'll have an excruciatingly fast putt. If you miss this green, always miss it right — you don't want to go left here.*

In the 1963 Ryder Cup, Arnold Palmer played it from 235 yards, about forty yards longer than pros today and over fifty yards longer than the back tee for members. When Arnold first saw it from that tee, the hole seemed to curve around a tall tree on the right about a hundred yards out that made the shot tighter. He turned to a friend, 'I've never seen a dog-leg par three before.'

Chad: *Jerry Kelly made the only ace in the Tour Championship here. They seem to happen all the time at Augusta National, but for some reason are rare on this course. The most unusual one here was when the bunkers were closed and large pieces of plywood were needed to get equipment in. A tee shot hit the plywood, bounced up on the green, and rolled in the hole.*

Charlie Harrison remembers that Ernest "Siege-Gun" Harrison (no kin) once hit it so far left the ball disappeared over the houses.

He explained, *I hit it perfect. I just aimed it wrong.*

From the member's tees in October of 1992, Tommy pushed a seven iron into the right bunker. He was disgusted with himself:

If a man can't hit a green with a seven iron, he ought to give up the game.

Despite a back brace, he had even par 72 that day, which was two weeks short of his seventy-seventh birthday. Tommy Barnes was one of the few men alive who had a bad day when he shot his age.

In 2015, this green was the site of a crucial birdie putt by Jordan Spieth in the final round of the Tour Championship, and if there's no pressure from behind, it's fun to re-create it. It was the beginning of the back nine, and both Jordan and Henrik Stenson were red hot. On this hole, Henrik hit a perfect tee shot within a few feet of the pin and Jordan was front left, forty-five feet away. The pin was cut back left, beyond the bunker on that side, just over the elevation. The long uphill putt had to be hit close to the second cut by the bunker. It broke four feet to the right at the end and dropped, dead center.

Henrik's face on TV was almost as priceless as the putt. He had a wry smile that said, *Are you kidding me?* As he went to line up his own birdie try, he gave Jordan a fist pump and a little pat on the shoulder.

Later, Henrik said, *You're feeling like you've got a good chance to make up some ground, but he just poured that in the middle. It's fun to watch and say well done.*

Jordan's putt was similar to Bobby's birdie putt to win the 1930 U.S. Open. That was a forty-foot uphill putt that also broke sharply right at the end.

Jones Scholar David Roemer outdid Jordan here in more relaxed circumstances. He had his first hole in one on March 15, 2015, eighty-eight years after Bobby's.

I was playing with my friends Dan Costa, Michael Seminer, and Vijay Makar. Vijay lives in the neighborhood, so he walked over with his wife and daughter to watch from behind the fence by the green.

We played from the green tees (147 yards), and I hit an eight iron into the wind that felt good. It tracked for the pin and bounced once. For a split second there was doubt — it either dropped in the hole or rolled behind the flag. We didn't see it again, but we heard cheering, first from Vijay's family, then even louder by my friends. My caddy said he clubbed me down — that I had asked for a seven-iron because of the wind — but I don't remember that. Chad rode up before we knew it and gave me the flag, which I still treasure. I had never had a hole-in-one, but friends and family members who struggle to break 90 had done it. I'd always thought it was pure luck but changed that day — it's all skill.

Photo © 2015-2017, Dave Sansom

The position of the pin when Jordan Spieth's
forty-five foot birdie putt surprised Henrik Stenson

THREE

Photo © 2015-2017, Dave Sansom

There are two illusions to consider here.

Golfers turn to the west on the third and get their first look at Atlanta's skyline, but it's only a preview of the views coming up from the sixth green and seventh tee. From this tee, a flicker of gold in the top of the trees is the sun's reflection off the dome of the State Capitol, six miles away.

Alexa was usually not challenged here: *380 Yards, Par four — My game here is a drive and a pitching iron to the green. I get a four there frequently.*

Bobby: *390 Yards, Par four — Drive. Mashie-niblick to eight feet from cup. One putt.*

It is harder now. Seventy-five years after Alexa, Rees Jones added a wide front bunker and a fast, tricky green. This peaceful-looking 379-yard downhill par four has picked up some drama.

Rick: *I like short, downhill par fours, and I love this one. There's an illusion concerning the slope of this green that tricks golfers. From the fairway, it looks like the green is slanted to hold their shots, but the center of the putting surface is basically flat, and the grain goes towards the lake. Balls tend to keep going and roll off. Instead of a birdie putt, the third shot may become a tough chip from Bermuda rough.*

Chad: *On the tee shot, you should not challenge that big bunker by trying to go over. The best drive is left center, but most people think they'll be rewarded by driving over the bunker. From the tee, players can't see how far to the left the rough comes over beyond the bunker. They think it's all fairway there. If that rough is deep, the hoped-for birdie may become a bogey. I like the way this fairway is shaped, especially the way it looks from the green, curving downhill around the bunker. If you overcook it and get it in the rough on the left, you may be blocked by the tree. I'd rather be long than short here — that's a really deep bunker.*

Bobby was almost killed by lightning while putting on this green. After the first three legs of the Grand Slam in the summer of 1930, a bolt of lightning struck the ground only forty yards away, and another struck the next tee. Bobby and his group ran for the clubhouse. The next bolt struck the large double chimney just before they reached cover. That last strike threw bricks one hundred yards, and one barely missed doing serious damage. The falling debris tore Bobby's shirt and opened a six-inch cut on his shoulder.

Charlie Harrison had the first birdie of his life on this hole in 1945 when he was fourteen. There was a large grass trap in the center of the fairway 150 yards from the green. He hit his second shot over the hazard but was well short of the green. He holed out the third with his hickory-shafted seven iron.

Robert Hamilton hitting from the rough beyond the bunker in the Amateur final

In 1990, after hitting his tee shot well over the old fairway bunker 200 yards from the white tees, Tommy Barnes was asked if Bobby Jones could have carried the bunker from the blue tees, fifty yards behind.

Easy. Bob Jones could hit a golf ball as far as he needed to. But I never heard him say that he'd hit it just right. After a drive of 250 yards, I'd say: 'Great drive, Bob.' All he'd say was, 'a little on the heel' or, 'a little on the toe.' He was never satisfied with his own game.

In 2017 Nic Cooper, an English visitor, finally got to play after a long wait. When he got his first look at the curving, mouth-like bunker in front of this green, he said, *Look, it's laughing at us.*

FOUR

Photo © 2015-2017, Dave Sansom

Next up is a 382-yard par four which winds up a gentle hill. There are dangers here. Professionals will have a tee shot between two pines that look like goal posts. A drive from any tee that drifts right might bounce through the trees and finish far down the hill in the next fairway. That would require a difficult recovery shot over trees.

Rick: *There's another illusion here that will frustrate golfers who want to open up the hole by hitting to an apparently flat area 100-130 yards from the green. It's hard to believe, but some of the pros actually hit their drives up to this area. It looks flat from a distance, but the fairway actually slopes to the right. Those shots may run down to the right off the fairway into difficult rough. Since the rough is much higher during the tournament, that slight tilt of the ground could turn a birdie into a bogey.*

Looking back through the goal posts

Chad: *From the members' tees or even the black, I use a three-wood, because if I use a driver and lose it right, I'll run out of fairway real quick. The line for the drive is along the walking path toward the last tree on the left up by the green.*

81

The prevailing breeze here is behind the player, and there's not much room between the back of the green and fence. Since the Bermuda greens are usually hard, a long approach shot over the bunkers can bounce through the green up against the fence or off the course. Many members wind up short and pitch from the front.

Alexa: *400 Yards, Par four — A drive, a brassie, and a mashie or mashie-niblick puts me on. I can count on a five.*

Bobby: *380 Yards, Par four — Drive 260 yards. Spade mashie to twenty feet from the cup. Two putts.*[6]

This is the first of several holes where golfers can compare their drives to his. It was 377 yards in the Ryder Cup, shorter than the hole played by Alexa and Bobby, but has now been stretched out by a new tee farther down the hill that adds those two pine trees. In 2016, the pros played from 479 yards, seventy-nine and ninety-nine yards longer than Alexa and Bobby and 102 yards longer than in 1963.

Charlie's 1932 Pontiac

Over the years, Bobby Jones made many birdies on this hole, the thirteenth back then, and Charlie Harrison and Tom Cousins were here for one. In 1945, Charlie and Tom were spending a perfect summer day for Georgia teenagers.

Charlie: *We were doing a little life-guarding and a little swimming when the word got to us that Bobby Jones was playing the back nine. I called to my friend, 'Come on Tom, we're going to see the best golfer in the world.' We rushed out to my 1932 Pontiac, drove out behind the thirteenth green and got there just as Bobby Jones was walking up to his ball. Now in those days, there was a big tree guarding the left side of the green, and since Bobby's drive was to the left, the shot required a hook around the tree. I remember the shot. There was no practice swing, and he hit the perfect shot. The ball hooked just like it needed to and ended up a foot from the hole. I turned to Tom, 'See, he does it every time.'*

6   Bobby drove the ball a long way in 1922 with wooden clubs. During the course-record 63 (Appendix), his seven measured drives varied between 250 and 310 yards. He had great length, but the fairways were harder and balls rolled farther — there was no underground watering system at East Lake when he was competing. Los Angeles CC installed pipes during WWI, but the first complete sprinkler system with pop-up heads appeared in 1932, ten years after the round at East Lake (Kurtz 2003).

No one can remember Bobby Jones taking practice swings, whether over the ball or other times. He liked to play quickly and was always serious about the game at hand. He hated having his concentration broken. A short passage in *Bobby Jones on Golf* speaks to both points.

The ethics of the game allow each person a reasonable opportunity to play each shot carefully, but they demand also that the player step up promptly to do his bit without unnecessary delay.

The habitual practice swingers, and there are numbers of them, have an uncanny talent for taking their swings at precisely the wrong times. Everyone has had the experience and knows how annoying it is hearing the swish of a club behind him just as he is in the midst of his swing. He has to be very fond of the culprit to restrain a desire to bash him on the head with a club, even when he knows that the guilt is only of thoughtlessness (Jones 1966).

In 1990, Ed Garner reported what the young Jack Nicklaus did here in the early 1960s:

Jack drove into the fairway bunker that used to be on the right, 250 yards from the tee, then hit an eight iron to the green and sank the birdie putt.

Hardy, the main character in *The Legend of Bagger Vance*, played this hole at East Lake while recovering from his service as a battlefield surgeon in WWII. One shot on this hole restored his positive attitude. Unfortunately, the important story at East Lake was not included in the movie.

The Atlanta Athletic Club had generously given provisional memberships to all returning officers … The only physical activity I could bear was golf. I started just putting. I would pedal out to East Lake alone and putt in the dark … Gradually I began to go out … Not surprisingly, I began to play pretty well … Finally, the Georgia Amateur came to East Lake. 'They're closing the course for ten days for the tournament,' Jeannie said, 'so if you want to play at all, you'll have to compete.'

… I breezed through the quarters playing well over my head, squeaked out a one-up nail-biter in the semis, and came to the thirty-six-hole final against Temple Magnuson, the defending champ … He had me four down at the turn and added two more by lunch … I stayed even through the third nine, and in fact picked up a hole on the thirtieth. I came to the thirty-first [today's fourth] five down with six to play … and promptly bombed one into the deep timber. The ball was wedged under a root, unplayable. Magnuson strode in mid-fairway, already accepting congratulations. I had reached my end … waves of despair rose to overwhelm me … I heard Bagger Vance's voice … I knew exactly what to do … I still had my ball,

my Spalding Dot ... I stepped to the shot. Two-ten to the flag, a knock-down hook off half an inch of pine straw that would have to be drilled between two trees no more than four feet apart and somehow stop on a shallow green with deep-lipped bunkers ... I settled the two iron in my grip and sank my spikes into the crusty, needle-strewn dirt. Something made me look up. There stood Mike, my caddie's kid brother ... 'Hold nothing back,' his voice said out of nowhere. 'Knock the s ... out of it.'

[Years later in the story] *Michael turned to me,' You holed the shot, right?' I nodded:*

I birdied the two after that, winning them both. That was too much for Magnuson. He handed me the thirty-sixth with a bogey and the match was mine, one-up on the thirty-eighth (Pressfield 2000).

FIVE

Photo © 2015-2017, Dave Sansom

The fifth is a straightaway, downhill 429-yard par four that usually plays into the wind. In 2016, at the second annual East Lake Cup, the fifth and the seventh were the two holes that honor caddie Greg Edwards heard the players praise most, typically as soon as they reached the tees.

Chad: *This has always been my favorite hole. After the U.S. Amateur in 2001, the USGA gave out the flags used in the tournament, and I chose the flag from this hole. Eighteen was the most popular but not in my case. I have that flag in my office behind my desk so I can see it while I'm working. My favorite drive here is to hit toward the left bunker with a little cut. This has everything you want on a golf hole, and it epitomizes East Lake — no tricks, it's all right in front of you.*

There's an illusion on the green, a little knob back-right that makes a putt to a pin back there look more uphill than it is, especially the farther the pin is to the right.

Alexa: *450 Yards, Par five — This is a drive, a brassie, and a short approach. She made many birdies here.*

Chad and Carrie Parker in 2018 with the 5th green in the background

Bobby: *465 Yards, Par five — Drive 300 yards down alley. Mashie short of green, pin in front of green, and a wee pitch failed to stop promptly and rolled fifteen feet past pin. Two putts.*

One of the strangest events in East Lake's long history happened here in 1993. After Dick Boyens hit his approach, he noticed something moving on the green, and when he got closer, he was amazed to see a big catfish frantically flopping around. He knew it couldn't have "walked" all the way up the hill to that spot. A man who had been mowing nearby told him what had happened:

A few minutes ago, an osprey grabbed it out of the lake and flew over the green but couldn't hold on. That fish dropped right out of the sky. It's the damnedest thing I ever saw.

Everyone who played at East Lake before the renovation in 1994 remembers the special quality of the bunkers. The sand was always thin, and special care was needed to avoid sculling the ball.

In 1935, in what O.B. Keeler called, *The greatest match I ever witnessed,* Joyce Wethered, the English woman champion, was paired with Charlie Yates against Bobby Jones and fifteen-year-old Dorothy Kirby, who was destined to win the U.S. Women's Amateur.

The match was described in *The Bobby Jones Story.* This hole, one of the bunkers, and the valley to the right of the green were featured.

Miss Wethered's driving was simply tremendous. The wind was coming up, and

when facing it she was hitting a low, raking drive of great carry and astonishing run. And at the fourteenth [now fifth], a hole of 448 yards, there was, for the moment, a half-gale coming out of the west, straight in her face. Bobby and Charlie Yates struck off two of their best, and Miss Wethered's ball was well in front. Against the sweeping wind, Miss Wethered was flag-high with her second shot, the ball curling off to the left into a bunker. And here ensued the most whimsical play of the afternoon. Miss Wethered, of course, was unfamiliar with East Lake bunkers in summer, or at any other time. This was her first recovery off what looked to her as if it might be sand. She essayed a good, substantial half-blast with the niblick, and the blade, ricocheting from the sun-baked surface under a thin layer of sand, clipped the ball fairly in the back and sent it flying fifty *yards over the green and the gallery, to the frank amazement of the latter and no less of Miss Wethered herself. But she trotted down into a little valley, found the ball in a difficult place, pitched back beautifully, almost hitting the flag and holed a twenty foot putt for a five, to be a stroke above par, while Bobby won the hole with a four* (Keeler and Rice 1953).

Many years later, Bobby paid Joyce Wethered a great compliment:

The first requisite of a truly sound swing is simplicity. In this respect, I think that the late Horton Smith and Lady Heathcoat-Amory, who as Miss Joyce Wethered played superb golf in my day, excel any golfers I have seen … I have found many to agree with me that Miss Wethered's swing was the most perfect in the world (Jones 1966).

This is the third hole where players can compare their drives to Bobby Jones. High school and college golf team members are usually eager to try to

Joyce Wethered

Hamilton's approach to the 5th green

Eventual champion Ben Dickerson, playing from "Miss Wethered's bunker."

The valley to the right of the 5th green — "Miss Wethered's Valley."

out-drive him, and they will not know how long he was. It shows them the effect of his tempo and timing.

On March 26, 2016, Wilson Belk, a member of the University of Colorado golf team, got his first look at East Lake. He was twenty, the same age as Bobby in 1922, but several inches taller, and his driver was state-of-the-art. After a little time to loosen up on the practice range, he was driven out to this tee to test himself against Jones, but there was only time for one drive. He enjoyed the experiment and hit one of his best drives. After pacing off his distance as 280 yards, he smiled and shook his head — Bobby had beaten him by twenty yards.

Michael Jordan on the tee during the 1996 Olympics

87

SIX

© Chet Burgess

This short, uphill par five is Charlie Harrison's favorite hole. It rises sixty-five feet to the highest point on the course, but the walk up is rewarded by a special view of the clubhouse and skyline. Seeing the downtown buildings from here in the morning sun was an unexpected result of the re-routing in 2016.[7]

Arnold Palmer and his team in the Ryder Cup played it as a 483-yard par five, but in 2016, the PGA lengthened it to 525 with a new and lower tee. Today, members play it from 496, a short par five similar to the pros in 1963.

Charlie Harrison remembers that after the Masters in 1963, twenty-three-year-old Jack Nicklaus came to East Lake to help promote the Ryder Cup in October. He had not been a pro long enough to be on the team. When he came to this hole, he asked his host, *What should I do here?*

After being advised to hit it left to right around the tall pines on the right at the point of the dogleg, he said, *What if I go over?* He was told it was too dangerous, but he teed it up high and tried. After it cleared the treetops by several yards, he smiled: *What's dangerous about that?*

---

7   The Bank of America building is the tallest. Some call it Atlanta's Eiffel Tower because of its unusual metal top, and because the two buildings are similar in height. Also, the distance from the street to the top of its spire is 1024 feet, about equal to the elevation of Atlanta above sea level (1050).

There are large fairway bunkers on each side, perfectly positioned to catch good drives from the back tees and the weaker shots of those playing it forward. Since it bends left to right and has a right-sloping fairway, a fade is the shot of choice. That's one thing most older golfers do well.

Building the left fairway bunker | Sodding the fairway in 1994

Alexa: *480 Yards, Par five — To my mind, this is one of the hardest holes anybody ever played. If the green wasn't so well guarded I might get on in three, but as it is it takes all I have, and more, too, to put the third on the green. A six does very well here.*

Bobby: *505 Yards, Par five — Drive 260 yards. Brassie to edge of green, thirty feet from pin. Two putts.*

From the winter tee, the hole that Bobby played after 1913 was almost straight. Member Roger Cordes remembered he liked to hit a long, right-to-left draw over the trees on the right that would climb the hill when it landed.

Rick Burton also likes this hole. He said the pros in the tournament usually hit three woods off the new tee and frequently carry the bunkers, leaving an uphill second under 200 yards. When he arrived at East Lake, there was only one bunker on the right. Adding the second one on that side made the landing area smaller.

The approach shot is blind, and if a ball goes into that last fairway bunker, golfers face an impossible shot. I'm always surprised that so few eagles are made on this hole and think it's because the green is so hard to putt. When the pin is back left, putts from below will break hard right, and the front positions always result in very fast putts from the back or center.

Red-tailed hawk to the left of the 6th fairway

The woods between six and seven have concealed a number of small animals. Rick once saw six coyotes crossing this fairway in the snow, and the pair of red-tailed hawks he named Bobby and Alexa frequently show themselves here.

Charlie Elliott wrote about Bobby's father on this hole:

This was an intra-club tournament held between the golfers of East Lake and those of another club in a town near Atlanta. The other club had a golfer who was every bit as proficient in the use of profanity as the Colonel, so the tournament committee arranged to pair these two against one another in the same foursome. It was agreed among the intra-club committeemen that both the Colonel and his opponent would be told the same story — that he was playing against a preacher and to keep from embarrassing his club, it would be necessary to watch his language during the round.

Everyone who was in on the joke declared that it was probably the most hilarious round of golf ever played. When one of the contestants missed a shot — which was often — instead of going into his usual verbal barrage, he would turn red in the face, controlling his temper with obvious effort. This went on for fourteen holes, with the other members of the foursome and the gallery scarcely able to contain their hilarity. On this hole, the Colonel's opponent missed a short putt. As he stooped over to pick up his ball on the edge of the cup, he said under his breath, '@#$%&!!!&%^*#.' The foursome froze for an instant. Colonel Bob, only a step away, reached over and caught the man by the arm.

'What did you say?' he asked.

'Why it was nothing — nothing,' the golfer stammered.

The Colonel was persistent. 'What did you say?' he demanded.

His opponent faced him, red to the tips of his ears. 'Look, preacher,' he apologized, 'I couldn't help it. It just slipped out. I'm sorry.'

'Preacher?' Colonel Bob roared. 'Who's a preacher?'

'They told me you were,' the man mumbled, and the two studied one another, the light beginning to dawn. Those who followed the match later declared the air was blue from that point on to the clubhouse (Elliott 1984).

VIII

THE MIDDLE HOLES
SEVEN THROUGH TWELVE

SEVEN

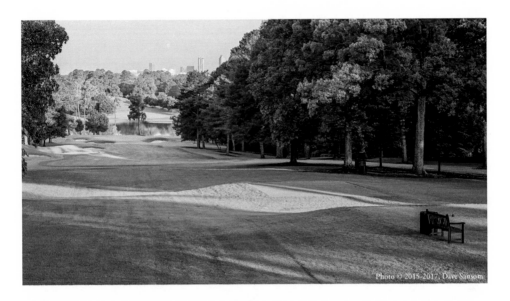

Photo © 2015-2017, Dave Sansom

This is the highest part of the golf course, but golfers playing the Bendelow course did not come up here. Everything changed for the better in the summer of 1915, when two beautiful holes were added to this corner of the property. It was just in time to handle the developing golf games of the two young golfers who were destined to bring so much attention to this course.

Alexa's swing was described in 1919. She was the reigning U.S. Women's Amateur Champion and was playing more frequently than usual to prepare to defend her title in three months, which she did successfully. The length of the hole was 375 yards.

She teed the ball low and stood well away, bending forward a bit in a position suggesting Chick Evans's play. Her stance was almost square but inclined to be a little open. She played the ball off her left foot and used the overlapping Vardon grip. Her back swing was full and easy, her body pivoting smoothly, and every motion lithe and free. The club swung down with a full, sweeping stroke, just brushing the clipped grass. There was the sweet smack every player joys to hear, and as the club head swung in the arc of a complete follow-through, the ball went flying over the bunker, well beyond the 200-yard marker and stopped 230 yards down the course.

Miss Stirling chose a jigger for her second and played the ball off her right foot, taking plenty of turf. The shot went well into the air, flag high, and stopped a little to the right in the well-cropped grass at the edge of the green. A chip shot with a mashie-niblick ran slightly over. A putt, easy and deliberate, yet without any uncertainty or over-waiting, put her down in one — a four for the hole. This was in a recent foursome in which Miss Stirling was paired with Bob Jones against Perry Adair and Tom Prescott. Miss Stirling wasn't on her game that day, neither were the others, yet in nineteen holes — an extra hole to decide the match — she had five drives of over 200 yards ("Alexa Stirling's Game" 1919).

Bobby: *405 Yards, Par five — Drive 260 yards. Mashie-niblick twenty feet from pin. One putt.*

In 1963, Arnold Palmer and his team played it as a 470-yard par four, but after that event and for thirty years (1963–1993), members played it as a friendly, downhill 463-yard par five. Rees Jones changed it back to par four again, and in 2016, the best pros played it from 481 yards. It's a little shorter for members, but still a long par four — 461 yards. Older members look wistfully back, wishing it were the par five it used to be. It was a treat to have two short par fives together so close to the end.

The skyline of Atlanta can also be seen from this tee, six miles away, reflecting the morning sun, but in 1922 and 1935, there was no evidence of a city. The Candler, Hurt, and Healey buildings, at seventeen stories, were the tallest in town and hidden by trees.

Many golfers like this view more than any other, and it's a good place to rest after the climb. If they're struggling, they can look over to the back nine across the lake and think positive. There are many holes to play. [1]

---

1   This tee is a good place for distance comparison. The length of the hole as played in the tournament, 481 yards (1443 feet) is similar to the height of the Empire State Building (1454 feet).

Although he prefers the view from the sixth green, Tom Cousins says this is his favorite hole to play. There is a wooden bench with a plaque:

> IN HONOR OF THE 50TH WEDDING ANNIVERSARY
> OF ANN AND TOM COUSINS, WITH LOVE AND
> ADMIRATION FROM THEIR CHILDREN
> AND GRANDCHILDREN
> MARCH 17, 2006

While riding down the fairway from the tee, Rick pointed out the view across the lake to the fourteenth tee. At the last fairway bunker, which was added in 2008, he pointed to a spot on the fairway only a yard or two from the sand.

These days many of the professionals hit their drives over the bunkers, but for those who don't, the drive has to be up here to avoid running down across the fairway into rough.

And at the green: *When I came, there was only one bunker on the left, which is the last one now. Rees made the new one in front and bought it forward so it comes over to make the entrance smaller. The last few feet aren't obvious from the fairway.*

On the green: *The elevation slanting across the middle is a real challenge. If golfers get in the second bunker on the left and the pin is tight on that side, they'll have trouble stopping the ball and face a long first putt. I like the far back and front pin positions, especially back right, tucked behind the bunker, and front left. If they fly it anywhere back there, they'll risk going over. When they putt from back right to front left, they will need to cross the ridge diagonally, making it a treacherously fast, downhill putt that breaks sharply right to left.*

Chad: *My favorite caddie story was on this green. On an earlier hole, a young caddie had heard honor caddie Charles Steppes say a putt was a ball or two outside the hole. On this hole, the new caddie got down behind the hole and leaned forward just like Charles. After thorough analysis, he called out the line, 'Play it about twenty-two balls to the right.'*

Back to O.B. Keeler and the match with Joyce Wethered in 1935:

Going down the fairway toward the sixteenth green, I was walking momentarily with Miss Wethered, and, naturally, I was complimenting her on her brilliant play. She smiled and then became suddenly grave.

'I had to play well here, she said simply. Bobby arranged the match, you know. And he's said and written so many kind things about my game. And then he was ill, and then he insisted on playing ... I wish I were sure he should be playing now ... It's — it's the most sporting thing I've ever known. I had to play well at East Lake. I couldn't let Bobby down, you know.'

Yes — I knew. And I know, too, that I saw something that afternoon at East Lake that will stand out as the prettiest picture of a lifetime in sport — the two greatest golfers, playing all they knew in every shot, in generous and gallant complement to one another, in the greatest match I ever witnessed (Keeler and Rice 1953).

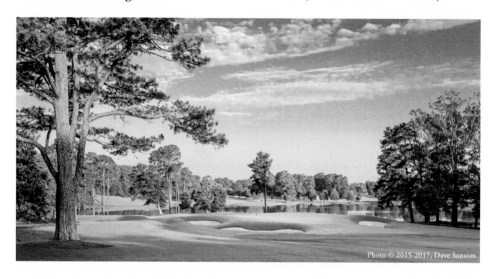

Photo © 2015-2017, Dave Sansom

THE BEAST OF EAST LAKE

In November of 2005, three new Jones Scholars from St. Andrews, Gordon and David Jones and Fergus Neville, were playing this hole when something happened that made them run to the clubhouse.

Gordon Jones: *Just after nightfall, we saw what appeared to be a large cat-like creature behind us after we had reached the green. It suddenly disappeared into the woods, only to appear to follow us up the next hole, its eyes giving away its position when they caught the light of the moon. This creature, this beast, gathered speed and seemed to be trying to cut us off. At that point, we abandoned our great scores, took out defensive five irons, and hastily made for the clubhouse, lest the beast beat us to it. When finally safe and secure, we asked for Kummel, which we prefer in Scotland, but it was not available. We settled for John Beale's special recommendation.*

A consensus was reached ten years later — the East Lake Beast was a coyote.

EIGHT

Photo © 2015-2017, Dave Sansom

For members, this is a 411-yard par four along the lake that demands a drive over a finger of the lake to the right center of the fairway. Long hitters either drive a bit to the left, which brings the lake on that side into play, or boom it over the large bunkers on the right. The entire hole is easy to see from the clubhouse, and from this tee there's a panoramic view of the clubhouse, practice green, par three fifteenth, and back nine.

Alexa: *406 Yards, Par four — I usually clear the bunker on my second and stand a chance to pitch to the flag and take one putt.*

Bobby: *400 Yards, Par four — Drive 250 yards. Mashie twenty feet from pin. One putt.*

There have been major changes over the years.

Rick: *From the tee, it's easy to visualize how it was before Rees Jones did his work. The Ryder Cup fairway was probably thirty yards farther from the lake, over the bunkers on the right. It was a slight dogleg right to a green up behind the third green.*

An after-work golf lesson on the edge of the road in 1994.
The tee on the dam was two years in the future.

There used to be trees between the fairway and lake from tee to green, but now, water is all the golfer sees to the left from the tees. At first we didn't plan to remove all the trees, just the unhealthy ones, but every time we took one out the hole looked better. When the lake was low, Bill Haas hit that great shot from the bottom of the lake up to three feet from a tight pin in the 2011 playoff. He made his par putt and won the next hole for the Tour Championship and FedEx Cup.

Ralph Kepple: *In 1995, Larry Mize played the hole and said it was too short; the next year Rees built the tee on the dam.*

There was no tee on the dam in 1963 when Arnold Palmer and his team were here. They played from 410 yards, but in the Tour Championship, professionals hit from the new back tee — 471 yards. This hole and the next were the final two holes during the Ryder Cup, and there was drama on the last day in the match between Palmer and Peter Aliss. After Palmer won the sixteenth, he was one down with two to play. When his approach here was only a yard from the hole, there must have been a wild celebration.

Undaunted, Aliss ran down a putt of twelve feet. The silence from the crowd was deafening. 'It was the loudest silence I've ever heard,' quipped Aliss. He halved the eighteenth and vanquished the American captain in the only bright moment of the championship for the British team (Matthew 1999).

Member Richard Kessler made the only hole in one on this par four that anyone can remember. He was playing with Ed Mitchell in the mid-1990s after the renovation. Work was being done on the tees that day, and Dick hit from a temporary tee across the lake 287 yards from the green. When he was on the tee, Carter Yates was putting on the green, but Dick couldn't see him. The hole was easier back then since the green was at the level of the fairway, lower than

Ralph Kepple, Director of Agronomy (hand on mower), and his team beside the 8th tee: (L-R) Dustin Bucher, Charles Aubrey, Wesley Holsenbeck, and John Julian

today, with a small bunker front left. The entrance to the green was open on the right, so it was a good place for run-up shots.

Carter Yates: *I heard a ball drop behind me in the fairway, and while I was putting it rolled right across my line and plopped into the hole. When Dick appeared in the distance, I could see he was just as surprised to see me standing there as I was at that moment. At first, he looked worried and apologized, but when I told him what had happened, he really got excited. We played in together.*

Robert Hamilton pitching to the 17th green (now 8th) in the U.S. Amateur. The match was all square with two holes to play, and Ben Dickerson won them both.

NINE

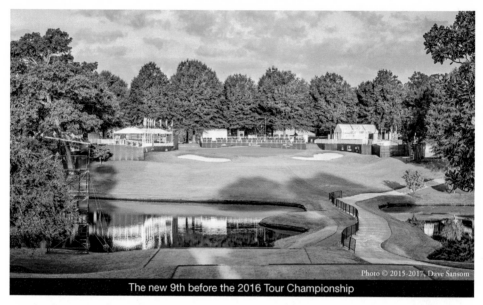

The new 9th before the 2016 Tour Championship

Photo © 2015-2017, Dave Sansom

Today, members play this par three from 207 yards, similar to Alexa (190) and Bobby (205). It was longer for the pros in 1963 (230) and 2016 (235). Since it was the eighteenth for over a hundred years, this hole has seen some drama.

Given the circumstances, the greatest shot ever played at East Lake may have happened here. On Sunday, November 1, 1998, Hal Sutton's four-wood from 240 yards stopped six feet from the cup. When he made the birdie putt, he won the playoff with Vijay Singh, captured the Tour Championship, and completed a long, hard comeback. Only two years before, he had been ranked 109th and thought his career might be over. Grandstands surrounded the green and hundreds of eye witnesses cheered the long tee shot and putt. It was televised live, seen over and over, and written up everywhere. It was Hal Sutton's day.

There was no tournament and no hoopla when Alexa and Bobby played here in 1919 and 1922.

Alexa: *190 Yards, Par three — I quite often get a three here. My drive, if nothing happens, puts me close enough for a short approach and perhaps one putt. My scores haven't been as good this summer as last year, but I think my game has been more consistent. I had some good holes this morning ... I only played nine holes and took a 43 with a seven on five and six on six.*[2]

On September 16, 1922, this was where twenty-year-old Bobby finished his course-record 63. There was no crowd watching and no tournament pressure, but when the young Jones stood on this tee, O.B. Keeler wrote that he became distracted by being nine under par with one to play. He got his par, but the short loss of focus made him scramble. With a cleek, similar to a one iron, he pushed the tee shot to the right of the green and bunker. But by the time he reached the ball for his second, his composure had returned. His niblick pitch cleared the bunker and landed softly next to the pin.[3]

Bobby wrote about the round, but it wasn't in a tournament, and he attached little importance to it. He was having a friendly round with his dad and two friends before leaving for Harvard. The round was written up the next day in the paper then promptly forgotten. After seven years of national competition, Bobby had not won a championship, but that was destined to change in nine months (Jones and Keeler 1927 and Keeler 1922).

Alexa was in a different world. That day in 1922 was eleven days after her twenty-fifth birthday, and she had already won three straight U.S. Amateurs and one of her two Canadian titles.

In 1935, the match with Joyce Wethered wound up all square, thanks to Bobby's uphill fifteen-foot putt for par on this green. He had a medal score of 71 that day despite abdominal pain. Miss Wethered had 74, Charlie Yates 76, and young Dorothy Kirby 84, all playing from the back tees. Miss Wethered was right to worry about Bobby's health — shortly after the match, he had surgery for appendicitis.

In October 1950, Alexa came full circle here. Her final appearance in a national championship was at East Lake, and this was her last hole. It was the Golden Anniversary U.S. Women's Amateur, and Bobby had urged her to come so they could visit. He came out to watch her play.

There was a lot of local interest, and newspaper reporters were present for her homecoming. Television existed, but 1950 was twenty-six years before the first portable, broadcast-quality TV camera and forty-five years before the Golf Channel (Suptic 2009, Beacham 2014, and Winfrey 1995).

---

2   That would be a double bogey seven on today's fourteenth and a triple on the par three fifteenth.

3   See Appendix

Like Bobby's Grand Slam at Merion in 1930, her career ended in style, but there was no dramatic victory. A large gallery had come out to watch her play, sensing this might be their last chance. She was fifty-three and decided to end her career at East Lake, directly in front of the house in Atlanta where she grew up. She conceded her first-round match by picking up her ball here.

After she walked off the green, she told her friend Patty Berg, *This is their time, Patty, I've had mine.*

Patty was quoted in the paper:

I only hope that when I leave competitive golf, I can be like Alexa. I've never met a golfer, or a woman I thought so much of. She has the sort of sportsmanship you just do not see any more on golf courses.

Not long after Alexa's last visit, Charlie Yates and Tommy Barnes were battling each other in a tight match that Tommy enjoyed thinking about the rest of his life. They had been partners and opponents over the years, and this one had come down to the last hole, like many others. Tommy hit to the green. Then Charlie stepped up and hit a low hook that dove into the water. He didn't throw his clubs or show much anger, just disappointment, but Tommy was flabbergasted by what happened next. Charlie calmly dropped his club, walked off the tee toward the green, then picked up speed, started running, and made

Robert Hamilton on the last hole of the Amateur

a beautiful racing dive from the tee by the lake. After a high-speed crawl to the other side, he threw up his arms in surrender, smiling widely.

On January 13, 1985, Scott Hansen was playing with Tommy Barnes against Don Russell and Bill Blalock. Scott took out his driver and hit a draw into the wind. The ball bounced on the green and ran in the hole — Scott and Tommy finished one up.

TEN

Photo © 2015-2017, Dave Sansom

Number ten is a 411-yard par four usually played into the prevailing breeze. Back to the match with Bobby and Perry Adair:

Alexa had two drives of about 220 yards on this hole, and each time pulled her brassie around the left of the trap that ended in the short grass at the edge of the green. The first time she chipped close enough for a four and the next time took a five (Alexa Stirling's Game 1919).

Alexa: *400 Yards, Par four — On this hole, I'm usually far enough with my drive for a good second to carry the trap and put me on. It's a hard one because it's trapped, and you aren't left much room. I suppose I'll average a five there.*

Bobby: *400 Yards, Par four — Drive. Spade mashie* [six] *to twenty feet from cup. One putt.*

Bobby described a situation on this hole in the 1927 Southern Open and wrote about how the decision to play a difficult recovery is affected by whether the issue is match or medal (stroke) play.

Starting the third round of that competition, I pulled my drive to a peculiarly difficult situation behind some trees at the edge of the lake, which encroaches upon the left edge of the fairway some 240 yards from the tee. I found the ball lying well on the bank of the lake, with a decently large opening through the trees in the direction of the green. In an informal match some days

(L-R) Scott Putnam, Rob Remar, Bob Guido, Chad Parker,
Eddie Gasperini, and Hunter Hughes

*previously, I had driven to almost the same spot and had played through the trees
to the green for my par four. This was different. A championship was at stake, at
medal play. So I looked over the situation, concluded that I assuredly would not
be as well off after a failure of the recovery shot — it almost certainly must have
wound up in the lake, unless it came off. I turned my back on the flag, and chipped
modestly to a safe place in the fairway. From there I had a comfortable shot to the
green, and a five; not so good as a four, but infinitely better for my state of mind, as
well as for the card, than a six, seven or eight* (Jones and Keeler 1927).

Charlie Harrison saw Bobby drive on this tee after World War II:

*I was struck by how he positioned his club head on the ground inside the ball.
I thought he was going to use a practice swing since the toe of the club was an inch
inside the ball. There was no practice swing, he quickly hit away. I don't know now
whether he always did that or only did it late in his career.*

Charles and Comer Yates, the sons of Charlie Yates, were asked about their
dad's shots at East Lake, but he did not talk to them about his own shots.
They said he had been thrilled by the work of Tom Cousins and architect Rees
Jones to renovate the Ryder Cup course. Charlie was also touched by Rees's
generosity — he designed the new short course at no charge. Comer said one
of the greatest honors of their dad's life came when Tom Cousins named it the
Charlie Yates Golf Course.

Comer remembers two shots from the Yates family from this tee, one by his older brother Charles and one by their uncle Dan:

I have a clear and favorite memory about the two best Yates family shots at East Lake. The first was when Charles was honorary starter at the Tour Championship a few years ago, sharing the honor with a young woman golfer, a teenager who had grown up in the East Lake community. When I looked over to the tee, I noticed he was getting ready for his big moment by spending time putting her at ease. He was joking with her, finding out about her interests and holding her attention during all the distractions: The U.S. Army band, the Color Guard, the TV audience, and the large crowd in the grandstands. All attention was focused on them.

In a few minutes, after watching her hit a great shot, Charles smiled, nodded his congratulations to her and relaxed a little more himself. Then he quickly walked over to tee up his ball, took a perfect stance, looked down the fairway for a second, and calmly crushed it right down the middle. Following the ceremony, someone said that my father would have been proud of that shot. I answered that he would have been prouder of what had happened before the shot.

Another memory is when Uncle Dan [Dan Yates, Sr.] was in exactly the same high-pressure setting another year. He was not at all happy with his first drive, but instead of walking away discouraged, he reached into his back pocket for a Mulligan. He drove that one straight down the fairway and walked off to smiles and loud applause. When we all filed out of the grandstand, I told cousin Carter I was happy Uncle Dan had hit his second ball so well. Carter smiled.

'Me too,' he said, 'and did you notice he had a bunch of other balls still left in that pocket?'

A week after the 2016 Tour Championship, Rick Burton rode out onto the new back nine. It was a bright windy day. He was proud of the way the course had looked, that it had challenged the best golfers in the world, and that everyone connected to the tournament had enjoyed the new par-five finishing hole.

He was impressed with the subtleties Rees Jones built into all the greens:

The little bitty undulations they don't really see are the main reasons these greens are so hard to putt.

His first stop was in the bottom of the landing area in the right rough.

These maples came from the driveway. They were dying up there but are doing well here. Before the trees were here, golfers could drive it into the right rough and have a shot to the green, even with a back right hole location. Now, when they drive it right at all, they have to contend with these trees. On the tenth green the most difficult hole location is back right. The little mound guarding that area makes the green slope away from the player. The grain also runs that way, so when they go for the pin on their approach, it will be hard to keep the ball out of the rough behind the green. With that back-right pin, if the ball is on the back of the green on the left, they'll have a fast putt coming across the green. But the next toughest pin position is the front right. If they hit it past or left of the hole, they'll have a giant break or fast downhill putt that frequently means three putts. The slope is back to front, so if they hit anything up on the green with the pin on the front, they'll face a treacherous run downhill. Also, if the pin is left front and the ball is in the left bunker, they'll have a shot they can't stop.

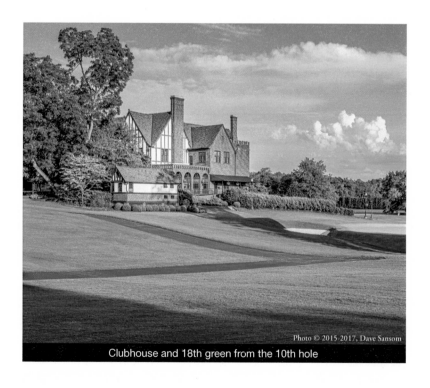

Photo © 2015-2017, Dave Sansom

Clubhouse and 18th green from the 10th hole

ELEVEN

Photo © 2015-2017, Dave Sansom

The eleventh is a 195-yard par three played over a pond. Like many old courses, the holes at East Lake are close to each other — a hard pull from this tee can reach a group standing on the next tee left of the bunker. The closeness adds interest. It's easy to visit with your friends and fun to watch them struggle.

In the summer of 1908, six-year-old Bobby Jones lived in a rented house beyond today's green that was described by Charlie Elliott. *Robert* is Colonel Robert P. Jones, Bobby's father.

This second summer his family again moved to East Lake for the season, but instead of living with Mrs. Meador, Robert rented a building on club property. It was a two-story frame structure between today's eleventh green and parking lot.

The ground floor of this building was arranged to house livestock used to pull fairway mowers and other equipment, and it had been used for this purpose before the house was renovated as a summer residence. It was then and forever after, as long as it stood, known as the mule house (Elliott 1984).

After following Stewart Maiden for a few holes, the young Jones would come home to the green in front of the Mule House and *spend hours pitching a capful of balls* to the flagstick and putting them out.

Through all my career, he once said, *I've never been able to pitch a ball as accurately as I could pitch it to the flagstick on that green* (Elliott 1984).

Alexa: *130 yards — I very often play a jigger. I find it a little too long for a mashie, and, besides, a jigger and a pitching iron are two clubs I prefer. I'm usually on, and I think I average a three.*

Bobby: *150 yards — Spade mashie to one yard from the pin. One putt.*

Charlie Yates enjoyed describing a shot he hit here because it gave him a chance to poke fun at himself. He was young and full of himself when he played with Bobby one day on this par three. Like many others, when playing with someone they wanted to impress, he tried to show off. It seems that Bobby had just hit what was for him an ordinary shot, a five iron 160 yards to the center of the green. After seeing what Bobby had used, Charlie took out his seven iron, hooded the club for extra distance and swung harder than usual, hoping to hit a big hook to the green. The shot came off, and the ball wound up on the green.

Charlie waited for congratulations, but Bobby just looked at him and deadpanned, *Charlie, don't you have any club in your bag other than that seven iron?*

When Chad Parker was quizzed about his own memorable shots, a story on this hole came out. He is the only staff member on the hole-in-one board, and ace-magic touched him here.

Rick and I played many times at 7:30 in the morning, and that day our caddie was Heath Stroud. It was March 11, 2001, and about 7:45 I hit my seven-iron from the blue tees, 170 yards that day. It was a good shot that never left the flag, which was back right, probably six paces from the right edge. Our view was partially obstructed by sunlight, but we all saw it bounce once and go in — no second bounce. The great thing is that two months later, I was a witness to Heath's hole in one on the Yates course. We went crazy when that went in — it's rare for two people to witness aces by each other.

Two holes from the 1908 course can be visualized from this green. The old thirteenth played along Alston Drive in the opposite direction from today's twelfth, and young Bobby practiced pitching *to a green in the hollow now occupied by the pond. Fourteen was along the right side of the* [current tenth] *fairway to a green at the eighteenth tee* (Elliott 1984, Appendix).

BILL RICE PLAYS AN ACE

Early one morning in the late summer of 2014, ninety-two-year-old Bill Rice walked onto this tee with Ray Ramirez, Jack Glenn, Jr., and Dick Snyder. As soon as they turned east after their work on the previous green, they realized they would be shooting straight into the sun.

Bill Rice in 2017

Bill had to face it first. As a courtesy, no matter who had won the previous hole, his friends asked him to lead off. Able Aklillu, his tall caddy, handed him the club Bill had made from parts he'd found in a catalogue. He had ordered a metal hybrid head with a 23-degree loft, glued that onto the new shaft, and personally wrapped and glued the grip. It was the perfect club for this shot.

As soon as he hit it, he knew he had given it his best swing and hit it exactly on the sweet spot, so he was disappointed when he looked into that dazzling sun. He couldn't see the ball, but he remembers the sounds of that moment.

Ralph Kepple was working behind the green. Like Bill and his friends on the tee, he had come to East Lake before the transformation by Tom Cousins and Rees Jones in the early 90s. When he saw Bill getting ready to hit, he froze, knowing he was in his line of sight to the pin. He did not know he was in the sun and invisible to Bill.

The green slopes back to front and left to right, and that day the pin was right center.

Ralph: *The ball landed in the opening between the two bunkers, on the upslope, rolled up the left side, then turned and curled down the hill ever so slowly to Bill's right, finally falling into the north side of the hole. He could not have hit it in a better spot, given the trajectory and alignment of the strike.*

When it finally dropped ... pandemonium! Ralph hopped off his cart and started jumping and yelling. On the tee, no one could see it, but they all knew what had happened.

While the hugging, congratulations, and hand shaking continued on the tee, Ralph got on the phone to Chad Parker, who dropped what he was doing and rushed out to the green to remove the flag for Bill. When he saw a few spots of mildew, he apologized. He wanted to clean those off to make it perfect, but Bill wouldn't let him. He wanted it to stay the way it had been when he made his greatest shot.

It is the only hole in one at East Lake anyone can remember by someone over ninety, and is extra special because it was Bill's first and only one … so far. The plaque by the entrance to the golf shop gives the essentials — the distance was 102 yards, and the date was August 30, 2014.

Rick: *That shot is the best thing I've seen or heard about on this hole.*

Photo © 2015-2017, Dave Sansom

Ralph's view of Bill's hole in one

Ralph: *This is the large bunker on 11. The flat area between the bunker and the swale behind it is where golfers walk to the 12th tee. The red brick in the background is the practice range service building.*

TWELVE

© Chet Burgess

The twelfth is a 390-yard par four with three fairway bunkers. The one on the right was built in 2016 to offer more of a challenge to professionals in the tournament. The one it replaced was much closer to the tee. The second bunker on the left had been added earlier to catch drives on that side carrying 250–300 yards. A slight fade is preferred here.

Alexa: *320 Yards — If my drive is 200 yards or more, I use a jigger for my second, otherwise I play my pitching iron, unless, of course, I dub my drive.*

Bobby: *320 Yards — Drive of 290 yards. Wee pitch with mashie-niblick to four feet from the pin. Missed putt. Took a four.*

Rick: *The key here is to drive in the fairway and not go out of bounds. In the tournament, most golfers choose to hit a three wood or iron here. From the fairway, there's an optical illusion in front of this green — it looks like there are four bunkers instead of two.*

Here again, the toughest hole location is probably back right, but the front right is also extremely difficult. If the pin is in front and you hit it a little long, you will have a big-breaking, very fast putt. Back left is also tough because if you reach the bunker back there, you'll come out running downhill.

BEFORE THE GOLF COURSE

This fairway crosses the site of the old Fayetteville Road that ran south from Decatur to Fayetteville, and Charles and Sylvia Harrison live across Alston Drive from the landing area. Their white-frame, old-fashioned house, Meadow Nook, has a distinctive surrounding porch and is easy to spot. A close look shows it sits slightly askew to the road — it was built to face that old road, long before either Alston Drive or the golf course existed. The old road crossed the golf course in front of the twelfth green and occupied the space between the thirteenth and seventeenth fairways. It exited the course beyond the thirteenth green.

Robert Alston built Charlie's house on his 400-acre farm that included the land of the golf course and Doolittle Creek, which feeds the lake today.[4] Over the winter of 1863/1864, the house was used as the headquarters of his military unit in the Civil War, the Second Kentucky Calvary, and 2,000 troops camped out all over the farm. Today, if you shank your approach over the fence into Charlie's front yard, you can blame the ghosts of those soldiers over 150 years ago.

CHARLES R. DREW SCHOOL

The imposing modern building at the corner of Alston Drive and Second Avenue is the Charles R. Drew Charter School, which was named for a widely admired African-American surgeon. Dr. Drew helped establish an early blood bank at Presbyterian Hospital in New York, supervised the "Plasma for Britain" project early in WWII, and "became the first director of an all-Red Cross blood program" (Schmidt 2003).

The man who named the school at East Lake for Dr. Drew was Asa Yancey. While serving as Medical Director of Grady Hospital, he was president of the all-volunteer Atlanta School Board. Dr. Drew had been his mentor at Howard University.

---

4   East Lake is located at the top of the Ocmulgee and Altamaha river basins. The land north of the golf course rises gently to the railroad between Decatur and Atlanta then falls away to the north. Water from the lake flows into the Atlantic, but the flow on the other side of the railroad is to the Gulf of Mexico. The railroad and Marta line mark the Eastern Sub-Continental Divide.

The 12th in 1994

Meadow Nook in the summer of 1996

IX

THE FINISH
THIRTEEN THROUGH EIGHTEEN

THIRTEEN

Photo © 2015-2017, Dave Sansom

When golfers turn this corner of the course, the pressure of the competition will ramp up. There will be a tendency to think things through all the way to the end, six holes away, and not only because of the situation. Both the seventeenth green and eighteenth tee are literally at their feet a few yards away, and the ones in between are easy to imagine. If they look to the left while walking down this fairway, they will see the entire eighteenth hole and clubhouse in the distance.

Rick added practical information here:

Just a few years ago, the fairway was thirty-five yards to the right, closer to the road. About ten balls a week were hit into the road, occasionally knocking out a windshield. We added extra trees to keep them in bounds and chose cryptomerias. They're perfect for the job because the foliage is so thick. This fairway is probably the narrowest fairway on the course, about twenty yards.

Professionals played this hole at 470 yards in the Ryder Cup and 440 in 2016, but for members it's shorter at 421. It plays north to south today, but in 1913, it was the par four twelfth of the first course and played the other way, to the north.

Bobby described an exhibition match that year, when he was eleven, between the two greatest golfers of the day, Englishmen Harry Vardon and Ted Ray:[1]

Looking south in the wooded area between the 13th and 17th fairways, the site of the Fayetteville Road

Vardon got the birdie at number twelve, but Ray, in getting his par four, produced this astonishing shot. His drive was the longest of the four, as usual, but right behind a tree. The tree was about forty feet in height with thick foliage, and the ball was no more than the tree's altitude in front of it, the tree exactly in line with the green. As Ray walked up to his ball, the more sophisticated members of the gallery were speculating as to whether he would essay to slice his shot around the obstacle to the green 170 yards away, or 'pull' around on the other side. As for me, I didn't see anything he could possibly do but accept the penalty of a stroke into the fairway. He was out of luck, I was sure.

Big Ted took one look at the ball and another at the green, a fair iron shot away, with the tree between. Then without hesitation he drew a mashie-niblick and hit that ball harder, I believe, than I have ever seen a ball hit since, knocking it down as if he would drive it through to China. Up flew a divot the size of Ted's ample foot. Up also came the ball, buzzing like a partridge from the prodigious spin imparted by that tremendous wallop — almost straight up it got, cleared that tree by several yards, and sailed on at the height of an office building to drop on the green not far from the hole. The gallery was in paroxysms. I remember how men pounded each other on the back, and crowed and cackled and shouted and clapped their hands.

---

1   East Lake was a stop on what was planned to be a triumphant national tour after the U.S. Open at Brookline, outside of Boston. They made the tour, but it wasn't triumphant. A young amateur, Francis Ouimet, upset them at the beginning. He was the first American to win our Open.

As for me, I didn't really believe it. A sort of wonder persists in my memory to this day. It was the greatest shot I ever saw (Jones and Keeler 1927).

Forward six years to Alexa, playing the new course in 1919 in today's direction. It was a 440-yard par five:

I use a brassie for my second here and a mashie or a jigger for my third. I can't get on in two. But sometimes, I get a four by taking one putt. I did that this morning.

Bobby: *450-yard, par five — Long drive that ran into the rough at the elbow of the fairway. Iron to twenty-five feet from the pin. Two putts.*

FOURTEEN

Photo © 2015-2017, Dave Sansom

In 1994, Rees Jones stretched what had been a 470-yard par four into a 544-yard par five, but it is not as long as the one Alexa (610) and Bobby (590) played with hickory clubs.

Alexa: *I seldom get on the green in three. Usually it takes me four, and I think I average a six here. My third is a brassie or an iron, depending on my lie.*

Bobby: *Drive 310 yards. Brassie* [two-wood] *260 yards to edge the green. Chip dead. One putt.*

Turning for home on the front nine.

It usually doesn't play as long as it looks because of the prevailing west wind and downhill roll, and professionals have always played it as a par four: 470-yards in 1963 for Arnold Palmer and his team, 520 in 2016.

The green and flag can be seen from the tee, and if golfers have lost their bets and are feeling gloomy, the view walking down this fairway will help. If they look over to the front nine across the lake and remember their best shots over there, they might start to think positive and propose a new bet.

In 1919, professional Jim "Long Jim" Barnes (no kin to Tommy) became the first Southern Open champion by beating seventeen-year-old Bobby Jones by one stroke. This new (1915) 600-yard hole was pivotal. Barnes scored an eagle three, the first one known here, and he used an unusual combination of shots. Bobby wrote:

He then pulled his drive far into the rough on the 600-yard fifth hole, pushed a brassie clear across the fairway into the rough on the other side, and then holed out a mashie shot [five iron] of 150 yards for an eagle three, while I was plugging along for a par five (Jones and Keeler 1927).

Barnes went on to win the 1921 U.S. Open by nine shots. Bobby finished fifth that year, tied with Alex Smith, the former East Lake professional.

Back to Rick Burton up by the tee: *This tee is eighty-four feet above the lake. It's usually the hardest hole in the Tour Championship, because it's such a long par four and may include a long iron shot off a downhill lie, except for Dustin Johnson, who usually hits a sand wedge from the bottom. That bunker on the left at the start of the downslope was added in the late 1990s, more to frame the hole than act as a penalty.*

From the landing area, Rick looked over into the space between the fourteenth and sixteenth fairways, where Long Jim hit his drive in 1919. The woods have been replaced by a new green with deep bunkers and large mounds. Rick likes how it looks:

I'm excited about this new hole but still haven't played it. It's a copy of the fifteenth hole on the old Donald Ross No. 2 course, where the Charlie Yates Course and Drew Charter School are today. The green is classic Ross with his signature bunkers and big mounds. It will be fun as a playoff hole, and will be a great practice

115

In April 2018, the new hole between the 14th and 16th was put into service when the 9th green was closed. It's being called hole 15½.

green. If the tee is west of the lake, it'll be short, but if it's played from the drop area for number fifteen, it will be over 200 yards uphill to the small green.

Rees redesigned and built it from the 1928 Ross design when we thought we were going to do major work on the fifteenth green and didn't want to use a temporary green.

Back to number fourteen: After Bobby returned from World War II he promised many good friends he intended to build a new course in Atlanta, the one that became Peachtree Golf Club. He knew the job would demand an enormous amount of time, and he procrastinated. On this hole, he had to wait to hit his approach because of a slow foursome on the green. They did not know that the Jones group had played through all the others and was standing behind them, ready to hit. They deliberately chipped and putted like they had the course to themselves. Bobby steamed and stalked back and forth across the fairway, kicking the ground and getting upset. Finally, he'd had enough of slow play. Tommy Barnes remembered he snatched his ball off the fairway and stormed off the course, saying angrily,

Let's go build that new course.

Jack Glenn and Charles Steppes where Long Jim was in 1919

FIFTEEN

Photo © 2015-2017, Dave Sansom

This is a 164-yard par three from an elevated tee to a peninsular green, frequently played with a cross wind from the left. The Ryder Cup version was longer at 180, but there were three bunkers that kept many errant shots out of the water.

The pros in the Tour Championship play to the same green, but everything else is different. Their tees on the dam are 211 and 220 yards away, lower than the green, and oriented into the prevailing breeze. The strip of land behind the green offers potential relief, but Rick said they rarely overshoot the green. There is no friendly feature from those new tees.[2]

Alexa: *165 Yards — I use a pitching iron on this hole if the tee is up toward the front and a mid-iron if it's further back. I can usually get on, and I don't find a three hard, though I took a five this morning* [in the match as Bobby's partner].

Bobby: *175 Yards — Mashie to ten feet from the pin. Missed putt. Took two putts. Par three.*

---

2   Since the Water Hole is now so close to the end, disappointment is frequent here. Sometimes a change of subject away from golf is welcomed, but judgment is required.

This tee is an interesting place to compare distances and areas. The full width of the property can easily be seen — 0.4 miles (2112 feet) to the traffic on Alston Drive. It is 960 feet from the dam to the closest point of land behind the clubhouse. If the sterns of the Titanic (883 feet) and Missouri (887) were against the dam, the bows would fall into the water about eighty feet short of land. The lake is twenty-seven acres, the same size as Ellis Island in New York harbor, and has a shoreline of one mile.

The Ryder Cup green in the early 1990s

Mariana Goldsmith was on this hole in 1920 when she saw a thunderstorm coming:

I left my clubs, ran around the green, and swam back to the clubhouse.

She was a powerful swimmer. She saved two teenaged girls from drowning and received the Carnegie Medal for heroism in 1916. Fifty years later, two women introduced themselves to her son, John Knox:

We want to thank you for your mother. If she hadn't saved the lives of our mothers at East Lake, we never would have been born.

During a round in the thirties, Bobby announced to his foursome that he had finally figured out how to play this hole.

The friend on the tee said, *Quick, what is it? I've never known what to do here.*

Bobby gave his quizzical smile: *Use a water ball.*

Chad: *From the tee on the dam, there's an illusion looking toward the green that makes golfers think the safe landing area is larger than it is. You can see it if you focus on the slope coming down to the water from the right side of the green. The apparent extension of a few feet is not safe, it's the slope to the lake from the back tee on sixteen, forty yards farther away. You have to concentrate to see they're two different points.*

In 1965, Charlie Harrison came out to qualify for the U.S. Open with three friends, Jimmy Cleveland, David Boyd, and Jimmy Gabrielson. He hit two perfect shots the same day with his six iron on this hole, a coincidence on

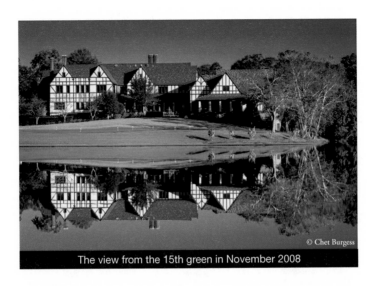

© Chet Burgess

The view from the 15th green in November 2008

its own, but they also came down in the same spot, one foot in front of the hole. In the morning round, the ball hit and hopped in for the ace. Four hours later the same shot stayed out.

There's a good story from the Yates family on fifteen from the Yates family.

Carter Yates, Charlie's nephew: *I was in a foursome in 1986 with Scott Hansen, Smoky Hicks, and Bill Hoffman. It was mid-afternoon on a beautiful day with no significant wind. I had just birdied the long par four to go one up on Scott. As we walked to this tee Scott said, 'I'm going to birdie this hole to square the match.'*

Then I said, 'It's not going to do you any good. I'm going to ace it!'

We played the back tees from 175 yards, and I hit a six iron. The shot had a little draw (all Yateses tend to draw the ball), hit ten feet from the hole, and rolled in.

Scott said, 'I can't believe you called that!'

There used to be a beach for swimming behind the clubhouse. Charlie Harrison remembers that from the elevation of the life-guard stand he could easily see where balls from this tee entered the water. Later, he took out his canoe and dove for the balls.

Bob Young remembers his own ball-retrieving strategy:

I would dive to the bottom and hold my hands together out in front so my forearms raked the bottom. I kicked as hard as I could. When my arm hit a golf ball, it made a distinctive 'thunk.'

© John Carlin

View of the 15th green from the dam in early spring, when the landing area to the right of the green looks larger. In summer, when the putting surface and grass banks are both the same color, the green itself seems much wider.

The 15th in 1994

SIXTEEN

Photo © 2015-2017, Dave Sansom

This is a 412-yard uphill par four for members that usually plays into the wind and is basically a monster. The approach, because of the wind, narrow opening, and big bunkers, is one of the hardest shots on the course, especially if a long iron or fairway wood is needed. The opening to the green looks flat from the fairway, but the slope to either side discards the short approach one way or the other into a bunker. It's hard to run-up onto this green.

Alexa: *380 Yards — Sometimes I can drive the bunker, but as a rule I play for the right side. My next shot is usually a brassie, but I went over the other day. Five is my usual score.*

Bobby: *380 Yards — Drive. Mashie to trap at left and in front of green. Niblick out to a yard from the pin. One putt.*

An event on this hole is mentioned in Harvey Penick's *Little Red Book*:

On the seventh hole [now sixteen], *there is a big canyon to the right of the green with a grassy hollow at the bottom. The weather had been nasty, and suddenly hailstones as big as marbles began falling. The whole green was covered with hailstones. Jones had been down in the grassy hollow and had pitched the ball just to the crown of the hill where he could hardly tell a golf ball from a hailstone. From there, he chipped the ball among the hailstones right into the cup for a par. Jones had a way of doing whatever was necessary* (Penick 1992).

There was drama here on Sunday of the 2016 Tour Championship. Rory McElroy holed out a 137-yard pitching wedge for an eagle two to help him shoot 64, make up a three-shot deficit, and get into the playoff. Then he won the four-hole sudden-death playoff and claimed the FedEx Cup on this green with a 15-foot birdie putt. His opponent at the end, a tenacious Ryan Moore, was finally beaten, but his play under pressure brought him a nice consolation prize. After the tournament, Davis Love chose him as his last captain's pick for the U.S. Ryder Cup team.

Michael Jordan driving on 16

Rick and Pam Burton in 2012. At dusk, this view of 16 is his favorite place on the course.

Ralph Kepple: *This big bunker was removed in 2008 when the green was moved back 40 yards. The current roll-off area to the right of the green was created in place of the bunker.*

SEVENTEEN

Photo © 2015-2017, Dave Sansom

The seventeenth is a 355-yard dogleg par four. Before the extensive renovation for the Ryder Cup in 1963, there were two greens on each hole because the different seasons required different grasses. Usually, the two greens were side-by-side and played the same distance, but they were widely separated here, and one was a par three.

On the days their details were recorded, both Alexa and Bobby played to the summer green, the 230-yard par-three version, that was a hundred yards to the right and 125 yards closer to the tee than the par four. Their green was on the hilltop now occupied by the upper practice tees.

Alexa: *I usually hit short of the bunker with my drive, but sometimes bounce over. I can count on a four and quite often have a three. Short approaches are one of the best parts of my game.*

Reporter from the Atlanta Journal: *In the recent foursome as Bobby's partner, Miss Stirling drove into the face of the bunker, but it bounced to the edge of the green. Her chip was too far to the right, and she missed her putt, taking a four.*

Bobby: *Iron off to right in rough. Niblick* [nine iron] *to eight feet from cup. One putt.*

Members usually play the seventeenth to the right to avoid the large fairway bunkers on the left, but long hitters may try a bold shot over the bunkers. If it comes off, the approach shot will be a short pitch over the bunker.

Ralph: *The drive is interesting in that the closer you play to the fairway bunkers the flatter the landing zone and the more roll-out you get. If you play to the safer right side of the fairway it slopes more toward you and kills the roll out, making that side of the dogleg even longer. The green is built like three greens in one. The left, center, and right areas all have different elevations and slopes.*

In the 2014 Bobby Jones Classic, high school golfer Brendon Doyle did one better. His partners wondered why he waited to hit until the team ahead had left the green, but they found out when he unleashed a booming drive that soared far over the fairway bunkers. Everybody thought it must be in the front bunker, but when they climbed the hill for the first look, there it sat, all alone in the first cut on the back of the green. The excited group walked onto the green, and James Watson made the eagle putt. They almost won the cup because of Brendon.

Less than a hundred yards from the green, the fairway is crossed diagonally by a depression that Dean Hudson, a deceased member of the Athletic Club, said was a trench in the Civil War.

Richard Courts described walking the course at East Lake with Bobby when they were caught in a severe thunderstorm on this hole:

We threw our bags away and ran, but the lightning was so close, we couldn't go far. We looked down into a gully [the trench] *hoping to hide, but it was full of water, so we had to give up and lay face down on open ground to wait for the storm to pass. It seemed like an hour went by with our faces pressed against that wet grass. We were scared to death.*

Richard was a businessman and tennis player who exercised with Bobby during the winter before his assault on the Grand Slam in 1930. They went over to the stage of an abandoned theater downtown several times a week to play a badminton-like game with heavy rackets and a huge bird that Bobby had learned in California. He called it Doug after its inventor, Douglas Fairbanks. Both friends lost weight because of the regular exercise; the tennis player lost fifteen pounds, but the golfer lost thirty-five. He must have had to work harder.

Richard and his other friends always knew Bobby as Bob. He said he was Little Bob at first for contrast and later to compliment his father, who was called Big Bob for the same two reasons. He never heard his friend called Bobby until he came back from a successful trip to Scotland.

'Richard, why don't you come with me? The people are delightful, and the golf courses are the best and most difficult in the world.'

'You mean you're going all that way just to play golf?' I asked.

When he was over there, he won an important tournament and was awarded what he called 'the most magnificent trophy I ever saw.' We read in the paper that after the tournament a big crowd formed around him for the presentation of this trophy. Bob told the Scots he couldn't possibly take such a wonderful trophy away and that he would be honored to simply have his name inscribed at the bottom and know that it was safe in that delightful place.

Well, those words touched every person in that crowd. When he finally had to leave, they began shouting 'our Bobby' and 'wee Bobby.' After that, every time Bob set foot in Scotland or England he was a sensation. There was something about him that let them pretend he was their own. He was unlike many Americans they knew; there was fire but no arrogance and no bragging.

Richard met Bobby the first time he played at East Lake. He was standing with his host on the practice tee watching a young man hit one beautiful arching shot after another.

He turned to his friend: *'I'm used to paying good money to see golf like that.'*

'Well, you're going to pay today,' his friend replied. *'That's Little Bob, and he'll be my partner. You're playing with his father, and Little Bob has just started to beat Big Bob.'*

Colonel Jones joined Richard's Board of Directors and became a close friend. Once, when the two men were visiting the Witham's on West Andrews Drive in Atlanta, they were gathered around a tub of potatoes boiling in resin out in the back yard. The Colonel burst into song. Richard remembered the details:

It happened to be the week the Metropolitan Opera was in town. Big Bob started singing 'Ole Man River' in his great baritone voice. He knew every word of every verse, and it was a wonderful sound. About halfway through, a messenger arrived with a note from Dr. Phinizy Calhoun's house next door. They wanted to know which opera star was singing and could they come over.

Back to the seventeenth: In September 2007, Charlie Harrison was out playing nine holes by himself on the last day before the course was closed for improvements. He had been taking his time. A foursome was in front of him, but he stayed back, not wanting to go through. It was getting dark, and he thought he would walk in after this hole. He hit a good drive, and when he came over the hill, he noticed the foursome had a young woman walking with them. They stopped to watch him from the ninth tee beyond the green. He thought he knew one of the men, and when he smiled and waved for him to hit to the green, he recognized him as James Watson, a Jones Scholar he knew.

He already had his pitching wedge and quickly indicated he would go ahead. He stepped to the ball. As soon as he hit it, even before his head came up, he knew the swing and the feel of the ball meant he had hit it as well as he could. The ball jumped off the grass, flew high and straight at the pin, bounced twice, and ran straight in for eagle two. The reaction from the young people was instantaneous.

Charlie: *I was excited by their enthusiasm and happily agreed to walk in with them. It's still fun to remember the last shot that day.*

James was playing with three other Scholars, Eric Teasdale, Oliver Gregory, and David Wilkinson. The young woman was Eric's sister, Elissa.

James texted his report: *We all watched it go in and cheered as loud as we could — it was dark and we knew it was the last shot of the day. We congratulated Charlie on the green, then we all walked together down the fairway as night fell. It had been a magical afternoon.*

Building the tees on 17 — looking back from the fairway

EIGHTEEN

Photo © 2015-2017, Dave Sansom

The eighteenth is the only hole with the same number in both the 1908 and 2016 courses, and it has always been a par five. The first version was 500 yards, but today members play it from 551 yards. New tees added several years ago make it possible to extend it to 600 yards. The length in the Ryder Cup was the same as Alexa and Bobby played — 525 yards.[3]

Two stories about Bobby's father happened here. After a practice swing, he said to his son, *There, what's wrong with that swing?*

Nothing, Dad, his son replied. *Why don't you use it sometime?*

Next, or at another time, the Colonel connected and hit a high booming drive over the trees on the left. At its highest point, the ball turned sharply right, crossed the entire fairway, and plunged into the woods on the right.

That's it, he roared. *Go on in there, you sight-seeing !!&@!%!^*#!*

Alexa: *I'm usually over the lake in two. If I have a reasonable lie, I use a brassie for my second. I can count on getting on in three. I got a four there today.*

Bobby: *Fair drive to heavy lie. Brassie short of the green. Niblick chip to eight feet from cup. One putt.*

---

3   In 2017 Greg Edwards measured the distance from the forward tee to the green. When he said it was 438 yards, something clicked. He told the group that in the recent WGC Dell Match Play at Austin Country Club, on the twelfth hole, Jon Rahm drove the ball exactly that distance in the championship match.

Chad: *There's another illusion from this tee. The hill on the right that's covered with rough makes you think the edge of the rough on that side continues on line, but the best landing area opens up to the right beyond the hill — it's the widest part of the fairway. The line for the tee shot is to the right of center, and a little draw is ideal. You should hit it farther right than you think to get all the way down the hill to a flat lie — into the mayor's office, so to speak.*[4]

The 2016 Tour Championship brought this old hole back into the spotlight. It was the site of the last hole in regulation and first and second holes in the sudden death playoff, and it proved to be as dramatic as everyone hoped. Rory McElroy hit the best shot here Rick Burton has ever seen. During the playoff, his drive disappeared into long grass on the left and settled ten to fifteen yards behind a tree. Branches blocked his line to the fairway across the lake. It looked like he would have to lay up short of the lake with a sand wedge, but that was not his plan. He managed to reach the ball with the clubface of a long iron, and it shot out under the branches with enough power to fly well across the lake. It settled in the fairway a pitch shot from the green.

Rick: *Almost always, in deep rough, a long iron will make the ball pop straight up. I've never seen anything like it.*

An eye witness reported that Ryan Moore won everyone's admiration during that playoff, and he also made three new friends. He was the leader in the clubhouse and had gone to the range to stay loose while waiting it out. Three spectators were across the lake watching the eighteenth when Rory finished in a three-way tie with Ryan and Kevin Chappell. They needed to get to the clubhouse, but the more direct way to the left of the green was packed with the large crowd. They checked the practice tee and only saw people walking behind it. Ryan and his caddie were not noticed against that moving background. They made a quick decision to hurry across the practice range to get back to the clubhouse. Half way across they heard a "whoosh" over their heads, then another, and that's when they saw him. They ran faster and made it to behind the range, now walking slowly with all the others. Then the call came for the players to board a cart and go to the eighteenth tee for the sudden-death playoff. Ryan and his caddie were coming up fast behind them on the special path.

---

4   If your drive ends at the top of the hill 280 yards (840 feet) from the green, as many do, you'll face a Titanic shot. The distance to the clubhouse from there is similar to the lengths of both the Titanic (883 feet) and the Missouri (887). When he heard this, James Watson suggested, *That shot should only be called a Titanic if it goes terribly wrong. If you like it, call it a Missouri.*

One of the men said, *Com'on Ryan, go get 'em ...* and, in a stage whisper, *Thanks for not hitting us on the range.*

Ryan and his caddie were now a few feet ahead on the right. At that, he turned around, and his face broke into a friendly smile:

It's not like I wasn't trying to.

Chad: *On the second shot, golfers who get it down here to the flat place before the lake will have a glimpse of greatness that will make them salivate. You can play it short to the flat place up the hill, but if you get sloppy up there, you'll either be in the lake or in the new cross bunker in real trouble.*

Several scenes in a movie about the beginning of McDonald's, 'The Founder' were shot at East Lake, and my friend Drew and I are in a scene on this hole.[5]

During the Ryder Cup Matches in 1963, a member recalled watching Julius Boros play his second from the Bermuda rough down near the lake on the right side:

He took a full swing with a wood, but both the ball and the club stayed in the rough. The grass pulled the club right out of his hands.

Over the years, East Lake golfers other than Bobby Jones have had outstanding rounds. Tommy Barnes finished a 62 at age 73 here, which may be the lowest score ever shot by a man that age. His son, Tommy Jr., also had rounds in the low 60s, and Charlie Harrison remembers a day in April, 1964, when the unexpected happened to him. Charlie had talked Allen Hardin into playing nine holes, but he changed his plan when his putt on the ninth spun out to give him an even 30 for the front nine. He turned to his friend:

Allen, I don't know what your plans are, but I've got to keep going.

He shot a 33 on the back to finish with 63.

Michael Jordan played thirty-six holes at East Lake on July 29, 1996, when he was in town for the Olympics, and a little group greeted him as he made the turn after twenty-seven holes. The younger professionals playing with him were hot and tired, but Michael looked cool and fresh.

In 1913, the last year of the Bendelow course, eleven-year-old Bobby sank a four-foot putt here to score 80 for the first time.

O.B. Keeler: *On this summer day, he was playing with Perry Adair as usual, but for once, and for the first time, he wasn't paying any attention to what Perry was doing. He was scoring better than he ever had scored before and he had no room in his mind for anything else. At the last green, faced with a four-foot putt for an*

---

5 Drew Dunn, East Lake's Head Golf Professional.

even 80, he must have wondered why his skinny little chest was so tight and why his hands were trembling as he stood up to that putt, not to beat Perry but just to score an 80. Down went the putt and on the card went the 80, with Perry's signature on the attested line.

And away across the golf course went Bobby Jones, setting off at a brisk trot to find his dad. He found Big Bob at the fourteenth green [the present eighteenth tee], *and he walked solemnly up to him and held out the card without a word — his hand still trembling. Big Bob took the card and looked at it. Then he looked at Bobby. Then he put his arms around him and hugged him hard.*

And so, before he was a dozen years old, Bobby Jones had discovered a new adversary in golf, the Great Opponent whose tangible form is only a card and a pencil. He had played his first round against the toughest foeman of them all — Old Man Par (Keeler and Rice 1953).

Michael had many caddies that day.

130

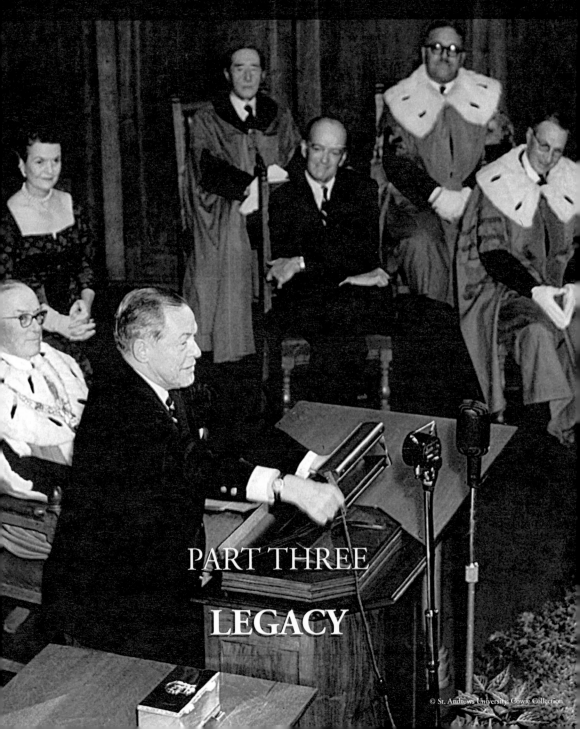

I could take out of my life everything except my experiences at St. Andrews, and I would still have a rich full life … Then it occurred to me to speak of my interpretation of the words 'friend' and 'friendship,' which are among the most important in our language, and yet are so often loosely used. Friends are a man's priceless treasures, and a life rich in friendship is rich indeed.

Bobby Jones, Freedom of the City speech
St. Andrews, October 9, 1958

PART THREE

LEGACY

X

REMEMBERING MR. JONES

In 1922, Bobby graduated from Georgia Tech with a degree in Mechanical Engineering. Then, during the same years that he won his national championships, he received a second bachelor's degree at Harvard in English Literature in 1924 and attended Emory Law School for one year. He passed the bar in 1927, joined his father's firm in 1928, and won his first case in 1929, the same year he won his third U.S. Open. He retired from competition after winning the Grand Slam in 1930. He was twenty-eight.

Those who practiced with him or knew him off the course didn't forget their stories.

HARVEY HILL

The first time I saw Bob was about 1920 in the Southern Amateur at East Lake. I picked him up on the fourth (new thirteenth) tee. He hit a ball off that tee which was the longest shot I'd ever seen, but nobody could find the ball. They looked all over and finally found it over by the fence on the right in the rough. Bob walked over, took a good look, and pulled out his baffy (approach wood, similar to a seven wood). Then he took a big swing, and the ball sailed clear up onto the green over 200 yards away. The crowd went wild.

I played lots of golf with Bob, but in the twenties and thirties we couldn't get him away from East Lake. He was always over there. Later, during the forties, East Lake began to get crowded, and he would play with us sometimes on Sunday morning at Capital City. One day, I played with Richard Garlington against Bob and Charlie Black. We played the back nine first that day, and they closed us out with three holes to go. After I paid my five dollars, I went up to Bob on the seventh tee and said,

Well, Bob, you've beaten us bad. Now I want to play you for five dollars a hole from here on in.

You mean that, Harvey? Bob answered.

I sure do, I said, *and you've got to give me a shot on every one since they're all 'stroke' holes for me.* I was pretending to be upset.

All right, then, I'll do it if that's what you want, he said. He looked real serious.

I played some of my best golf and shot three straight pars but it wasn't good enough. On the par five seventh, he drove to the top of the hill, hit a fairway wood onto the green, and sank the putt for eagle three. One up. On the eighth, a 350-yard par four, Bob drove the green by hitting up onto the hill to the left and having it trickle down to the green. He made that putt for eagle two. Two up. On the par five ninth, he drove almost to the top of the hill, reached the green with his second, and made the final putt for his third straight eagle. He pulled his ball out of the cup and he turned to me:

I guess that'll teach you a lesson. He was not smiling.

He never used people. His practice was a lot smaller than it could have been if he had taken advantage of his influence around the world to bring in new business.

I asked him many times, *Bob, why don't you call so-and-so and see if we can be of any help? You know him so well.*

I'll get around to it in a little while, he answered. But he never did.

We all admired him because he never used his influence to manipulate people and was lacking in affectation.

ANNE THOMAS

Mrs. Thomas is the daughter of Green Warren, a friend of Bobby's who helped him establish Peachtree Golf Club in Atlanta in 1948.[1] In 2017, she was interviewed by Johnny Vardeman, the retired editor of the Gainesville Times:

He was just plain Mr. Jones ... I don't know how they became good friends, but every Saturday my parents played gin rummy in a back room of the Jones's home in Buckhead. If I ever needed them, and they weren't home, I knew to go over there.

Mrs. Warren also played golf. When Jones misplaced his putter, Calamity Jane, he told her, *I've looked everywhere for it, at Peachtree and Augusta, and nobody can find it.*

Mrs. Warren responded that he had left it in her golf bag.

---

1   Green Warren was a dentist, and the dental part of the Good News Clinic in Gainesville, a charity-funded healthcare system, is named the Green Warren Dental Clinic.

Then just keep it, Jones said, and she became the owner of a Calamity Jane.

His original putters are described as beat up and rusty, their cracked hickory shafts repaired with glue and wire. One is displayed at the clubhouse at Augusta National. The other is in the United States Golf Association's museum in Far Hills, New Jersey.

The Warrens were so close to the Joneses that they stayed with them in Boston when he underwent surgery on his neck.

Once, they were staying at the Jones's cottage at Augusta National when Mrs. Warren heard something outside her window. She looked out and saw a man standing there.

What are you doing? she asked.

I'm looking for the paint brush Winston Churchill gave me, former President Dwight Eisenhower replied. Ike was an avid golfer, frequent visitor to Augusta National, and painted as a hobby.

FRAZER DURETT, JR.

Merger

In 1958, about two years after I started practicing law, mergers changed my firm from Bird & Howell to Jones, Bird, Williams & Howell. This was not necessarily for a better economic opportunity but rather for such soft factors as congeniality and shared values. Although we associates were not involved with either the negotiations or the decision to merge, experience has shown me that such justification for merger is indispensable to its success.

Our merger led to the first of many subsequent law office expansions. The most significant physical change was the location of Bob Jones's office next to the men's room, where a private bathroom was created for Bob. (I never addressed Bob other than as Mr. Jones, but that formality now seems unnatural). After having been chauffeured to the Haas Howell Building, Bob would laboriously walk to his office on aluminum crutches clamped to his arms above and below the elbows. Syringomyelia is defined as "a chronic, progressive disease of the spinal cord ... The cause is unknown ... Onset is insidious." In Bob it was first manifest in 1948, and was subsequently evidenced by an initial deterioration of feet and hands, progressing to severe atrophy of all limbs. When Bob first showed up in a wheelchair, it was a sad indication of the inexorable progress of his disease.

Bob, not a decorator, determined the contents of his office. Besides many books, none legal, I recall particularly the illustrated Grantland Rice poem:

For when the great scorer comes to write against your name, it matters not that you won or lost, but how you played the game.

Also present were the Alister MacKenzie layout of Augusta National, with today's front and back nines reversed, small monochrome portraits of his father, Big Bob, his friend Bob Woodruff, and a photograph of him with President Eisenhower. He permitted us to hang the portrait that Ike had painted of him in the hall. There were no trophies.

Most exciting in those early days was the frequent arrival of a simple but elegant envelope carrying the engraving, The White House. To have periodic personal communication from the President was only reflected glory, however. Bob kept his correspondence with Ike confidential, not wishing to exploit their relationship.

One day, Bob asked if my two sons, then four and two, had any interest in his dog, which he decided needed more active companionship than Mary and he could provide. Upon reflection and without consulting the boys, I decided that they very much wanted his dog and no other. When my wife Cree, the boys, and I drove to Bob's home to take possession, we discovered that the dog in question was a basset, with the meatiest body I had ever seen. The reason for the bulk was one of two hitherto undisclosed problems: Bob and Mary had begun feeding the dog ice cream, to which he had become so addicted that he would eat nothing else. The second problem was the dog's name — MacMillan — after the Prime Minister with basset eyes, or Mac for short. Mac happened to also be the name of our two-year old. When Cree called the child, the dog, gathering speed like a diesel-powered bowling ball, would scatter his tottering namesake like a tenpin.

It was too late to rename the child, so poor MacMillan was forced through the psychological trauma of being concurrently weaned from both ice cream and name. It is a testimonial to the stamina of the breed that MacMillan successfully adapted to both dog chow and a new name, Judge, forerunner of later bassets named Bailiff and Chancellor.

A short time after the merger, we were saddened that Ralph Williams, Sr. died of a heart attack. The firm gathered in our conference room to comfort each other and to acknowledge his vital spirit. One moment of that meeting remains vivid in my memory. Bob noted that most people engaged in conversation are not listening but concentrating solely on framing their response. Ralph, however, was a listener. Being a listener, Bob suggested, was not just rare but was of great value. It made the conversation better and the friendships stronger.

From that moment, I began to understand that friendship was one of the principal gifts Bob Jones, Ralph Williams, and Ed Kane brought to, and sought to find in, the merger with Bird & Howell.

Sale of Joroberts Corporation

In addition to the Augusta National and the Masters, one of the ventures Bob Jones and Cliff Roberts started was Joroberts Corporation, a holding company of South American Coca-Cola bottling plants the two co-managed for investors, including themselves. By 1960, Bob had decided that the burden of management had become too heavy, so Roberts, a New York stockbroker, found a buyer for the company, now listed on the NYSE as Standex International. For reasons still unclear to me, I was designated to accompany Bob and my senior partner Arthur Howell to New York to close the sale of Joroberts stock.

A sister of the new airplane we were to fly, a Convair 880, had been drilled into the ground by a test flight crew two weeks before our departure, killing all aboard. Therefore, we were more than a little apprehensive as we sat off the runway at Atlanta Airport watching the ground crew with dipsticks swarming over each wing. A flight attendant eventually informed the passengers that the fuel gauges were malfunctioning — too much fuel had been pumped into the tanks, and the captain was trying to decide whether to siphon the fuel off on the ground or jettison it from the air.

After ten minutes of silence, while we wondered how a plane with too much fuel could get into the air, Bob rang the stewardess. When she leaned over, he innocently inquired whether the captain was experiencing difficulty in making up his mind.

It was dusk when we landed at Idlewild (its name before its rebaptism as Kennedy) Airport and the plane stopped just off the runway, well away from the gate. The other passengers joined me in wondering why only the three of us were disembarking in the middle of nowhere. We descended on movable stairs and entered a limousine parked next to the airplane. Two motorcycle patrolmen already had their red lights flashing before and aft. As we gathered speed while still within the airport, Bob gruffly announced to his stunned companions that when one has received the keys to New York, they occasionally come in handy.

The closing was scheduled in the Wall Street offices of Shearman & Sterling. With just over 150 lawyers, it was the largest law firm in the world. (At that time, all major New York law firms were clustered around Wall Street.) When we arrived the next morning, we discovered a big problem. The senior associate responsible for preparing the documents securing Chase's loan to the buyer had experienced a nervous breakdown, and no security agreement had been prepared. It shortly became apparent that the only lawyer present with both knowledge of the deal and the incentive to get it promptly closed was me. Although I represented neither party to the security agreement, I started preparing it immediately.

At the closing that afternoon, attended by Standex's CEO Dan Hogan (who brought his golf clubs), Messrs. Jones and Roberts, and a bank vice president, I hesitantly suggested that the banker might wish to review his security agreement, since it had been prepared by a lawyer not representing the bank. He coolly informed me that he had no need to rely upon that document, since he required the borrower to maintain a corresponding balance at his bank. That was not the last time a banker's actions have caused me to appreciate the value bankers place on their lawyers and to wonder whether anyone other than a lawyer ever reads a loan document unless it must be enforced.

As we checked out of the Westbury Hotel, then more a club than a hotel, Arthur was called upon to perform a service for which he was uniquely qualified, checking the bill. I jumped when he exclaimed, *Good Lord, Bob, they've charged you a dollar apiece for Coca-Colas!*

Bob never hesitated with his reflective response: *You know, Arthur, this is the only place in the world where they charge what they're worth.*

For those unaware of the effect of inflation, a Coca-Cola in 1960 was selling for fifteen cents in Atlanta. For those who never had the pleasure of savoring Arthur's companionship, he spent much of his free time on trips to New York with Ralph Williams, Jr., Dick Allison, or me in tow, looking for men's dress shirts that could be purchased for less than their cost in Rich's basement.

But What Did He Do?

People are naturally curious about whether Bob practiced law. In his early career there is a story about a trial in Macon, when Bob represented an insurance company defending a tort claim brought by a widow. In mid-trial court was recessed, and the judge invited Bob to play a round of golf. After victory in the case and upon his return to Atlanta, Bob was rumored to have written his personal check to the widow for the amount she would have been awarded had she won.

After that he advised the firm, *I'll be damned if I ever try another case.*

After the merger, his time in the office was occupied in large part by writing several books on golf — his one earlier book was a joint venture with O.B. Keeler when he was twenty-five years old. He maintained the most varied and extensive personal correspondence imaginable. Everyone who had ever met him seemed to write him, not just the rich and famous. One day he called me into his office, where he had opened a letter from a caddy master retired from a Massachusetts club where Bob had won a tournament in the twenties. The letter informed Bob that the writer's son had just been named an administrative dean of The Harvard Law School. Bob wondered if I might know anything about the matter. When I responded that the son was a classmate and acquaintance, Bob relished the prospect of advising the father of that mild coincidence. I was struck with the force of a personality that after forty years still invited the father to share his pleasure.

Bob was also an officer of Spalding, the manufacturer of Bobby Jones golf clubs, still a top seller despite Bob's long-time absence from tournament competition. One purpose behind Bob's continued production of books on golf was doubtless to promote the purchase of his golf clubs in an inconspicuous way.

The Jones family businesses, a textile mill and a mercantile company, were located in Canton, Georgia. They were steady clients of the firm, particularly during the brief popularity of scrub denim and the violent times when the plant voted to join a union, threatening ultimate liquidation for the benefit of creditors.

One day I found the judge of the Superior Court of Cherokee County presiding over a boundary line dispute before a jury in Ellijay. As I waited for a recess to obtain an order enjoining picketing, I noticed that no surveyors

138

had been called as witnesses. As I handed over the order, I remarked to the judge that identifying a boundary line without a survey seemed hard to do. He replied that such a procedure was only recently adopted in that county.

What procedure preceded this one? I asked.

Feuds, he replied.

A legal matter I worked on with Bob was revising the bylaws of the Peachtree Golf Club, which Bob had been instrumental in founding. Like his predecessors, the current club president always deferred to Bob on matters involving governance of the club. It quickly became apparent to me that in the bylaw revision I was to author, those two shared one objective: that the document be purged of every vestige of members' rights against governing board authority. To a bleeding-heart liberal like myself there was not a shred of democratic instinct in either of them, although there was one big difference. The president was about as simpatico as Attila the Hun, but Bob emanated as much noblesse oblige as the entire Court of Versailles.

When golf was no longer possible, Bob was able to experience some pleasure in fishing. His frequent companion was Charlie Elliott, fish and game writer for an Atlanta newspaper. One day in South Georgia, two local men were watching Elliott hoist Bob clumsily into a fishing boat.

One said to the other, *They say that fella was a golf champion. Wonder how he did it?*

Overhearing but without looking up Bob muttered, *Lots of practice.*

My favorite picture of Bob is on the wall of the Jones Room at the Commerce Club. It is a 1930 photograph of the Walker Cup team on an English lawn. Three men are seated in front. As captain, Bob is in the center, flanked on one side by a prince who became Edward VIII and on the other by George VI. Bob had a regal bearing and may have missed his true calling. He would have been the consummate king.

Photograph of Bobby Jones at Sandwich, England in 1930
with King George VI (R) and Edward, Prince of Wales

Bobby Jones Golf Balls

People still recount Bob's reaction to the praise he received for calling a penalty on himself when no one but he could see the club move the ball:

You might as well praise someone for not robbing a bank.

He was equally dismayed at the criticism leveled at the 1968 Masters committee when the apparent winner was disqualified for wrongly adding up his score. The reason for the disqualification was to assure careful attention by the only person who can keep score accurately. Anyone with brains, Bob thought, should understand that a rule with reason deserves support, and soft-headed sympathy does not.

Less well known is the importance Bob placed on good taste. When he heard that a liquor store owner in St. Louis was selling Bobby Jones golf balls as loss leaders, he was as outraged by the low quality of the balls as by the clear theft of his name. The fact that the owner of the liquor store was also named Robert Jones arguably mitigated the theft but not the shoddy quality. During his life Bob permitted his name to appear on irons and woods he designed, but he had never designed a golf ball and would not permit his name to be associated with a commodity for which he had no responsibility.

Judge Bird recommended a lawyer in St. Louis, Bill Webster, a young member of the American Law Institute. Shortly before Bob and I were to fly to St. Louis for the trial, I received an apologetic phone message from Webster telling me that he had just been appointed to the U.S. District Court and therefore had to turn over the case to his partner. After a distinguished career on the U.S. District and Circuit Courts and as director of the FBI and CIA, Bill Webster is now retired with one regret. He lost the chance to represent Bob Jones in open court.

The trial took place over thirty years after Bob had played his last tournament. When I pushed his wheelchair through the hotel lobby to catch a cab to the courthouse, an army of reporters, photographers, and television cameras barred our way. Bob was still front-page news in St. Louis.

We also discovered something else about the status of an equitable remedy far from the eastern seaboard. Acting upon the person of a defendant, such as demanding a certain behavior or compelling an accounting, was viewed in the West as English law, entirely out of step with individualism and the self-reliant spirit of the American frontier, even a frontier that left St. Louis a hundred years before. Our St. Louis counsel was overjoyed to have obtained an injunction against the further marketing of Bobby Jones golf balls, but we had also wanted an accounting.

I returned from St. Louis with a valued insight on human nature. At the end of the day, Bob had asked if I would help him undress. He could handle most of the big things but not neckties, shoelaces and buttons. I was embarrassed, not for me but for him, that as great an athlete as anyone had ever known had to ask for such personal help. I tried to disguise my feelings and then realized Bob evidenced no embarrassment at all. He joked about our challenge, completely devoid of self pity. The next morning as we cooperatively dressed him, it was as if we were engaged in a carefree game in which neither was very accomplished. What I learned about human nature is that one can bestow a great gift in asking for help. The gift comes when the person asking for help also communicates that he harbors no resentment for being forced to incur an obligation. Bob appeared to harbor nothing but gratitude, and under the circumstances there could have been no more cherished gift.

Lousy

Never having known Bob as an athlete, I found his abiding interest was to find the best possible way to express a thought in the English language. His ability to write clearly was the result of his two years at Harvard studying English literature and his determination to publish books. Much of his time in the office after our merger was spent writing books and letters. Reading Bob's books is a pleasure, surprising to those whose image of a great athlete is that of a dumb jock.

It was while Bob was at work on *Golf Is My Game* that I made the mistake of including the word "lousy" in a memorandum to him. The word offended his sense of propriety. Mark Twain once said that the difference between the right word and the almost right word was the difference between lightning and a lightning bug.

Lousy, Bob informed me, *did not qualify as either.* Until now, I never consciously wrote the word again.

Shortly before Bob died, I asked his secretary, Jean Marshall, to ask him whether there was a time I could drop by his home and visit. Jean soon phoned to say that Bob appreciated my offer and would love to see me but just felt too lousy.

I knew he had used the right word but had no way of knowing whether he appreciated the irony.

Naming a Firm

In 1982, during the negotiations leading to Alston & Bird, we at Jones, Bird & Howell (except for the name partners who excused themselves from participating) were insistent that the new firm be institutionalized by having only two names, one from each firm to be selected by that firm. Once that was agreed, we focused on our one name.

It was Ralph Williams, Jr., the only surviving member of Jones, Williams, Dorsey & Kane, who proposed the name Bird. Ralph reminded us that the Jones in the firm name was that of Big Bob, dead before any of my generation even went to law school, that Bob's reputation was not that of a great lawyer, and that Judge Bird's name connoted all one could wish to project in terms of legal reputation. Someone suggested that the Jones name, however, had glamour no other name in Atlanta could match. Upon reflection, we decided to avoid exploiting Bob's name for the wrong reasons.

As I recall, we easily reached consensus on the appropriate name. I have no doubt Bob would have approved.

FRED RUSSELL

After his playing days, Bobby was frequently invited to appear with other figures from what has been called the golden age of sport, the 1920s. One event was recorded by Fred Russell, the longtime sports editor of the *Nashville Banner*, in his book, *Bury Me in an Old Press Box*. The occasion was a luncheon in September of 1953 in Nashville with Jack Dempsey and Red Grange. It was described by Bill Corum of the *New York Journal American*:

Red Grange, a still slim and racy-looking man with dark auburn hair, thinning a little now, moved into the big room. Once he had been as close to a darting, spinning shaft of light across the cross bars of a football field as any man has ever been before or since. Next to appear was the big fellow, Jack Dempsey. There's something about Dempsey, forever boyish. Then, through the archway came a man walking slowly with a cane, a proud man in the way a man should be proud in the face of whatever may befall him. Suddenly, every man in the room was on his feet. Hand clapping drew as close to a cheer as the clapping of hands can come. Tears jumped to sting a little behind your eyes. Bobby Jones smiled.

'Thank you, gentlemen,' he said.

And then, turning the moment deftly, as the champions and those who are born with such a knack can do, he said:

'But I know why you are applauding. I'm the only man in the room who had the foresight to bring his high-ball with him from the bar. It was a fine thing, a very fine thing. Not many men, whatever they may have done, ever got a tribute so totally spontaneous and touching.'

Even in Bob's sense of humor, there was always a certain softness. He had been intrigued by the veteran caddies at St. Andrews when he won the British Amateur in 1930.

In experience, wisdom, and dignity, they're in a group to themselves. There was one, perhaps in his seventies, carrying the clubs of an unpleasant fellow who was playing very poor golf and blaming it all on the caddie. The old caddie maintained a dignified silence, of course — until the man formally declared, addressing the other members of the match,

'For this round, I believe I've drawn the worst caddie in the world!'

'Oh no, sir,' said the caddie. 'That would be quite too great a coincidence.'

BOB FOREMAN

We all knew he was receptive to one of us leaning in his doorway to see how busy he was. He would drop whatever he was doing and invite us in with a friendly smile and genuine interest. He made us feel important. There was a natural sweetness about him that drew us to him.

An example of his thoughtfulness is a story about his need for secretarial assistance on a Saturday morning when his own secretary was out of town. He called me on Friday afternoon and asked if I could arrange it. I notified one of the firm's best secretaries, Mary Edenfield. That night Bob called me again to let me know the emergency had passed, and he would not need Mary the next day. I told him I would let Mary know she did not have to come.

Bob quickly said, *No, let me call her. I think she would appreciate that.*

I once heard another lawyer in the firm enthusiastically announce to Bob and some other friends that he had heard about an invisible cream to rub on golf clubs to make shots go farther. Bob immediately became serious and looked him in the eye:

If you use that I'll never speak to you again!

One feature of his office in the 50s and 60s was an ever-present, open six oz. bottle of Coca-Cola on his desk, a bottle that sat in a crocheted coaster and cost a nickel.

CY STRICKLER

I was an internist in Atlanta and played golf with Bobby at Capital City and East Lake. I was one of his friends invited to play with him at Augusta after the Masters in the 30s and 40s. Four foursomes were formed, and Bobby played in a different group every day.

I remember when the man I knew only as a great golfer became a friend. In 1924, I was eighteen years old and qualifying for the Georgia State Amateur at the Capital City Club. I was one under par when I walked onto a water hole on that course. I was surprised to see Bobby Jones sitting on a bench beside the tee.

Everyone knew Bob, but I knew he didn't know who I was. I tipped my cap to him on the way to teeing up my ball.

He said, *Hello, Cy.*

I was so flustered that I topped that ball right in the lake.

I only had one formal golf lesson of my life, and it was at East lake by Stewart Maiden. Several of my golfing friends had told me for months that I stood too far away from the ball. Since it felt right to me, I kept standing in the same position, but when I went to see Maiden, I expected him to tell me to stand closer. He gave the lesson on the first tee rather than down in the practice area, and I soon found out why. He was feeling the effects of some alcohol and was in an unusually expansive mood. While I hit ball after ball down the fairway, he stood out in the driveway greeting all the big shots driving in. He was stopping the cars and shaking their hands and chatting loudly while I worked away. It didn't seem he was paying me the slightest attention. Finally, when I'd finished a third bag I called over to him, *What do you think?*

He looked up from the driveway and yelled, *Stand farther away from the ball.*

EUGENE BRANCH

I was mainly a tennis player, and I remember Bob telling me that I ought to play golf because it was more relaxing:

You just can't think of anything else while you're playing golf.

Bob was a great friend of Robert Woodruff. Mr. Woodruff was a good golfer, and I remember his favorite Bobby Jones story. One day when Woodruff was playing the Old Course at St. Andrews, he had a caddie who said very little. On one hole he hit three great shots to a par five and was about three feet away. He turned to the caddie and said, *That was a pretty good shot, wasn't it?*

The caddie uttered his first words, *Bobby Jones was there in two.*

He thought he would pull the leg of the caddie a little and said, *Who's Bobby Jones?*

At that, the caddie just laid down the clubs and walked off. He never said another word.

I asked Bob how he felt about people calling him Bobby since he seemed to prefer the more mature Bob.

It's not any big deal, he said, *but let me show you something.*

He pulled out a letter he'd saved from a grammar school teacher. Apparently, the teacher had asked the students to write a letter to a famous person, and the letter went as follows:

Dear Bobby, I'm in the third grade, and when I grow up I want to be an engineer. What are you going to be when you grow up?

Bob said, *This kid thinks I'm his age.*

He was frequently asked about who the greatest player was, and he remembered that some Scots used to say Old Tom Morris could beat Bobby Jones if he had the same equipment and played the same golf courses:

I always thought this was a useless argument. The only thing you can do is beat the people playing against you. There's no way you can work on somebody who died before you were born or who was born after you died.

I had the great idea of naming one of our new courses at the Athletic Club Calamity Jane. I couldn't wait to go to work the next morning so I could tell Bob about it. He didn't like the idea at all. When I thought about it, I realized he didn't like anything that tended to glorify something about him.

An impressive piece of information about Bob was that when he was thirteen he won the championships of both the East Lake Country Club and the Druid Hills Golf Club. At first, I thought the person telling me must have meant the junior championships, but I was wrong. He won the real club championships at age thirteen. There is a gold watch at our club which was presented to him in 1915 by the membership in commemoration of those two victories.

RALPH WILLIAMS, JR.

There was a big difference in our ages, but I worked for him and certainly enjoyed getting to know him. One of the things I remember most clearly was how Bob always knew the name of any new secretary or young associate who joined the firm. As he was wheeled down the hall in his wheelchair, when the newcomers passed him, Bob would always call them by name and look them right in the eye. All those young people considered that a great compliment.

Bob Jones and his daddy were very close. They especially loved leaving work early in the afternoon to play golf together at East Lake. Occasionally, they would ask a third or a fourth to join them, but mainly they liked to be by themselves. They loved doing anything together.

He didn't practice at all, not even on business matters after the fifties, and for the most part managed his own investments. These included a string of Coca-Cola bottling plants up in New England. At that time, he had decided he wanted to sell the plants and he sent me up there to negotiate the sales.

I made many trips and spent all week talking to this or that person, trying to work out the proper deal. As soon as I got back, I always went over to his house and left off all the details on the trip. I used to dread Monday morning because I knew he would want the details word-for-word. It was a lot harder answering his questions than making those deals in New England. When it finally came time to close the deal, I spent many more hours negotiating the precise words of the contract with Bob than with the other side. He was an absolute perfectionist and a master of the English language. Also, he had an incredible memory and a wonderful capacity for complex details — he never forgot a thing. I remember one of Bob's favorite letters, in which a friend had written, *I apologize for writing such a long letter, but I didn't have time to make it shorter.*

DALE HARMAN

I was a 1962 graduate of UVA law school without many connections in Atlanta, and one of the reasons I wanted to look for a job there was I had heard Atlanta was welcoming to outsiders. Without writing a letter to introduce myself, I simply knocked on the door of Jones, Bird & Howell. I met with senior partner Arthur Howell, who introduced me to a few other partners.

Although Bob Jones had not interviewed me or been a factor in my hiring, it didn't take long to realize Mr. Jones and I had something in common — we were the only two Republicans in the firm. Because of my minority status, I didn't talk politics at work except with Mr. Jones, and I was told he played an important behind-the-scenes role near the end of the 1952 Republican Convention, which featured a back-and-forth battle between Ike and Senator Robert A. Taft from Ohio for the nomination. The delegation from Georgia, split between the two men, turned out to be the decisive vote for Ike, largely due to a few well-placed phone calls of support from Mr. Jones.

In the mid-to-late 1960s, Senator Charles H. Percy of Ohio, a favorite of President Eisenhower, was the featured speaker at the Dinkler-Plaza Hotel in Atlanta. Unexpectedly, Mr. Jones presented me with a ticket to sit up front at the head table. When I took his seat, I saw questioning expressions I interpreted as, *Who's this guy?* I made no effort to explain myself for two reasons. Since I had the right ticket, how I got there wasn't their business, and it would have made me uncomfortable to tell people I didn't know that I knew such a famous person.

Mr. Jones would never let a conversation center on himself. If his history came up in a conversation, he would immediately change the subject to my childhood or my military experience, anything but himself.

One day in the office, he was more pale and weaker than usual. I suggested he take a few days to rest at home.

Dale, he said. *If I ever quit coming because I don't feel good, I won't be back at all.*

That was Mr. Jones, quietly courageous. I revered the man and felt privileged that he seemed to enjoy my company.

JACK GLENN, JR

Mr. Jones was a friend of my father's, who admired him and trusted his judgment in complex business situations. My first face-to-face meeting was when I was manager of Qualco, an aluminum casting company owned as an investment by the Jones family's Canton Cotton Mills, then being run by Mr. Jones's first cousin Lewis. Mr. Jones had thought up the name Qualco and was chairman of its board.

When his hands became too weak to handle utensils, we made a large knife, fork, and spoon for him. Once on the way to Canton, Mr. Jones decided to drop by Qualco to thank those who had made them. He showed great interest in the manufacturing process and was pleased that they had been polished so well. We were all greatly complimented.

Before he left, many staff members asked for his autograph, but because of his hands, he could not sign his name without an effort, taking too much time for the situation. He smiled and greeted everyone but could not delay his trip.

Three months later, he arrived with a stack of signed index cards. Everyone knew it had taken many hours for him to sign so many; if they received one, it was treated like the treasure it was.

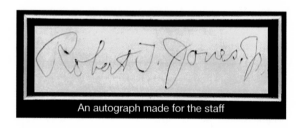

An autograph made for the staff

BILL ROOKER, JR.

The Last Swings of Bobby Jones

One day in 1953, I walked out the back door of Peachtree Golf Club and saw Bob was alone hitting balls on the small practice tee near the first hole. In those early days, we practiced with our own balls, and each of us had a bag boldly identified with our names so a caddie could find them quickly and meet us in that area.

Bob's crutches were leaning on a chair close to where I was standing, and he was standing without support, hitting balls with his seven iron. When he noticed me, he stopped and smiled, greeted me by name, and asked what I'd been up to. He asked me to put his crutches on the ground and sit down for a while.

Then he hit a few more balls, stopped to tell me some stories about himself, and hit three or four more. We talked again, and he hit again. We visited there until he was done.

During the conversation, the first time he turned to hit, I noticed his caddie standing down the fairway. All the balls I could see had stopped within a few yards of each other at his feet. After all were hit, the caddie gathered them into Bob's shag bag, walked back to the tee, and handed it to Bob. I was astonished by what happened next.

Bob turned to me, held out the full bag and said, *Bill, I will not need this anymore. I want you to have it.*

Later, in the clubhouse I told the story to three friends and showed them the bag. They thought I had just seen him hit the last balls he ever hit.

Sixty-five years later, that full bag of golf balls sits on the coffee table in Bill's living room, carefully protected in a glass cube. There is a small brass plaque:

> ### Robert T. Jones, Jr.
>
> This is Bobby Jones' practice bag that he gave to me at Peachtree Golf Club in the spring of 1953. After having the privilege of watching him practice, he said he wanted me to have the bag since he would not need it anymore. I may have seen him hit his last ball.
>
> Bill Rooker

JOHN IMLAY

In his book about his career in Atlanta's early software business in the 1960s, *Jungle Rules,* John described his only meeting with Bobby Jones. He had exploded in court after being called a liar by the opposing attorney.

I am many things, he wrote, *but liar is not one of them.*

John got into a shouting match, and the judge threatened to hold both men in contempt of court. His lawyer took him back to his office to see Mr. Jones:

There, sitting in a wheelchair, was this small, thin, hunched figure. I knew him instantly. It was Robert Tyre Jones, Jr. ... the finest golfer to ever split a fairway ... Jones now seemed to be shrinking under the weight of a debilitating spinal disease. But there was still a lively spark in his eyes, and this wonderful, calm wisdom in his voice.

'You know,' Jones said, 'I used to lose my temper with every bad shot. Once during the British Open at the Old Course in St. Andrews, the course had gotten the best of me. Finally I took an eleven on number twelve. I tore my scorecard in half, threw down my clubs, and walked away.

John Imlay and one of his stone bridges at North Berwick, Scotland

'After that, I began to think my temper was my trouble. When I finally got it under control, I began to win. My advice is, don't ever let that happen to you again.'

John followed that advice and said those few minutes with Bobby Jones changed his life. He became an effective leader and wrote,

At the end of the day, the battle done, it is civility that makes someone a winner (Imlay 1995).

Bobby died a few months after John's visit.

BOB YOUNG

I am not a golfer, but since I grew up at East Lake in the 1950s and worked at Jones, Bird & Howell, I've always had an interest in anything about Mr. Jones. In late 1970, I had a conversation with Harold Vassar, a man who played golf with him. It was at a wedding my future wife and I attended in Saratoga Springs, N.Y. When someone told Harold I was in Bobby Jones's law firm, he walked over and told this story:

In 1925, I was in the same group with Bobby Jones when he was playing every day in Florida to get ready for the much-publicized, head-to-head match against Walter Hagen. Bobby was the best amateur in the world at that time, and Hagen was the best professional.

Five years later, during the summer of the Grand Slam, he and Mary stayed with me in my New York apartment when they came up for his ticker-tape parade.

When I get back to Atlanta, I told him, *I'll let him know immediately that I met you.*

Oh, I'm sure he wouldn't remember me, he replied.

Are you kidding? Anyone would remember that!

That December or in January, I went up to Mr. Jones's office on the eighth floor. Jean Marshall, his secretary, was there, but he wasn't.

I'm sorry. Mr. Jones isn't in today, she said, *and I don't know if he'll ever be in again.*

The next Christmas, shortly after our own wedding, my wife and I drove back to Saratoga. In Greenville, South Carolina, an announcer interrupted the program to say that Mr. Jones had passed away. I never got to tell him.

BOBBY JONES HAS BEEN HONORED WITH TWO COMMEMORATIVE STAMPS, IN 1981 AND 1999.

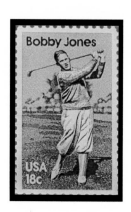

Dedication ceremony at East Lake in 1999 - (L-R) Historian
Sid Matthew, grandson Bob Jones IV, granddaughter Anne Laird,
and Robert J. Sheehan, USPS Atlanta District Manager

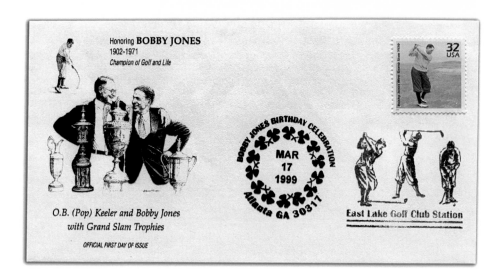

XI

THE FINAL YEARS

RESPICE FINEM

"Look to the End"

My soul, sit thou a patient looker-on;
Judge not the play before the play is done:
Her plot hath many changes;
Every day speaks a new scene,
The last act crowns the play.

EPIGRAM BY FRANCIS QUARLES

(1592–1644)

I

JACK S. SCHRODER, JR.

My story began as a mystery, soon became reality, and lives on today as an unforgettable legacy.

It was October 1968, not a very good time for our country when you consider the recent Robert Kennedy and Martin Luther King, Jr. assassinations, the Democratic Convention riots in Chicago, and the growing turmoil over the Vietnam War. But, as a young undergraduate at Emory University, my life was about to change for the better.

The Mystery

First, early in the month, and thanks to an unlikely substitute blind date, I met Karen Keyworth, the woman who was to become my wife for the next forty-five years.

Two weeks later, my college swimming coach, Ed Smyke, approached me at practice and asked if I wanted to make some extra money sitting with an elderly man who'd just been discharged from Emory Hospital.

He wouldn't tell me the gentleman's name, where he lived, the nature of his illness, or even the amount I would be paid. He just wanted to know if I'd take the job. Without much thought, I said *Yes*, and he instructed me to come to his office the next week to get directions to the man's house.

When Coach finally informed me my new employer's name was Robert Tyre Jones, Jr., my mind went temporarily numb.

Bobby Jones — the greatest golfer of all time, the only person to win the Grand Slam, the amateur who at twenty-eight resigned from competitive golf at the peak of his career to practice law and become a family man — was Atlanta's most famous native son, a paragon of civility and a source of pride for Atlanta for five decades.

And, he was going to spend his waning years with me?

The Reality

The next night I met Mr. and Mrs. Jones at their home on Tuxedo Road in Buckhead. After some discussion, Mr. Jones anointed me the "captain of his team." I was to organize and schedule a group of fellow college students to arrive at 8 p.m. every night, spend time chatting or watching television, and then put him to bed when he got tired.

Thus began my unforgettable journey as one of a few lucky college students who received lessons away from the classroom that changed our lives forever.

I was fortunate to assemble a team of dependable friends who went to Emory and Georgia Tech, including John Lambert, David Elizardi, Peter Ward, and Mike Baumgartner.

Our biggest challenge was Saturday night. After all, no self-respecting college student wanted to give up Saturday nights. But that problem was solved when we added to our team a married hospital orderly who agreed to cover every Saturday.

Curiously, although I sat with him for hundreds of hours over the next three years, that first night was the only time we talked about his golf career. He explained that the Grand Slam had never entered his head until he was selected for the Walker Cup team (the amateur equivalent of the Ryder Cup) to be held in England in 1930.

Since the Walker Cup paid for his travel expenses, he realized he could afford to stay abroad a bit longer and compete in the British Amateur and Open Championships. As any golfer knows, he won them both, and the Grand Slam became reality when he also won both the U.S. Open and Amateur Championships that same summer.

No one's done it since.

Despite my steadfast intention not to bore him with dumb questions, I couldn't resist asking the same inevitable query that had been asked of him a thousand times before, *Why did you retire?*

Because there was nothing else left to win, he said candidly, and that closed the subject of golf for the remainder of our years together.

But that was mainly because Mr. Jones was far more interesting as a person than a golfer. He was a true Renaissance man, a master of many subjects. Nothing was beyond his realm of interest — an astonishing fact considering his impaired physical condition.

With degrees from Georgia Tech, Harvard, and Emory, his interests extended far beyond golf. For example, I walked in one night as he was reading, and he exclaimed, *Oops, you've caught me with my favorite book!*

In his lap sat a dictionary, of all things. Our topics of discussion each evening ranged from current events to history, from World War II to Georgia Tech football, and from Shakespeare to the latest "Peanuts" column.

In the process, he became one of my greatest mentors. When writing, he explained, use as few words as possible, review your draft many times over several days, and each time strike out every word that isn't absolutely necessary.

When I nervously told him I was scheduled to give a speech to a large crowd, he coached me not to read my speech, but to simply jot a few key words for each thought on an index card, thereby making my remarks more relaxed and natural.

If you've ever seen one of his speeches on tape or read any of his books, you'll recognize how he practiced what he preached.

And his sense of humor was priceless. I vividly recall the night of December 1, 1969, when Selective Service held its first draft lottery in response to the Vietnam War.

It was televised live so those of draftable age (like me) could learn their fate. The camera started to scroll down the first list of birthdates drawn at random from a large glass container. The earlier your birthday was drawn, the more likely you would be drafted.

There I sat in Mr. Jones's living room, sweating bullets, wondering if I would spend the next year in law school or in a Vietnamese rice paddy.

All of a sudden I heard a shout from behind, *Ouch, they got me!*

I turned around to see Mr. Jones with an impish grin pointing at the TV.

They got me, he repeated. *There's my birthday at number thirty-three!*

With that one quick remark, he put everything in perspective. Here was a World War II veteran telling me not to worry, and at that moment, I knew everything would be all right (and it was, as my lottery number was well out of draft range).

There was another TV incident. Mr. Jones never used his lofty status to gain an advantage — well, almost never. To soften the blow of having to miss the Masters in 1969, he purchased a large new color TV, but when he tried to turn it on that Saturday morning, it didn't work. The young operator at Rich's assured him a repairman would come first thing Tuesday morning. He explained why Tuesday morning would not be soon enough, but she didn't budge. Flushed with irritation, he picked up the phone and called the store's owner, his friend Dick Rich. It was fixed later that morning.

The only time we ever argued was the night President Nixon announced yet another expansion of the Vietnam War, this time into an adjoining country.

After sharing our opposing views about the war, Mr. Jones instructed, *Go fix me another scotch — we've got to talk this out.*

Even though it was well past his normal bedtime, we continued our dialogue into the night.

Finally, he observed bluntly, *You know the guy that got us into this mess to begin with?,* and he pointed to a nearby bronze bust of his very close friend, President Eisenhower.

Speaking of war, few realize Mr. Jones was an officer in Army Intelligence and among only a handful of persons who knew the details of the upcoming D-Day invasion. He recounted waking up each morning petrified he might have talked in his sleep and revealed military secrets.

Even fewer realize that, despite his status as a world-famous icon, he landed at Normandy beach on D-Day plus one.

Once I graduated from Emory and entered law school at the University of Georgia in Athens, I wasn't available to see Mr. Jones as often, but every vacation or free weekend I was at his side, soaking up the magic. As time wore on, his condition worsened, and we weren't needed anymore. However, we were always welcome to stop by for a visit. (Incredibly, the most famous golfers were turned away several times, but we were always welcome.)

I vividly recall my last such visit, during Thanksgiving break of 1971. I had some personal news I wanted to share with him, face-to-face. I had just accepted an offer to join his law firm, Jones, Bird & Howell (later Alston & Bird).

When I told him, he gave me a big smile and shook my hand for the last time. He died ten days later. Several years later, Mr. Jones's personal physician told me his patient lived an additional six months because of his relationship with our group of college students.

The Legacy

Although thousands of people were inspired by Mr. Jones's character and integrity, my legacy is more personal. Whenever I prepare for a speech, I follow Mr. Jones's short notes regimen. Whenever I write a letter, memo or legal brief (and even as I write this story), I get out the red pen and try to delete every unnecessary word. Whenever I'm tempted to throw a golf club after yet another bad shot, I think of that young golfer who learned to control his temper (unfortunately, I sometimes still throw the club).

Perhaps the most accurate quote about Mr. Jones came from renowned sportswriter, Herbert Warren Wind:

As a young man, he was able to stand up to just about the best that life could offer, which is not easy, and later he stood up with equal grace to just about the worst.

We personally witnessed Mr. Jones confronting the worst life had to offer on a daily basis. He suffered from a very rare and still incurable disease of the spinal cord that slowly wasted his muscles, causing loss of sensation and permanent injury to his nerve fibers. His hands were withered fists, and he could only move his head and arms with great difficulty.

We viewed our job as diverting him from his physical infirmities by engaging his mind. We considered ourselves privileged to serve in this treasured capacity, and we respected Mr. Jones's understandable desire for privacy.

In deference to that intense (and well-deserved) desire for privacy, I have avoided even talking about my amazing experience with Mr. Jones except on rare occasions and then only when specifically asked. But almost fifty years after his death, I've come to realize my story needs to be told — not for self-aggrandizement, but so others can learn what a courageous, incredible man he was even if he had never swung a golf club.

Five decades ago, I was one of a few college kids privileged to get "up close and personal" with one of this country's greatest superstars. In his earlier years, he had been a strikingly handsome athlete who enjoyed worldwide fame, universal admiration, and a unique level of reverence that is still honored today. However, by the time I knew him, he was an incapacitated, cloistered person who shunned any type of publicity or exposure. To my amazement, his obvious physical debilities didn't diminish by one iota his mind, his sense of humor, or his character — in short, he was still a superstar.

While writing this story, I suddenly realized I am now the same age as that "elderly" man I met way back in 1968. He had only three more years to live, while I hope to have a few more. But regardless of what the future may hold, and even though someone else may finally win the coveted Grand Slam, there will never be another like Robert Tyre Jones, Jr.

II

JOHN M. MARTIN

My first meeting with Mr. Jones was in late 1970 or early 1971. Another SAE approached me, mentioned our fraternity connection to Mr. Jones, and explained the rotating schedule in play. He became an incredible blessing for me, and I thank God for him almost every night.

I came to Emory from Tennessee and have returned here to practice dentistry. When I was in college, I had never played nor even watched much golf. I was also ignorant in many ways, especially concerning the accomplishments of Mr. Jones. I have since become a golfer, although my golfing friends might debate this, and have now read virtually everything written about him and even played the Old Course at St. Andrews. Now that I've had my own miserable experience in the Bobby Jones bunker, I understand why he walked away the first time.

My evenings with Mr. Jones are some of the favorite memories of my life. Scotch and ice cream, two of his favorites, were shared on many visits. These were the Vietnam years, and as the owner of a very low lottery number, I was destined for the military. My grades at Emory would determine whether grad school could preclude my military service. Mr. Jones routinely asked about exams, both those I had completed and those coming up. He had a remarkable memory of my progress and sensed when I had done poorly. Mrs. Mary and Mr. Jones were my parents away from home, and their interest in me and my future are what I cherish most.

Bobby Jones was brilliant, gifted, and interested in all of us. I was in his last group of students, and his health was diminishing rapidly, finally ending his desire for visitors. He died soon after.

He had a much greater influence on my life than he could have ever known. He did not share golf stories with me. He shared himself with me, much more of a blessing. He never complained and did not discuss his regrets, but he made this young Emory fraternity brother feel valued.

III

JOHN LAMBERT

In the fall of 1968, Jack Schroder, my friend since third grade (sixty years), asked if I would be interested in being a night aide for Bobby Jones. He said that four of us would alternate sitting with Mr. Jones and placing him in bed if he was tired. He had two of his Sigma Alpha Epsilon friends of Emory University lined up and wanted me to join them. I was a Sigma Chi at Georgia Tech.

Sure, I said.

My first day and many of my experiences with Mr. Jones are described in Curt Sampson's 2005 book, *The Lost Masters.* The book tells the story of the 1968 Masters, the last Masters Mr. Jones attended. This was the year that Roberto DeVincenzo, having apparently won the tournament, signed his scorecard with a wrong score and thus was disqualified. Mr. Jones made the final decision in accordance with the rules of golf.

Later that year Mr. Jones had major surgery. After that he became too weak to assist his nurse in moving him from the TV room to bed each evening, so some young, strong college boys were recruited.

Day One

What does a twenty-year-old college student say to Robert Tyre Jones, Jr., one of Atlanta's most famous citizens. He was a Georgia Tech grad, the winner of thirteen major golf tournaments as an amateur, including the Grand Slam in 1930. Then he retired from competitive golf at age twenty-eight and co-founded Augusta National and the Masters.

If I had known then what I have read since and learned about him, I would have been scared to death. However, I was only moderately familiar with the above background and thus was not terrified. So there I sat next to him in a little ten by twenty-foot room upstairs at his large home on Tuxedo Road.

Mr. Jones sat in a green easy chair with an elevated hospital tray on a stand in front of him. On the tray were two tall cups with flex straws, one containing water and the other bourbon or scotch, two bottles of pills (Miltown and phenobarbital) and an ashtray with five cigarettes in thin holders. The holders allowed him to bend over and pick them up with his mouth.

This first visit was also a test/interview. Mr. Jones's wife, Mary, had told Jack that if her husband was satisfied and comfortable they would *accept the young man*, meaning me. In three years, Mary told us only one time that one of our choices was not acceptable and asked that he not be a part of the team.

Mr. Jones was very weak. He suffered from Syringomyelia, a disease similar to Lou Gehrig's disease, and was partially bent over in his chair. Our job was to sit and talk with him and assist him any way we could. We would also watch the "great" programs offered by the four Atlanta TV stations, without a remote control.

Occasionally, Mary Jones would show us historic items including a sterling silver, satin lined, hinged container holding the parchment given to Mr. Jones by the citizens of St. Andrews honoring him as a Freeman of the Burgh of St. Andrews. The only other American so honored was Benjamin Franklin.

When Mr. Jones was ready for bed, we would lift him up by his chest under his arms, swing him into his wheel chair, and take him to his bedroom where we would repeat the process.

St. Andrews

In March of 1971, I traveled to Europe with Frank Fidler from Augusta, Georgia, my fraternity brother and fellow Mr. Jones team member. We spent six weeks backpacking in nine countries, ending with a visit to St. Andrews in May. Before we left Atlanta, Mr. Jones told us that he was sending a telegram to Secretary Alister MacKenzie requesting that Frank and I be his guests at the Royal and Ancient Golf Club. His father, also Alister MacKenzie, was the famous architect who had designed the Augusta National course, home of the Masters. Frank and I brought nice windbreakers and ties to Europe just for this occasion which included a rare tour of the R&A clubhouse and archive vault.

St. Andrews was a small, quiet college town then without any of the present commercialism.

One amazing experience during our visit was seeing their reaction to the fact that Mr. Jones was still alive. On our train ride from Edinburgh to St. Andrews we shared a compartment with a middle-aged Scot. We mentioned Mr. Jones and our upcoming visit to St. Andrews.

He looked at us somewhat stunned and said, *You mean wee Bobby is still alive?*

The "St. Andrewsites" had the same reaction. The day we arrived, we walked down the main street and asked two senior citizens if there was a hostel in town. One lady, Mrs. Watson, gave us a good looking over and then gave us her address.

Come by my flat in one hour, she said, *and I will put you up for a pound a night — morning continental breakfast and evening 'hot toddy' included.*

When Mrs. Watson learned that her new guests knew Bobby Jones, she cried — her late husband had once met Mr. Jones and admired him greatly. During our walks through the town, people would come up to us to shake our hands and ask about *wee Bobby.*

Once word got out about our visit and our relationship with Mr. Jones, we couldn't pay for a meal. We stopped for lunch at Joe's Hamburgers [I'm not kidding] along the main street. A young woman named Shirley, the daughter of a RAF pilot stationed nearby, waited on us.

I know who you lads are, she said. *Lunch is on us.*

We ordered our first European hamburgers [You guessed it: burgers were a pound each] and I asked for iced tea. When I ordered that, Shirley gave me a quizzical look. About fifteen minutes later she brought our burgers. I asked about my tea.

Oops, she said, and ran back to the kitchen. Finally, she emerged with my iced tea. She had poured tea into a coffee mug and placed it in the freezer for fifteen minutes to cool — Scottish iced tea.

I have a great memento of this trip. Mr. Jones had copied my father on the R&A telegram. My father had once consulted Mr. Jones about changes to his course design of the Peachtree Golf Club. Dad had this telegram framed and on the wall of his den. When my father passed in 1988, I saved the telegram,

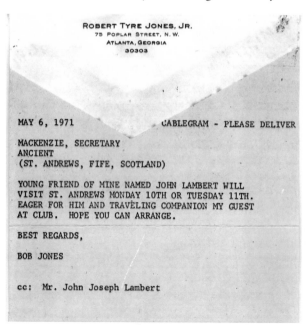

ROBERT TYRE JONES, JR.
75 POPLAR STREET, N. W.
ATLANTA, GEORGIA
30303

MAY 6, 1971   CABLEGRAM - PLEASE DELIVER

MACKENZIE, SECRETARY
ANCIENT
(ST. ANDREWS, FIFE, SCOTLAND)

YOUNG FRIEND OF MINE NAMED JOHN LAMBERT WILL
VISIT ST. ANDREWS MONDAY 10TH OR TUESDAY 11TH.
EAGER FOR HIM AND TRAVELING COMPANION MY GUEST
AT CLUB. HOPE YOU CAN ARRANGE.

BEST REGARDS,

BOB JONES

cc: Mr. John Joseph Lambert

and I have it on my wall. This telegram was the last contact Mr. Jones ever had with St. Andrews or the R&A.

We played two rounds of golf on the Old Course. Each day the tee time was 0500 hrs. Since St. Andrews is near the 60th parallel, dawn is very early. The greens fee was a pound a round, about $1.50. On my second round, I tied the course record. My 96 tied the course record of 1886. The R&A provided us with free golf bags, clubs, and enough golf balls to make it through two rounds — barely.

During our golf rounds I took some film of our play with my high tech, hand wound Brownie 8mm movie camera. When I returned home to Atlanta, Mary and I placed a white bed sheet over the TV as a movie screen, and I played the film for Mr. Jones. He just stared at the scenes of St. Andrews and my ungodly swing.

Afterwards, he asked if I would play the film again. I wondered what memories this film was bringing back for him. At his request, I played it four times.

His Last Trip

In the Fall of 1970, my Sigma Chi fraternity built a forty-foot long by fifteen-foot high model of a battleship for the homecoming display contest for the Georgia Tech-Navy football game. The wood and chicken wire leviathan was stuffed with colorful tissue. A four-foot long Yellow-Jacket torpedo came out of the ground, crossed the grass and speared the vessel amidships. The huge ship rolled over on its side. The tissue on the underside of the hull spelled out the words "Beat Navy" in eight-foot high letters.

I told Mr. Jones about our display. Mary later said it was all he could talk about. He asked me if he could come down and see the display, and I was delighted to invite him.

The next day, while standing in the front yard of the fraternity house, I noticed a powder-blue Cadillac drive by. It was Mr. Jones, unannounced. I chased after the car.

Hoyt, his driver, looked in the rearview mirror and told Mr. Jones, *There's a guy running after the car waving his arms. I think it's John!*

I rallied the display operators, and we ran the entire program for him. He was amazed and laughed hard.

That was the last time he left his Buckhead home.

The End is Near

In 1970, Jack Schroder graduated from Emory and started law school at the University of Georgia. As the senior team member, I became the leader for the final year.

I was scheduled to enter the U.S. Army OCS program in February 1972. Therefore, I was the only team member to be available for all of the final three years of Mr. Jones's life. He died on December 18, 1971.

As the end drew close, Mr. Jones was too weak to leave his bed, yet Mary asked us to continue our visits. Mr. Jones's doctor, Ralph Murphy, told Mary that our visits each evening probably kept Mr. Jones alive for months, maybe a year. It was important to give him something to look forward to every day.

During these last months, we would sit next to his bed and watch a smaller TV and talk with him. His favorite program was *It Takes a Thief,* starring Robert Wagner as Al Monday, the thief turned sleuth. We continued to do this for about two months until Mary told us that Mr. Jones was slipping fast and that he did not want us to remember him in this failing condition. Weeks later he passed. He is buried in Oakland Cemetery, yards from one of my family's sections.

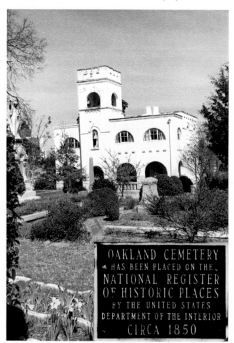

I saved the front-page section of the December 18, 1971, Saturday *Atlanta Constitution* with the lengthy article by Furman Bisher about Mr. Jones's life, accomplishments, and character.

In 2013, I played a round of golf with John Capers, club historian and curator at the Merion Golf Club in Ardmore, Pa., where Mr. Jones won the Grand Slam. I gave the club museum that newspaper section as well as other memorabilia I had collected through the years. These items included a copy of the St. Andrews telegram and an original print of William Steene's painting of Mr. Jones, *The Concentration of Championship*. I was honored to be named a Friend of Merion.

Reflections

I remember Mr. Jones sitting in his chair, his body a mere relic of the great athlete he once was. While winning the U.S. Amateur at Merion in 1930, he was racked with stomach pain, exhausted from winning the first three majors, and under enormous pressure. At Merion he still played over 220 holes of golf in eleven days: Charity golf rounds, practice rounds, and then the tournament play — the equivalent to playing three U.S. Opens in a row without a break.

I still think of him often whenever I am down or upset about something. The memories I cherish most are the sharpness of his mind until the very end and his smile when I arrived each night and walked into the room.

In the three years with him, I never saw him sad or upset, and he never complained about his condition or his pain. Thinking of this always makes my troubles disappear. One night, when leaving his bedroom, I turned around at the door and looked back at him. He was smiling and watching me leave.

He appeared to be saying to himself, *Thank you, John, for helping me get through another day.*

His gravesite is unusual. When Charlie Harrison was speaking to a group there, he noticed four men dressed for golf. One of them said, *Excuse us for interrupting, but we're on the way to Alabama to play and want to place golf balls on his grave for good luck.*

XII

ONE DOWN WITH
ONE TO PLAY

by Henry A. McCusker[1]

The sign on the fence read "Private Property — No Trespassing." But one side of the gate was open, so I drove through and continued down the driveway toward the clubhouse. This was my first visit to the East Lake Country Club, and I was surprised to see such an unbecoming sign. It put the place on the defensive, I thought, and then with my first glimpse of the clubhouse — a huge Tudor-like structure, dark and brooding in the distance — I was at once reminded of similar signs and structures I had seen twenty-two years before, in 1959, when I first came to Atlanta.

Those signs were along Washington Street in front of large decaying old houses which three quarters of a century earlier must have been the residences of the fashionable establishment. The houses still possessed traces of their once-grand character and were unwilling to yield to the hard use and neglect by generations of other occupants. But nothing remains of those old houses now, not even their ghosts.

Fortunately, the notion which got into my head far exceeded the extent to which East Lake had deteriorated. Its best days were long past to be sure, but clues to its built-in high quality were instantly visible, and unlike those old houses, this crusted old diamond was now being nurtured rather than abused.

I decided to park the car and walk around in order to get a closer look at things, and I began to feel a little ashamed for having allowed twenty-two years to go by before coming out here to see Bobby Jones's home course. I have played golf since 1945, and I love the game; I have seen all the current great players many times, and I never miss the Masters. Why did I not come out here long ago to see where Bobby Jones started playing golf — where he grew up, practiced, and perfected his game. He was born an invalid and died an invalid,

---

1   This story was the result of a visit to East lake by Harry McCusker in 1981. That was in the middle of the twenty-five-year period between its time as the golf course of the Atlanta Athletic Club and the formation of East Lake Golf Club. His story has been edited for him to play the holes in proper order.

but he became the greatest player of his time, a super person, and a genuine national hero?

There was not a good answer to that question, but I consoled myself with the thought that now I would appreciate East Lake even more. I had read more about Bobby Jones during those years, and had become a better player and gained some small awareness of the pressures in tournament golf. For those reasons, my feeling of appreciation and esteem for the spirit of his old place would be keener and of greater value.

After leaving the car in the lot behind the clubhouse, I walked around to the front without seeing anyone. It was late October, and the weather was cloudy, windy, and damp — not a good day for golf. When I drove in, I passed the first tee up near the gate, and the tenth was to the left of where I stood directly in front of the clubhouse, but there were no golfers around. Then a lone middle-aged man emerged from some shrubbery behind me. He had been picking up bits of paper trash and showed a little embarrassment from being observed tidying up and the place needing it. He smiled, said good morning, and we introduced ourselves and shook hands.

What brings you out here? he asked.

The memory of Bobby Jones, I answered.

It crossed my mind that he might take what I said to mean that I had known the great golfer personally, so I was quick to correct a possible misunderstanding. But he had not misunderstood at all and seemed to know that what brought me here was a feeling of profound respect and awe for a man he felt the same way about. The difference was that he had known Bobby Jones and played several rounds of golf with him right here at East Lake. That was after the war when Jones was in his forties and near the end of his playing days.

I felt comfortable with this man I had just met, and as we talked we walked around some. I gauged him to be typical of the men who are still members of East Lake — loyal and proud of the club's distinguished past, honored and inspired by the courage and deeds of its great hero, aware of the club's decline, but determined to continue the struggle against almost overwhelming economic and social forces threatening to end its existence. And I could understand it all, especially after seeing as much as I did of the course. I felt that the course was getting hold of me somehow, through its sheer showing of itself. Just as a star creates its own light and warmth, this place created its own aura of time and patience and beauty. East Lake was old, artful, and surprising. The cult of haste and greed could never see it as I did, but, taken on its own terms, I believed that Nature had accepted this course and that it deserved to be restored and preserved, not destroyed in the name of progress.

We returned to the area between the first and tenth tees, and still there were no golfers around. The member told me that two of his friends would be here soon and asked if I would like to make it a foursome and play as his guest. I said that I would like nothing better, but I could not, and I explained that I was expected home soon, and besides I did not have my clubs with me. But I made a strong bid for a raincheck, and he readily obliged me. We exchanged business cards, and he said that whenever I could play I should call him. I thanked him, said that I definitely would, and left.

A little more than three weeks went by before I called him at his place of business downtown — a brokerage house. He seemed glad to hear from me. (East Lake was looking for new members and he might try to sell some stock for me as well.) We wasted no time getting to the point of my call.

When would you like to play? he asked.

Today. I answered.

Today? he exclaimed. *There's no way I can play today.*

That's all right, I said.

In order to give him time to think about that, I went on talking, and I told him I was calling from the lunchroom at the Stone Mountain course; that I had taken the day off and came over here intending to play; but when I arrived I thought of East Lake; and the more I thought of it the more I felt compelled to call. (Ordinarily, playing golf alone is no fun for me, but I knew the first round at East Lake would be more than just golf. It would be a trip into the past that did not have to be shared to be enjoyed. In fact, by playing alone I would be better able to feel the aesthetic depths of the place.) He asked for a number of the phone I was using and said he would call me right back. After a few minutes, he did call.

It's all set, he said. *I just talked to the pro, and there's not much going on out there today. You can start playing as soon as you get there — just check in at the golf shop and he will take care of you.*

I thanked him, and when I hung up the phone I exclaimed, *Hot Damn,* so loudly I startled several people in the lunchroom.

Stone Mountain State Park and Downtown Atlanta are connected by fifteen miles of Memorial Drive, and East Lake is situated along this route two-thirds of the way in. I covered the ten miles in what must have been record time for that time of day, and while I felt exhilarated over the prospect of playing, I was also somewhat depressed by the neighborhoods along this toward-town direction. It was, after all, East Lake's nearness to the inner-city that brought on its present-day plight. And it was also in my mind that if I were to continue on Memorial Drive the remaining five miles I would pass Oakland Cemetery, the city's oldest burial ground, where Bobby Jones was laid to rest in 1971. His grave is just inside the cemetery's south wall, which runs along Memorial Drive a few blocks from the State Capitol and City Hall. It seemed that Bobby Jones and East Lake were inseparable in my mind now, and my thoughts of them had become a little sad, almost mournful.

But that brief heavy feeling evaporated when I drove through East Lake's gate. The disagreeable sign on the fence went unnoticed this time, and upon seeing the clubhouse and grounds, I felt a little like Hugh Conway must have felt when he reached Shangri-La the second time. Nobody was on the first tee, and I could not wait to start playing. The weather was something like it had been the first time I was here — very cloudy and damp, but not windy or cold. However, a cold front was due to move through later in the afternoon or evening, bringing with it clear skies and dry, much colder air.

Within a few minutes I had parked the car, changed shoes, checked in with the pro, strapped my golf bag to the electric cart he had waiting for me, and driven up to the first tee. I did take time to loosen up instead of hitting practice balls and, in honor of the occasion, broke open a pack of three new Wilson Pro Staffs. I must have been feeling reverence for the place, which resulted in excellent concentration, because I hit a good solid drive up the center of the fairway about 240 yards. I had the feeling I was going to play very well.

The second shot presented no particular problem. The ball was sitting up, and the distance to the pin looked to be about 250 yards. The scorecard showed the first hole to be a 493-yard par five, and what I had left was more than my typical three-wood distance, but maybe it would run and get close. The pin was on the right side behind a trap, and I intended to hit the ball to the left of the pin between the two front sand traps. But the ball went straight at the flag and rolled into the sand. Before getting back into the cart, I noticed there was a flag farther up the hill beyond some trees. The second must be a par three, and I drove the cart toward that green, thinking that I would just see how far back that pin was before having to play that tee shot.

When I drove back down to the first green, my vision and attention were carried beyond the green to the adjacent fairway where a man stood, waiting. I was surprised to see him there, or anyone, and thought it strange that the pro made no mention of another single golfer being out here a hole or two ahead of me. Neither of us waved nor made any gesture to indicate the other's presence.

I continued on my way to finish the first hole, parked the cart near the tee, took my sand wedge and putter, and walked over to play my third shot. My golfer friends know me to be very good at getting out of sand. In fact, one of them once said that I must be the guy who taught Gary Player how to use the sand wedge. The shot I played here was in keeping with that. I blasted out three feet from the cup and left myself an easy uphill putt, which I sank for birdie four. Today would be especially good for playing out of traps because the surface of the sand was smooth and hard, left that way by a day of light rain. A good trap player can really put "stop" on balls hit from wet sand.

I was not thinking about that as I moved on to the tee. My back had been toward the first green for a while, and I wondered if the man was still waiting. I turned and looked in his direction. He was there all right, still watching me, but he had begun to walk back uphill, probably to see where my tee shot landed. I believed he had seen where I hit my first drive, watched my second shot, my third from the sand, and the short putt, and probably concluded that since I was not a hacker, it would be worth his while to wait for me and not have to play alone. Or maybe he was a hustler waiting to catch a "fish" — me.

The distance to the pin on this par three was 181 yards and slightly uphill, a five-iron shot, but my ball fell short of the green. However, the chip shot was good, and the ball stopped six inches away, so close there was no need to putt out. I picked up the ball and walked to the third tee. The man had not taken his eyes off me and when I got close to him he smiled and said, *Would you like some company, sir?*

His voice, looks, and demeanor were those of a well-bred young man. This was no hustler, I thought, not the usual kind anyway.

Sure thing, I said. He had a carrying bag, so I told him he could strap it next to mine and share the cart with me.

That's swell, thank you sir, he said.

My name is Harry McCusker, I told him and held out my hand.

Mine is Bob Clara, he said with a very firm handshake. I was about to ask him to spell his last name because I had not heard Clara as a last name before,

Bob Clara's view of the 2nd green from the 3rd tee —
the site of the first meeting

and I thought the spelling might be something else. But he was already saying I should take the honor and hit first because anyone who played the first two holes as well as I did deserved it. I knew he was being polite. Nothing had been said about our playing a match, but my instincts told me that one was about to begin, and that he would be some kind of player. His first words to me, Would you like some company, sir? were a challenge, I felt, as well as a question — conveyed in the way a medieval knight would have gone about enticing a stranger into friendly combat. He looked very fit, in the prime of life, and about twenty-eight years old.

The third hole was a 379-yard par four which ran straight back down the hill beyond the first green. Hitting to the left had to be avoided because of some trees, and there was a large trap on the right curving out into the fairway. The best place seemed to be fairway just left of that sand, but a ball hit too far in that direction with a draw would clearly run into those trees. I judged that distance to be not more than I could hit with the three-wood, especially today with the course being as soft as it was, and I hit a good straight shot to the desired spot. Being unfamiliar with the course, it had taken a few moments for me to figure all that out before I hit, but Bob Clara required no time at all. He took his three-wood from the bag and slammed the ball on the same line mine had taken, but it landed ten yards ahead of mine and ran down to the left just short of being in the trees. I hit an eight-iron second shot twelve feet from the flag. He hit a pitching wedge to the back of the green and two-putted for a four. I sank the twelve-footer for birdie three.

He was sincere in the compliment he paid me, and as we rode to the next tee, it was in my mind that I should be the one to somehow make it official now that we were playing a match, since I had taken first blood so to speak. The stakes, if any, were unimportant, but pride and one-on-one competition were important and, I suspected, more so to him than to me. As I stepped onto the tee, I turned to him and said, *I'm one up.*

There you go, he said, smiling at me. Long ago I came to know that is a Southern response meaning complete affirmation.

From that point on occurred some of the best golf I have ever seen or will ever see. While I played better than I'm really capable of playing, Bob Clara was absolutely unbelievable. He hit a drive on the fourth, a 382-yard uphill par four, the likes of which I had not seen before. The impact sounded like a thunderclap, and the ball leaped off the clubface as if it had been fired from a cannon and carried over 250 yards.

He had a little more than a hundred yards left, and his wedge dropped the ball on the soft green two or three feet from the pin. My second shot landed in the trap on the right side of the green, and although I managed to get down in two from the sand, my par was one stroke more than his birdie three.

That was really something — the way you played that hole, I said to him. He looked very pleased but said only, *Thank you,* and seemed to want to let it go at that.

Only a very unusual golfer can hit shots like those, I continued, and was again about to inquire into the spelling of his last name as a means of getting to his identity as a golfer. But he had walked onto the fifth tee, a 429-yard par four, and was getting ready to hit. It was not necessary for either of us to say anything about the match being even again. I watched him carefully as he hit his drive and realized that his golf game was like a Rolls Royce with mine a Chevrolet.

There was really no comparison — he was definitely world-class, and I could live to be a hundred and never hit the ball the way he did. What perfection he had in timing, balance, concentration, grace, and power. Still, golf is a game of how many, as they say, not how, and after the fifth hole, the match was still even — halved in fours. I had missed the green with my second shot but chipped to within eight feet of the cup and made the putt. He drove 300 yards down the alley, but he hit an easy nine iron too far and missed the twenty-foot birdie putt. I knew that if I were to stay in this match I would have to be lucky, stay cool, and take advantage of whatever small opening might come my way. After all, the best golfer in any tournament or match does not always win and, as Bobby Jones himself used to say, anything can happen.

At this point, the pace at which we were playing came to a halt for several minutes. We were in no hurry to leave the fifth green. It may have been that I felt the need for a breather before taking on the uphill par five I had seen riding down the fairway. But a more likely reason was from this spot we had an irresistible view of much of the East Lake course, the lake and clubhouse as well. In addition to all which lay below us in the foreground, we could see on the horizon that the promised change in weather, the cold front, was indeed coming. Dark clouds had covered the sky, but now a great horizontal band of brightness appeared, growing and moving toward us as though a gigantic shade was being raised across the heavens. The land was being flooded with the oncoming light, and it was a majestic sight. We sat there in the cart and watched the approaching light illuminate everything, including the far reaches of the course, and as it continued onto the lake and the clubhouse, Bob Clara was moved to say, ... *this little world ... this blessed plot ... this earth ... this realm ... this East Lake ...*

Well, I said, *very good — how clever of you to have the Bard say it for us.*

Then we felt the wind and the sudden change in temperature. I released the brake, and we drove to the sixth tee.

The wind out of the west was behind us now, and he went one up on the uphill 496-yard par-five sixth hole with an eagle three while I plodded along for par. His drive landed well on the upslope about 190 yards away, and he drilled a two iron uphill that landed between the traps and ran up to fifteen feet below the hole. My drive was to the bottom of the hill, my second ran into the left front trap, and I came out poorly. After my first putt finished a foot short, he sank his fifteen-footer.

When we turned to the west on number seven, a straightaway 461-yard par four, the wind was strong against us. He reached with a drive and three wood, but my three wood landed fifteen yards short and ran into the sand on the right. I was happy to see the ball was sitting up. If I could just get down in two, I would probably halve the hole, because he would most likely two putt. I was about thirty-five feet from the pin, and the green sloped upward. I wanted to hit the ball about twenty feet beyond the pin and have it roll back down the slope. I had a clear mental image of what I wanted to do and pulled it off. The ball spun backward almost hitting the pin and stopped two feet below. He had seen my sand shots on number one and number four and now with this one, which could have a real bearing on the match, he had to be impressed. He did not say anything, and I did not look at him, but I knew his eyes were on me, so as I smoothed out the sand, I put my hand to my mouth and yawned — as though a shot like that one was rather routine and tiresome. That broke him up. He laughed and was really amused, and it was a minute or so before he was able to collect himself and play his next stroke.

He had to compose himself again after his putt for a different reason. The pin was in the center below a long ridge, and his ball had run up into the far right corner. He intended to putt to the top of the ridge and let it trickle down fifteen feet close to the hole, but his putt stayed on the top. With that, he blew up, let out a string of curse words, and looked like he might try to throw the putter into the lake about fifty yards away. He did not like losing his advantage, and with that shot he may have blown the chance to stay one-up.

He had shown an explosive temper, but his next putt, as much as anything else, convinced me he was a real champion. It was a delicate, curving, and hard-to-understand putt that would have to be struck with surgeon-like precision or it would not go in. A real good putter might make it once in fifteen tries. He studied and stared at it from all angles, stealthily moving around in total concentration like a jungle cat stalking its prey. When he got into putting position, he stood over the ball for a few moments appearing to be in a trance, then tapped it so perfectly that its movement seemed to be still under his control, and it disappeared into the cup. It was a marvelous moment, but all I could say to him was *Bravo.* I knew that putt could no more miss going in than the moon could move out of its orbit.

We moved on to the next hole in silence, an indication of one way we were alike. We believed that golf should be played as a contest with concentration and competition so keen that it was not possible to think of anything else. To relax or talk of other things would detract from the game. We were deeply in this match but, at the same time, I was preoccupied with wanting to know who he really was, but as long as we were playing, there would be no opportunity to find out. Perhaps when we finished the first nine, we could stop for a sandwich and a drink, and that would give me the chance I wanted. The trouble with that was I had to depend upon him to suggest it. Since I was not a member and was here as a guest of someone else, I could hardly do the inviting in a no-cash situation. He was the member I was sure, and would suggest it.

His one-up position was still intact as we teed off on number eight, a 411-yard par four. I played a very poor second shot, but it turned out to be a good miss and reached the edge of the green about forty-five feet from the pin. His second shot was struck with the usual authority and stopped ten feet from the hole. The thing I had to do now was to try to get this first putt as close to the hole as possible to then make a par four, so he would have to sink his putt to win the hole. "Anything can happen" happened — my first putt went in. It was so unexpected that I lost control of myself and went wild for a minute. He just stood there shaking his head slowly from side to side in utter disbelief. This was the first time that dumb luck had become a factor in the match, but what a factor and what a time — unless he made his putt he would go one down when a minute before it looked like he could very well be two up. Again he was faced with a must-make putt to stay even, and again he went about it in his champion's way. His concentration became intense, evidenced by the way he glared at the ball and its line to the cup. I was sure that he would make it, and he did.

The ninth hole was a 207-yard par three over water back to the clubhouse, and I stayed even. The pin was down front, and after he hit to the center of the green, I pushed my two iron right of the bunker but hit the best sand wedge shot from the rough I've ever hit. After a full swing, the ball jumped out and flew high over the bunker, landed softly a few feet above the hole, trickled slowly down toward the cup but stopped, dead for a par. He managed to smile and congratulate me. Maybe he thought my good shots weren't only luck. His downhill putt didn't drop this time so at the halfway point the match was even. I shot 33, three under par; he was also three under for the seven holes he played. When we got into the cart and started moving, he said something

175

about how much he was enjoying the match and my company, and as we reached the driveway he pointed to the right.

The tenth hole is this way, he said.

I had intended to go straight toward the clubhouse, or the half-way house, but now that was out. Damn, I thought to myself, there goes the sandwich, the drink, and, most of all, my chance to get some information. Now I would have to wait until we finished the back nine.

When we drove up to the tenth tee, two other carts were already there and four men were standing on the tee. This foursome had played the front nine well ahead of us, had stopped for a break, and now was ready to go again. I remembered noticing these men on two occasions when the hole they were playing was close to where we were, and they interrupted their play long enough to watch the shots we were about to make — or at least it seemed that way to me. We remained seated, and then one of them looked at me.

You can play through if you like, he said.

I thanked him, and both of us bounced out of the cart. Bob Clara moved quickly to the tee and hit a tremendous drive. I had become used to seeing him hit and did not say anything. But I could not believe these men would not break out in some kind of spontaneous reaction to such a sight. But they did not — not one of them said a word — like they had not witnessed anything. And then I was again shocked when they complimented me on my drive, which was all right but not nearly the caliber of his. Something was mighty strange here. As we drove away, I was about to ask him for an explanation, but it occurred to me that if he knew them and they knew him, and because of that, acted with such total mutual indifference, the explanation might be something of considerable and unfavorable significance or embarrassment, so I decided to let it go. It was not likely that any other players would be out ahead of us on such a day.

We halved the 411-yard tenth hole with par fours and the 195-yard eleventh with par threes. I was playing extremely well — swinging confidently and with unusual smoothness from start to finish, and my putting stroke, which comes and goes, was definitely with me today. I could see no reason why I would not continue to play at my peak for the rest of the match, and while I could not seriously expect to win it, Bob Clara would know that he had been in a dogfight. But it is when you start thinking one way that things often start going another way.

On the twelfth tee, for some reason I lost my concentration. I had been so fascinated with the play of Bob Clara and the closeness of my match with him that now I was beginning to think I was not fully appreciating the special qualities of the course itself, which to begin with, was my main reason for being here. Maybe it had something to do with crossing the driveway and seeing the entrance again, because my mood changed. I tried to recapture and exploit the feeling that had taken hold of me the first time I came through that gate.

How stupid I was. It did not work, and I should have known that it would not. No one can make things like that happen — you just accept them on their terms, thankfully, if they come to you at all. It was just a short time that I had been out-of-tune, but long enough to have played the twelfth hole. I lost the hole, making my first bogie of the day and going one down for the first time. But on the thirteenth hole, my head was clear again, and I tore into the tee shot like a liberated tiger.

Well, welcome back, said Bob Clara. *Where have you been?*

For a moment I thought of attempting a real answer, but then I decided, no way.

It's a habit of mine to fall asleep for two or three holes on the back side, I said. *I ruin more good rounds that way. But I'm telling you that today I have limited my nap to that one hole.*

I'm one up, he answered.

There you go, I replied.

The thirteenth hole was a 421-yard par four, and I hit a seven iron ten feet from the cup. While he was preparing to hit his approach, my thinking started to race ahead, and I figured that I had to win this hole or the par five fourteenth to stay in the match. The fifteenth was a par three over water, and sixteen was a tough uphill par four. If he were still one up after the fourteenth and won the next two, the match could very well end at the sixteenth, with his margin of victory being 3 up and 2 to play. I needed a birdie soon. While I was visualizing all of that, his pitching-wedge shot stopped less than a foot from the hole. His putt was so short I had to concede it, and now I had to make a ten-footer just to remain one down. There was no way I could afford to go two down. I looked the putt over very carefully and struck the ball solidly into the center of the cup.

He drove first on the 544-yard downhill par-five fourteenth, and it was something to see. The ball rose only about thirty feet above the ground and was hit so straight that the sight of it against the dark sky made me think of a tracer-bullet — something I had not seen nor thought of since 1944 when I was flying bombing missions over Germany.

We were both disappointed with our pars on fourteen. Since I thought he would birdie eighteen, I needed to birdie and get even, and his two-putt from eighteen feet took away his hope to go two up with only four holes left.

From here on the wind would be an important factor in our play. Strong and gusty, it would enter our thinking before every shot and putt. We would have a cross wind on fifteen, a head wind on sixteen, a cross wind on seventeen, and a tail wind on eighteen. But concern for the wind could not have been the reason for the change that had come over Bob Clara. He tried not to show it, but I knew that something important was very much on his mind now. Whatever it was it did not affect his play to my advantage; in fact, his concentration seemed to intensify, and he played like he had to dispose of me in a hurry, not just win. He had been the most considerate and mannerly person I had ever played golf with, and still was, in spite of whatever was troubling him. He did not say anything, but I got the feeling that he had remembered some urgent thing. Perhaps he realized that he was supposed to be somewhere else now or within a very short time. He wasted no time hitting his tee shot on the 168-yard fifteenth. I noticed that he closed the clubface of his seven iron intending to hook the ball, hoping to hold the line against the wind, which he did. It landed on the front and ran back to within six feet.

I was impressed, but was determined and energized now despite missing that birdie. When I saw him hit that laser on the fourteenth, I thought I might be finished. Pumped up with new hope, I knocked the ball stiff. He made his putt so we halved the hole with birdies.

But I could not do it again on the uphill sixteenth. I did manage to make a par four despite the wind and thereby made him earn his win and two-up position. He birdied the tough 412-yard hole all right. He hit two wood shots uphill against that strong wind, which was howling now, reached the putting surface, and made the ten-foot uphill putt. I would not have believed it possible, and I don't know how the ball could stand being hit so hard. It is not often that a Rolls Royce has need or opportunity to display its amazing power, but it is there.

I was two down with two holes to play, still alive but barely. It would be all over if I lost or even halved the 355-yard seventeenth. I had to win it to keep the match from ending. Bob Clara did not say he was two up. He did not say anything, nor did I. He hit his driver down the left side that the wind moved over to the middle of the fairway, about 115 yards from the green. I must have lost my concentration for a moment, rushed the swing, and hit a poor drive into the rough on the left side, between the first bunker and the trees.

The lie was not good enough to attempt hitting a wood club even though the distance to the green called for it. The green was long and shallow and guarded by a deep, long front bunker. The pin was on the top end to the left. Most of the green was to the right and below where the pin was. I took the two iron from the bag, concentrated on making a good swing, and did make solid contact with the ball. The shot felt as good as any I had ever hit, and the ball carried onto the green, stopping about forty feet below the cup. I could very easily have failed in that situation, but I did not come apart, and Bob Clara rewarded me with a friendly grin and a casual salute, as if to say well done. He also seemed to be thinking that this match is not over yet.

If my ball had not reached the green, I believe he would have quickly played his second shot into the fat part of the putting surface below the pin and settled for a par four, which would either win or halve the hole for him, ending the match. But my ball was on the green, and that gave him pause. He took some time to think. He may have thought to himself I might get unconscious again and sink that long putt like I did the one on number eight. At last it appeared that he had made up his mind and had decided to go for the pin — probably concluding he had to be inside my ball and have a putt for a birdie three in case I made mine. But the shot he was going to attempt was extremely tough. There was very little putting surface to hit to around the pin; the wind would make club selection difficult; and the consequences for a less-than-perfect shot could be extremely unfortunate. Having made that first decision, he now had to decide how to play the shot. I figured that he could use an eight iron, nine iron, or pitching wedge, depending upon just what he intended to do.

He had taken time to plan the shot, but then executed it without delay. He hit the pitching wedge high and to the left. The wind did not seem to affect the ball while it was rising, but when it started down it drifted to the right, appearing as if it would fall in perfect alignment with the flag. Near the end of its descent, a strong buffeting gust of air pushed the ball back toward us, and it dropped short of the green, hit the steep bank between the green and the bunker, and kicked down onto the sand.

Anything can happen was happening again. He sat down heavily on the cart, and as we rode, I told him that it was the worst bit of luck I had ever seen. He looked bewildered and did not seem to notice I had said anything. Whatever it was that had been bothering him the last few holes was worse now. In no way could it have been worry over the eventual outcome of the match. After all, he was the better player by far, he was still two up, and even if he were to lose this hole, he would still be one up with only one to play. And, of course, we were not playing for the U.S. Open title. It had to be, as I had guessed before, that he had remembered some urgent thing requiring him to be somewhere else, but his time was running out, and I was still hanging in there.

I drove the cart around the green to the left and parked beside the eighteenth tee. I took my putter, and he took his putter and sand wedge, and we walked the few yards back to finish the seventeenth hole. The sand trap he was in, like all the others today, was perfectly smooth. From end to end the sand was completely free of footprints or any other markings — the way sand is at an ocean beach after high tide. However, the last half hour of sun and wind had dried the surface sand and, although Bob Clara played a good shot, the ball came out of the sand more easily than he thought it would, and skipped past the pin about twelve feet. While he was smoothing the sand he had disturbed, I had time to line up my forty-foot uphill putt that looked like it would break right at the end. I was ready to go. I wanted to get this first one close and I did. The ball stopped even with the hole and just ten inches to the left, and rather than mark the ball I tapped it in for par four. He was lying three, and if he made his putt the match would be over. He studied it with the same intense concentration he had shown on number seven and number eight, and then he struck his putt just as perfectly as he had those. I was sure the ball was going in and so was he. It was rolling perfectly and straight for the cup — it could not miss. But somehow, it did not go in. It stayed out, appearing to have been prevented from going in by some invisible barrier that guided it to the left, an inch past the hole.

I could not believe what I had seen, and when I turned to him, the look that came into his staring eyes revealed that he was much more troubled by the why of the ball not going in than he was by the fact of it. I could see he was fumbling, fearfully, and that something within him was going out of control. But he regained his composure, partly for my sake I believe, and said he hoped he had not upset me and asked that I go on ahead. I assumed he meant to stay there alone for a minute or so, and perhaps try that putt again a time or two before continuing with the match. I was going to ask if there was anything I could do for him, but he was trying so hard to hide the problem from me I thought it better not to.

As I moved on alone to the eighteenth tee, my thoughts were mixed, to say the least. I felt good about still being alive in the match. Being one down with one to play against such a formidable opponent was praiseworthy indeed, but I felt bad about Bob Clara's problem and the effect it was having on him. Everything had been great through fourteen holes, then suddenly this change came over him. Why? Of course, I had no knowledge or understanding of what was causing his mental state, but if, as I suspected, he remembered some other pressing engagement, why didn't he just tell me so and leave? That would have been a disappointment for both of us, but it would have been better than his suffering the way he was now. Or, having made the decision to continue to play despite the other pressing engagement, why could he not just make the best of it now and worry about the consequences later? Maybe he remembered when it was already too late to do anything about it, but could not help dreading the consequences. Maybe that last putt was some kind of omen. Maybe the cutting edge of the cold front that came through after we played the fourteenth hole had something to do with all of this. Maybe it would be better if I just stopped thinking about it.

The eighteenth hole was a 551-yard par five. We had the wind with us now, and I had the honor for the first time since the twelfth. I teed the ball up for a higher drive hoping to ride the wind. It would take my best shots, and then some, to win this hole from Bob Clara.

For the first time, I looked back toward the green. He was not there, but I assumed he had gone down into the bunker to try that shot again. I walked up on the green so I could look into the bunker. He wasn't there — he was not anywhere to be seen. When I looked back at the cart I could see it was where I'd left it, but I noticed his bag was no longer strapped to it. At this point I was only puzzled, not alarmed. I looked around in all directions and saw no one. I stayed there for a while, dumbfounded, but there was still no one to be seen. Then I saw two carts parked beside the seventeenth tee. The four men who had let us play through were now leaving the sixteenth green. I caught up to them before they started to tee off. As I approached, one of the four spoke first.

How's it going? he asked.

O.K., I said, *but have you seen my playing partner?*

All four of them looked at me with blank expressions and then looked at each other.

The one who had spoken before said, *Playing partner?*

Yes, I said, *the fellow who was with me when you let us play through back on the tenth hole.*

Again there was a pause and they exchanged questioning glances.

He said, *You are the only golfer we have seen out here today, other than ourselves.*

I said nothing more, and all of us remained as we were for several seconds. I began to feel something strange happen inside my body — like the pull of gravity had suddenly been greatly increased and was dragging on my insides. I remember looking at my fingernails to see if the flesh underneath had become blue. (During the war we made this simple test to check for shock or oxygen loss, and I did it now automatically.) Then I must have started to shake and tremble, because two of the men rushed toward me as if to assist me. But I caught hold of myself, and the violence of the sensation subsided. I told them I would be all right now, and left. I got back onto the path, which took me past the practice area down toward the clubhouse, and as I continued on, I noticed a man standing alone near the last green. Closer now, I could see that he was my host, the stockbroker. He left work early and stopped here on his way home to see how I liked the course.

When he saw my face, he asked, *What is the matter?*

I was not able to say anything yet.

I was inside a minute ago, he said, *and they told me some new guy was out here playing alone and really tearing the course apart. I figured it was you.*

I played very well, I told him, *but I was not alone. I started out alone, but I met a fellow on the third tee, and he and I played together through the seventeenth hole. Now he's disappeared. He must be the best golfer in the world.*

Come on inside and have a drink, the member said. *I want to hear about this — and I want Doc Cameron to hear it, too.*

Doc Cameron was introduced to me as being East Lake's oldest and best member. He was a fine old gentleman and a lifelong member of the club. He could not play golf anymore, but came out to the course almost every day to talk golf with the players and drink scotch. He especially loved to tell about the long-ago experiences that remained in his memory.

I told them everything — starting with my love for the game that brought me out to East Lake in the first place, and ending with my conversation with the foursome a little while ago. I gave an almost stroke-by-stroke account of what had gone on, and I included facts of special significance relating to Bob Clara's play, as well as my thoughts and opinions concerning his character and personality. They listened most intently and interrupted only occasionally to ask for clarification of some particular thing. When I finished, we sat there for a while without anything being said.

Then my host said, *Doc, what do you make of it?*

Doc Cameron lifted his glass to his lips and swallowed what was left in it. A third round was ordered.

There's only one thing I'm sure of, he said, *and that is who the other player was.* He looked me square in the eyes. *You played that match with Bob Jones.*

Bob Jones? I gasped.

Yes, he said. *Of course, the world knew him as Bobby Jones, but he was never called that around here. His family and friends always called him Bob, never Bobby. He hated to be called Bobby.*

Somehow I knew he was right, but I said, *How the hell could I have played golf today with Bobby Jones?*

I don't know how, he answered, *but I am more sure of that than I am of anything. From the very beginning — when you were on the third and fourth holes — I knew it was Jones, and everything else you said afterward just confirmed it. That was Bob Jones you played golf with today — or his ghost.*

Wait a minute, I said. *Let's consider the facts and examine this thing rationally. One, Bobby Jones — I mean Bob Jones — was born in 1902 and died in 1971. If he were still living, he would be eighty years old on his next birthday. Obviously, I did not play with that Bob Jones. Two, the person I played with could not have been a ghost; ghosts are not real — they are spirits and don't have bodies. I shook hands with this man and I could feel his weight when he got in and out of the cart, etc. Believe me, he was real.*

My host said, *How do you account for the other people in the foursome not seeing him?*

I can't account for that, I said.

Did Bob Clara leave anything of his in the cart, like a golf ball, a sweater, a head cover, or anything? he asked.

I had to answer *No* to that. Then I remembered something I wanted to ask Doc Cameron before but had forgotten.

So I turned to him and asked, *Why would Bob Jones tell me his name was Bob Clara?* Doc Cameron smiled a little.

Yeah, I've thought of that, too, he said, *all I can tell you is that Bob Jones's mother's name was Clara, one of his two daughters was named Clara, and when Jones was a little boy he named his pony Clara.*

There was no more conversation concerning the name.

Then a thought came to me and I asked both men, *Could a ghost leave footprints in a sand trap?* Both heads shook *No*.

Doc, you wait here, I said, *we'll be back in a few minutes,* and I motioned for my host to come with me. We went outside, and the cart with my bag on it was still there.

Come on. I said, *We're taking a little ride.*

On the way, I told him what the traps were like today, that I had been in several, but Bob Jones had been in only one — at the seventeenth green. I said I would show him just where his ball had been in the trap. While Jones had smoothed out the sand after hitting his shot, we would most certainly be able to tell whether a shot had been played from the spot. We left the cart on the path and walked down around to the side of the trap away from the green. It had started to get a little dark outside by now, but there was still more than enough light to see the entire trap had not been touched. It could not have been more evident that nobody had set foot on that sand today. We rode back to the clubhouse, and my friend explained to Doc Cameron the what, where, and why of our absence.

After another drink and a long period of silence, I said, *What kind of trouble do you suppose ghosts can get into? Bob Jones was certainly stewing about something. I hope I didn't cause his problem. Do you suppose spirits have laws and rules they have to abide by? I wonder who it is that they have to report to.*

My two drinking partners did not show any interest in pursuing this kind of talk. In fact, Doc Cameron looked like he was thinking of something else.

In the summer of 1930, he said, *I played a round here with Bob Jones. It was just a few days before he left for Philadelphia to play in the United States Amateur, and he was trying to keep his game tuned up. He shot a sixty-three that day and went on to Merion and won the Amateur, completing his famous Grand Slam. Man, was he ever ready to play.*

I got the feeling Doc was just getting started and could go on all night. Perhaps some other time I would really enjoy hearing him, but not now. I had to get away soon. The two of them were really relaxed now, and I did not get much response when I said I had to leave. So I stood up, and while that was a mild surprise for them, it did not cause them to move. I thanked them, said how much I enjoyed being in their company, and I told my host I would call him. They wished me well. At the door, a young fellow was waiting to help me with my golf gear.

It was almost dark outside, but the weather was beautiful. The air was crisp, bracing, and clear as a bell, and the eastern horizon was aglow, brightened by a harvest moon rising beneath. The evening was something to be thankful for, as was the entire day, a day for which I felt most privileged and grateful as well as astonished. I accepted what it had brought, trauma and all. The match with Bobby Jones was the golf highlight of my life. I thought again about that problem of his, but what I thought was, how could he possibly have a problem now? The ways of fate are strange. Was the problem really mine and not his, as it had appeared? I drove slowly along the driveway and through the gate, and when I had left the grounds there no longer seemed reason to worry, but all of my life I would wonder.

© Chet Burgess

The 17th green and 18th tee, where Bob Clara disappeared

XIII

GOLF WITH A PURPOSE

America's Greatest Untapped Resource

By Thomas G. Cousins
Purpose Built Communities
Revised May 15, 2016

Philanthropy in the United States holds one of the keys to life-changing possibilities. The constant challenge is how to make a measurable difference. I think especially in terms of America's poorest children. Lifting them out of the pain and degradation of poverty is rewarding and contributes enormously to the economic vitality of our nation.

Americans contribute $335 billion or more to charitable organizations every year, and every year our federal, state, and local governments combined spend a trillion dollars combatting poverty. Why, then, do we not see results that match the scale of these efforts? I suggest two reasons:

• One, we have yet to fully recognize and respond to the crucial fact that poverty is rooted in geography. Specifically, in isolated neighborhoods of concentrated poverty. In every city, a handful of such neighborhoods account for the lion's share of crime, violence, joblessness, high school dropouts, failed schools, and neglected children. Yet, we tend to take piecemeal approaches to jobs, housing, health, and education when the challenge is to engage simultaneously on all of these fronts in one depressed neighborhood at a time.

• Two, we have yet to fully understand and exploit the transformational capacity of our nation's public charities, which oversee $3 trillion in assets. Philanthropy needs to be much more entrepreneurial — that is willing to take risks to discover solutions, and then demand measurable, sustainable results. In other words, the same results-driven spirit that built America's storehouse of philanthropic wealth to begin with.

186

A lot of data challenges philanthropy as usual. There are 72 million children in the United States, and four of every 10 live in low-income families — 16 million of them in families below the poverty threshold. Every year, a million and a half students drop out of school. In our 50 largest cities, only 59% of students graduate from high school. Every year, dropouts commit 75% of crimes. These markers suggest either that we have grown too satisfied by the act of giving to demand results; or worse, that we have lost faith in the possibility of significant progress.

We accomplish a lot of good. No doubt, the numbers would be far worse without our work. But I worry that we get better and better at managing money without making a comparably bigger impact. I've been at this for nearly 60 years now, and every step of the way I've found it easier to make money than to give it away with true impact

That's why, in the 1990s, we decided to concentrate our foundation investments and time in one geographic area. We wanted to take on a single implacable challenge and see if we could make something happen that we could measure, sustain, and adapt, and therefore create a model for the rest of the country.

The Challenge

The breakthrough for me came when I read an essay in the *New York Times* by a scholar from Rutgers University, Dr. Todd Clear. He did a study of New York State prisons, and I was astonished at one result: nearly three of four inmates in the state's prisons came from just eight neighborhoods in New York City. That hit me hard. Our company had experience in neighborhood change. We had

helped turn around Ansley Park and Grant Park in Atlanta — grand old neighborhoods that had descended into rooming houses and instability.

But the New York study challenged us. What would happen if we took on a neighborhood of concentrated, inter-generational poverty? See if the cycle could be broken. The geographic dimension struck me as an advantage in tackling the problem. If a handful of neighborhoods generate the majority of crimes, ill health, high school dropouts, teen-age pregnancies, and lost children, then turning around one of those neighborhoods would not only improve those lives, it would improve the health and economy of the city, and perhaps the entire state.

Seen in this light, a neighborhood of concentrated poverty becomes a place of concentrated opportunity — one small geography with every need imaginable. You can drive around it in a matter of minutes. You can map it like a military campaign. It tells you exactly where charitable muscle needs to be focused.

You can visit, see and measure results. The eyes of the children will tell you if you're making a difference. It's not abstract and remote — it's local, specific, and human.

One Struggling Neighborhood

The big question, of course, was: Is anything like this even possible? Well, after decades of distributing charitable dollars to so many separate, wonderful causes, we were ready to find out. We decided to focus our attention on one neighborhood, its people, and their children.

187

The East Lake Meadows public housing development before its demolition in 1995

Long story short, that's how we arrived at the old East Lake Meadows. One policeman told me it was the most dangerous neighborhood south of Newark, N.J. (often in the headlines at that time). At the least, East Lake was arguably the most dangerous neighborhood in metro Atlanta. Gunfire was so frequent the police called it "Little Vietnam." They wouldn't go there in fewer than two cars. Drug dealing. Prostitution. Teenage mothers. A neighborhood in ruins, and children all over the place.

America's greatest untapped resource is the human capital trapped in neighborhoods of concentrated poverty

Here's what East Lake looked like when we first studied it:

- 5% of 5th graders meeting math standards
- Only 13% employment among public housing-assisted families
- Median household income: $4,536
- No new commercial or residential investment in more than 30 years
- Crime rate 18 times the national average
- All residents had a 9-in-10 chance of being a victim of crime every year

Riding through East Lake then, I thought: if I'd been born here, I'd be in prison. The kids scrambling around in there had no choice where they were born. They wouldn't even look you in the eye.

After 15 years of hard work, here's what we saw:

- More than 90% of 5th graders meeting or exceeding math standards
- 70% employment among publicly-assisted families — (the other 30% were elderly, disabled, or in job training)
- Average household income of public housing-assisted families: $17,260
- Home values rising in surrounding neighborhoods; a major bank and grocery, and other retail shops and services returning to the area.
- A 90% reduction in crime — to a point 50% lower than the city overall.

Based on the most recent test results, Charles R. Drew Charter School consistently ranks near the top among Atlanta public schools and is often No. 1, with Drew's students out-performing the excellent schools in the city's upper-income north side. They are the bright faces of a better future. Happy faces. And smart. A young woman who grew up in the Villages of East Lake recently graduated summa cum laude from Georgia Tech.

Hard-earned Lessons

How did all this happen? Well, it took some money and a lot of hard work by many good people, and totally focused, involved leadership — including a lead organization, the East Lake Foundation, that gave its undivided attention to the holistic revitalization of the neighborhood. To capture and share our many hard-earned lessons with local leaders in other cities, we formed Purpose Built Communities in 2009, with the backing of philanthropists Warren Buffett and Julian Robertson. We stress three major lessons:

Children at the Charles R. Drew Charter School in East Lake

No. 1 — It can be done. It has been done, now. Neighborhood-based solutions are powerful. Working on multiple fronts within a defined geography generates an entirely different spirit and energy. A kind of stubborn will to get things done.

No. 2 — A holistic approach — once underway and gaining traction — multiplies the inspiration and progress. By that I mean the Drew Charter School, alone, could not achieve such high levels of success. But a quality place to live, a secure environment with adult role models created by mixed-income housing, and a great school with specially-trained teachers — all together — awakened their capacity to learn; made them <u>hungry to learn</u>.

In Indianapolis, where Purpose Built Communities is participating in a similarly tough neighborhood turnaround, the new school is making the same impact. The principal and teachers have banners of dozens of colleges across the walls. Students are invited to visit college campuses. Every child has reason to believe he or she can make it, can go to college or continue developing skills — and can succeed.

I see these children and I think: They have more incentive to learn than my own children. I believe the real motivator is that these children <u>see a way out</u>. Out and up.

Everyone has a reason to believe he or she can make it — up and out

No. 3 — A third big lesson is the importance of mixed-income housing. At East Lake, we worked closely with the Atlanta Housing Authority and re-built the place entirely. Every other unit was reserved for public housing-assisted families, the others for working people who could afford market rate. We wanted people of varying income levels to be next door neighbors. We wanted children to be around adults who go to work and take care of property — solid role models, rather than the drug dealers, prostitutes and their customers, who prey on the very poor.

Negotiating with the School Board to build the city's first public charter school was difficult. But it was important for the school to be designed and staffed specifically for children who had been deprived of so much opportunity. Today, you can walk the halls of the Drew school and see children studying math, reading, and science with the same eager look they bring to swimming and tennis lessons, soccer, golf, art and music. You can step into the early childhood academy and see teachers reading and singing to children in diapers. You can see instructors from the YMCA we built on campus, working with students in physical education.

Imagine what the impact would be if every city in America had a holistic, neighborhood-based, child-focused reformation effort

When it comes to poverty, education and the economy, I believe answers can best be addressed through creative combinations of philanthropy and private enterprise, like East Lake. Governments at all levels can help facilitate these developments, but <u>local leaders must plan, execute, manage, and sustain them.</u>

The Villages of East Lake today

The Biggest Lesson

Looking back, I think of my own hard lesson about good intentions and high expectations. In the late 1950s, my company built a thousand new homes for the very poor, which they could own on very favorable terms. We thought home ownership was the answer. We didn't think to work with the city on a specialized school, or to consider health and wellness opportunities. In other words, nothing else in the environment was improved, and within a few years those families were living in slum houses again.

Maybe that's the biggest lesson of all. Decent housing alone doesn't redeem a neighborhood. A better school, alone, will not do it. Nor just job training. Nor just more health and

wellness opportunities. It takes all these things, simultaneously.

East Lake is not an exception — it's a demonstration model

Imagine hundreds of thousands of adults coming into the work force. Millions of children staying in school to graduate with dreams of their own.

Almost every day, I meet with someone or get on the phone, making the case with anyone who will listen. People hear me talk about East Lake and say, well, that's a pretty story but I can't believe you can do this just everywhere, or get it to scale across the country.

East Lake is <u>not</u> an exception. Neither is the Bayou District development in New Orleans, nor the Meadows Community development in Indianapolis, nor Northside in Spartanburg, nor Renaissance West in Charlotte, nor Woodlawn United in Birmingham. Neither are the communities in Omaha, Houston, and Columbus, Ohio that are working with Purpose Built Communities. If you think these are exceptions vs. genuine, tangible opportunities operating with inspired local leadership, we say let us show you. Come see for yourself.

Columbia Parc at the Bayou District, New Orleans

Then imagine what the impact would be if your city — if every city in America — had a holistic, neighborhood-based, child-focused reformation effort going on in at least one (if not two or three) of its own neighborhoods of concentrated poverty.

Income being earned, taxes being paid, innovative minds flowing into the work force. Crime going down, prison populations shrinking, family health improving, etc. etc. etc.

Liberate Human Capital

It is simply true: America's greatest untapped resource is the human capital trapped in neighborhoods of concentrated poverty. These people — these children — represent trillions of dollars in unrealized economic productivity. Liberate this human capital across the nation, and economic benefits will accrue on a scale that could pay off the national debt in a decade or less.

It has become so obvious to me. I feel confident in saying that the moral imperative and the economic imperative are one and the same. It's not just the scale of the problem — it's also the scale of the opportunity.

People buried under generations of poverty are like oil beneath the Saudi desert — only more valuable, because their spirits and energy are renewable. Burn a barrel of oil and it's gone. Educate a child in poverty and he or she will grow up pursuing dreams, working and paying taxes, and raising children who will do the same.

A McKinsey & Company study documents how closing the education gap between the privileged and the poor could add $2 trillion or more to the GDP every year. That's more than four times greater than our nation's annual budget deficit.

Other studies — exhaustive ones — have demonstrated that every $1 invested in early education returns $7 to $12 to a community. Other scholars document how third grade reading levels determine a child's life path and opportunities. On the darker side, recent science has proved that younger children living in abject poverty are subjected to "toxic stress," a condition similar to what soldiers experience from repeated combat. A recent study determined that a child living in poverty is likely to hear 30 million fewer words spoken or sung to them by age three. Is that not a heartbreaking call to action?

Our nation needs collective urgency about this — about the suffering, yes, but also the understanding that restoring these lives and sparing these children so much pain and misery will strengthen and grow our nation's economy. The education gap between advantaged and disadvantaged children has doubled since WWII and is getting bigger every day, leading to poor health outcomes that translate into poor cognitive skills. The number of Americans living in neighborhoods of extreme poverty grew by a third in the first decade of this century .

Leadership is Key

We have wrung our hands forever, it seems, thinking there is no solution. But there is a solution. It can be done. East Lake proves it. New Orleans and Indianapolis prove it. And if it can be done in these neighborhoods, it can be done anywhere. There's only one real secret to it, and that is leadership. Philanthropists know the leaders in their communities. The

191

businessman or woman with a big heart and a lot of influence. People who can pull other leaders together from the neighborhood, the business community, and governments. Every city and town has one or several key leaders like this.

And every city and town has one or more East Lake Meadows kind of neighborhoods. The opportunities are huge. East Lake has taught us one adaptable way that is proven to work. Every city has the challenge, and every city has the resources — if some leader, some group of leaders, will just get mobilized.

I tell everyone: use East Lake as your R&D lab. East Lake/Purpose Built Communities will test any reasonable idea. If your state

doesn't allow charter schools, talk to us. We don't charge for these services. Maybe there are ways to get exceptions, or ways to get a public school designated as a special school eligible for additional resources in a private-public partnership.

Government, philanthropy and private enterprise — with the right leadership — can move mountains. It happened in East Lake, it's happening in New Orleans and Indianapolis, Spartanburg, Charlotte, and Birmingham. More than 15 other cities are talking with us about getting underway.

It can be done. We know at least one proven way for getting it done. Every day, I ask myself, what in the heck are we waiting for?

PUTTING EDUCATION FRONT AND CENTER   Drew Charter School opened its doors in 2000, providing the cradle-to-college education pipeline for the holistic community revitalization of the East Lake community in southeast Atlanta. The success in East Lake led to the creation of Purpose Built Communities, which is taking the East Lake model and replicating it in communities around the country. Drew Charter School has served as the cradle-to-college education model for several of these other revitalization initiatives, and after fifteen years of success at Drew, it was determined that Purpose Built Communities should create a special entity dedicated solely to providing this innovative approach to education. Purpose Built Schools was created to fulfill this need.

OFF AND RUNNING   In 2016 Purpose Built Schools entered into a first-of-its-kind partnership with Atlanta Public Schools to operate four schools within APS's Carver Cluster — two elementary schools, a middle school, and a high school. Purpose Built Schools has reopened Thomasville Heights Elementary (July 2016), Slater Elementary (July 2017), and Price Middle School (July 2017), and it will add Carver High School in 2018. The completed feeder pattern of schools will have more than 2,000 students.

The Purpose Built-APS contract creates a middle ground between traditional public schools and charter schools. Under this "partnership school approach," all schools remain traditional APS neighborhood schools — accepting every child living in the attendance zone — but Purpose Built Schools has the flexibility and autonomy of a charter school. The first year of the partnership showed remarkable progress at Thomasville Heights: out-of-school suspensions decreased nearly by half; the transiency rate was cut by one-third; parent engagement (as measured by attendance at parent-teacher conferences) increased seven-fold; and most significantly, the school had the second-highest gains in student achievement among all APS schools.

Purpose Built Communities has eighteen network members and roughly forty-five communities that are in discussion about the model.

Greg Giornelli, President of Purpose Built Schools, and
Eytan Davidson, Purpose Built Communities

November 2017

XIV

EAST LAKE HOSPITALITY

The success of East Lake has depended on people – Rick Burton

The one word that unites all positions and all people at East Lake is hospitality – Chad Parker

Few members of the staff know about Bobby Jones before coming to East Lake, but they are quickly introduced to a style of hospitality and mentored in ways that reflect the principles and values that defined him. He did not invent them, but the men and women who knew him well saw them in him, and his clubs and the programs named for him reflect them.

The nine core values taught to children in the programs of the First Tee describe his character and can be applied to working in any group. Honesty (truthful, not deceptive), Integrity (as a standard of conduct, a value), Sportsmanship, Respect, Confidence, Responsibility, Perseverance, Courtesy, and Judgment. His friends and the students who spent so much time with him in his last three years also saw his intelligence, positive attitude, and sense of humor.

These are the timeless principles of success in any career.

William Campbell | Larry Riley | Chris Mulgrave | Chris Arthur | Angelo Simmons

Cameron Batey | Paul Parkinson | Jeremy Avery | Brandon Roberson | Michael Simons

Cameron Lilly | Peter McClain | Drew Dunn | Mark McCartney | Dave Purdie

Scott Putnam | Rick Burton | Chad Parker | Caroline McGill | Lauren Rosenzweig

Krista Cardinal | Nick Auten | Terry McClendon | Najah Walcott | Susan Hazel

Robierre Fluker | Ron Shinholster | Chef Nick Barrington | Kevin Bean | Dot Kelley

Jamaal Ali | Beate de Priest | Mae Searcy | Tracy Kelley | Jesse James

Stacy Kelley | John Beale | Michael O'Brien | Sashah Bozeman | Andrew Pless | Tim Rawlings

(L-R) Lisa Tuggles, Henry Bierenfeld, Arthur Whitaker, Charlie Harrison (seated), Sheralyn Feezell, and Melanie Grimes

Briean Byrd | Jon Lothner

Rico Jones | Anwar Rahgman

Greg Edwards   Drew Hinesley   John Garbe   Charles Banks   Miller Gantt   Joe Sanders

Chris Smith   Kyle Barry   Stephan Moday   Steve Watkins   Walter Williams   Ransom Lutz

Ismael Mergan   David Drust   Javon Hutchinson   Brian Salmon   Earl Singleton   Young Park

Darrell Shedeger   Nick Wade   Craig Wilson   Philip Gore   Randy Buckner   Brandon Boucher

Chris Jackson   Lloyd Barneby   Kevin Yancey   Jesse Mitchell   Jon Gray   Peter Von Feilitzen

EPILOGUE

What does the future hold for East Lake? Will the names and accomplishments of Alexa Stirling and the other Hall-of-Fame members gradually disappear? Will Bobby's friend Charlie Elliott be remembered? What about Bobby Jones himself?

East Lake Golf Club is here to stay. It is now a safe place and has become the home of the season-ending PGA Tour Championship, the finale of the FedExCup Playoffs. Well-managed nonprofits benefit from the annual tournament.[1]

The Hall-of-Fame golfers? The Georgia State Golf Association and Georgia Golf Hall of Fame will be centrally located in Atlanta on Northside Drive as part of the new Bobby Jones Golf Course. It will offer championship golf to the public, serve as the home course for Georgia State, and attract all ages. It was the last course designed by Atlanta architect Bob Cupp, and a short course reserved for young golfers, the Cupp Links, will honor his memory. Golf House will be the first home of the Georgia Golf Hall of Fame, which will feature the images and accomplishments of the five master-golfers in this book and ninety-seven others. The project is the newest chapter in Atlanta's long golfing story.

The Charlie Elliott Wildlife Center, an hour east of Atlanta, includes a large nature preserve and honors Charlie's memory by emphasizing teaching and research. Inspired by Charlie's commitment to teaching children about the natural world, teachers from the center are taking wild animals into classrooms within a ninety-mile radius that includes Atlanta, Macon, and Athens. Bobby and Alexa would approve for a special reason — the Center offers programs for homeschooled children.

Bobby Jones himself? The USGA's highest honor is the Bob Jones award, presented annually since 1955 in recognition of sportsmanship in golf. Large numbers of golf fans learn about him during the Masters, the Tour Championship, and the tournaments held at the Athletic Club. Also, the interest of students and faculty members at Emory, Georgia Tech, and St. Andrews in the Jones Scholarship has given him a presence in the academic world; and the Jones Program in Ethics in the Laney Graduate School at Emory has broadened the reach of his principles of behavior.

There are two Bobby Jones historic sites in Atlanta east of downtown, and an impressive exhibit is only a few miles away.[2] His birthplace, on St. Paul Avenue in Grant Park, is now the home of the Atlanta Preservation Center. His gravesite in Oakland Cemetery is less than one mile north of his birthplace, and is marked by a horseshoe-shaped arrangement of flowering trees and shrubs representing every hole at Augusta National. The Atlanta History Center in Buckhead offers *Fair Play: The Bobby Jones Story*, a permanent exhibit on his life and career.

He lived to enjoy the popularity of the Masters through the 1960s and to inspire the USGA to bring the U.S. Open to the Atlanta Athletic Club, his life-long club.

---

1   The East Lake Foundation, the First Tee, and Purpose Built Communities.
2   The new Bobby Jones Golf Course and Hall of Fame on Northside Drive will be the fourth.

Although he could not know what would become of East Lake, he inspired hope. Before he died, he met with Paul Grigsby, the leader of the partnership that bought East Lake from the Athletic Club. A few words were enough.

Don't worry Paul, he said. *The Athletic Club is my club, but East Lake is my golf course.*

Birthplace in Grant Park, now the home of the
Atlanta Preservation Center

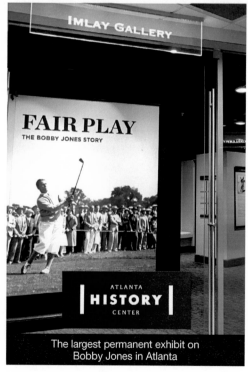

The largest permanent exhibit on
Bobby Jones in Atlanta

THE NEW YORK TIMES   *Sunday, December 19, 1971*

Bobby Jones, Golf Master, Dies;
Only Player to Win Grand Slam

ATLANTA. Dec. 18 — Bobby Jones, the master golfer who scored an unparalleled grand slam by winning the United States and British Open and Amateur Tournaments in 1930, died today at his home. His age was 69.

Mr. Jones, a lawyer by profession, who competed only as an amateur, had suffered from a progressive disease of the spinal cord since 1948. By the middle of last December, he was no longer able to go to the offices of his firm, Jones, Bird, & Howell, although he tried to continue working at home. Death came from an aneurysm in his chest. Surviving are his widow, the former Mary Malone; a son, Robert T. 3d of Nashville; two daughters, Mrs. Carl Hood Jr. and Mrs. Clara J. Black; and seven grandchildren.

Bobby Jones in 1930

Star of a Golden Age
BY FRANK LITSKY

In the decade following World War I, America luxuriated in the Golden Era of Sports and its greatest collection of super athletes: Babe Ruth and Ty Cobb in baseball, Jack Dempsey and Gene Tunney in boxing, Bill Tilden in tennis, Red Grange in football, and Bobby Jones in golf. Many of their records have been broken now, and others are destined to be broken. But one, sports experts agree, may outlast them — Bobby Jones's grand slam of 1930.

Jones, an intense, unspoiled young man, started early on the road to success. At the age of 10, he shot a 90 for 18 holes. At 11 he was down to 80, and at 12 he shot a 70. At 9 he played against men, at 14 he won a major men's tournament, and at 21 he was United States Open champion.

At 28 he achieved the grand slam — victories in one year in the United States Open, British Open, United States Amateur and British Amateur championships. At that point, he retired from tournament golf.

A nation that idolized him for his success grew to respect him even more for his decision to treat golf as a game rather than a way of life. This respect grew with the years.

"First comes my wife and children," he once explained. "Next comes my profession — the law. Finally, and never as a life in itself, comes golf."

His record, aside from the grand slam, was magnificent. He won the United States Open championship four times (1923, 1926, 1929, and 1930), the British Open three times (1926, 1927, and 1930), and the United States Amateur five times (1924, 1925, 1927, 1928, and 1930).

"Jones is as truly the supreme artist as Paderewski is the supreme artist of the piano," George H. Greenfield wrote in the *New York Times* in 1930.

Felt the Tension

Success did not come easily. Though Jones was cool and calculating outwardly, he seethed inside. He could never eat properly during a major tournament. The best his stomach would hold was dry toast and tea.

The pressure of tournament competition manifested itself in other ways, too. Everyone expected Jones to win every time he played, including Atlanta friends who often bet heavily on him. He escaped the unending pressure by retiring from competition.

"Why should I punish myself like this over a golf tournament?" he once asked. "Sometimes I'd pass my mother and dad on the course, look at them and not even see them because I was so concentrated on the game. Afterward, it made a fellow feel a little silly."

The quality of the man projected itself, too. He was worshipped as a national

hero in Scotland, the birthplace of golf. Scots would come for miles around to watch him play.

In 1936, on a visit, he made an unannounced trip to the Royal and Ancient Golf Club at St. Andrews for a quiet morning round with friends. There were 5,000 spectators at the first tee and 7,000 at the 18th. Businesses closed as word spread that "Our Bobby is back."

In 1927, when he tapped in his final putt to win the British Open there, an old Scot stood by the green and muttered: "The man canna be human."

Off the course, Jones was convivial in a quiet way. He was a good friend and always the gentleman, though he had full command of strong language when desired. He had a fine sense of humor, and he laughed easily. He smoked cigarettes and drank bourbon.

He was besieged by people who wanted to play a social round of

Jones, at left, with President Eisenhower and Gene Tunney at the White House in 1955

golf with him. When they talked with him it was always golf. He managed to tolerate their one-sided approach to life. He also learned to put up with the name of Bobby, which he hated (he preferred Bob).

He was not always so serene. As a youngster, he had a reputation for throwing clubs when everything was not going right. When Jim Barnes, the 1921 United States Open champion, watched him let off steam, he said:

"Never mind that club throwing and the beatings he's taking. Defeat will make him great. He's not satisfied now with a pretty good shot. He has to be perfect. That's the way a good artist must feel."

The defeats Barnes spoke of were frequent in the early years. For young Jones, though he had the game of a man, had the emotions of a growing boy. He never won the big tournaments until he got his temper under control.

At 18, he learned that his greatest opponent was himself. He was playing at Toledo one day with Harry Vardon, the great English professional, and was his usual brash self. They were about even when Jones dribbled a shot into a bunker. Hoping to ease his embarrassment, he turned to Vardon and asked:

"Did you ever see a worse shot?"

"No," replied the crusty Vardon. It was the only word he spoke to Jones all day.

Jones matured, so much so that O.B. Keeler, an Atlanta sports writer and his longtime Boswell, once wrote:

"He has more character than any champion in our history."

He also had the dream of every golfer — a picture swing. No one taught it to him, for he never took a golf lesson in his life. He learned the swing by watching Stewart Maiden, a Scottish professional at the Atlanta Athletic Club course. He would follow Maiden for a few holes, then run home and mimic the swing.

His putting was famous. So was his putter, a rusty, goosenecked club known as Calamity Jane. His strength was driving, putting and an ability to get out of trouble. He was an imaginative player, and he never hesitated to take a chance. In fact, he seldom hesitated on any shot, and he earned an unfair reputation as a mechanical golfer. The game often baffled him. "There are times," he once said, "when I feel that I know less about what I'm doing on a golf course than anyone else in the world."

When he was an infant, doctors were not sure that he would survive, let alone play golf. He had a serious digestive ailment until he was 5, and he stayed home while other children played. In his later years, he was crippled by syringomyelia, a chronic disease of the spinal cord, and he had circulation and heart trouble.

Robert Tyre Jones, Jr. (named for his grandfather) was born on St. Patrick's Day 1902, in Atlanta. His father was a star outfielder at the University of Georgia, and the youngster's first love was baseball. He also tried tennis. At the age of 9 he settled down to golf.

His parents had taken up the game after moving to a cottage near the East Lake course of the Atlanta Athletic Club. Young Bobby would walk around the course, watch the older folk play, and learn by example. He was only six years old, a scrubby youngster with skinny arms and legs, when he won a six hole tournament. At 9, he was the club's junior champion.

In Philadelphia Tourney

He was 14 when he journeyed to the Merion Cricket Club near Philadelphia for his first United States Amateur championship. He was a chunky lad of 5 feet 4 inches and 165 pounds and somewhat knock-kneed. He was wearing his first pair of long trousers.

After qualifying for match play, he defeated Eben M. Byers, a former champion, in the first round. He beat Frank Dyer, a noted player at the time, in the second round, after losing five of the first six holes. Then he lost to Robert A. Gardner, the defending champion, 5 and 3.

In 1922, he reached the semifinals of the United States Amateur before losing. That ended what he called his seven lean years. Next came what Keeler called "the eight fat years," as Jones finally achieved the heights.

In 1924, Jones decided that he was worrying too much about his opponent in match-play (man against man) competition. He vowed to play for pars and forget about his opponent.

This was a turning point in his career. He started to win match-play competition. That year, at Merion, Pa., he won the United States Amateur for the first time. In the final, he defeated George Von Elm by the overwhelming score of 9 and 8.

Also in 1924, he married Mary Malone, his high school sweetheart.

All this time, golf was a sidelight to education. Jones wanted to be an engineer, and he earned bachelor's and master's degrees in engineering at Georgia Tech. Then he decided to become a lawyer. He went to Harvard and earned another bachelor's degree, then to Emory University in Atlanta for a Bachelor of Laws degree. In 1928, he joined his father's law firm in Atlanta.

In 1929, Jones had a close call in the United States Open at the Winged Foot Golf Club, Mamaroneck, N.Y. He sank a 12-foot sloping, sidehill putt on the last green to tie Al Espinosa. The next day, Jones won their 36-hole title playoff by 23 strokes.

Then came 1930 and the grand slam, Lloyds of London quoted odds of 50 to 1 that Jones wouldn't win the world's four major tournaments that year. He won them.

First came the British Amateur. He started his opening match by shooting 3, 4, 3, and 2. In the final he beat Roger Wethered, 7 and 6.

Next was the British Open at Hoylake, England, and his 72-hole score of 291 won that championship.

Back home, Jones got his sternest test of the year in the United States Open at Interlachen near Minneapolis. There were 15,000 spectators in the gallery as he played the par-4 18th hole. He got a birdie 3 by sinking a 40-foot undulating putt, and his 287 won by two strokes.

He had become the first man to win three of the four major titles in one year. The last of the grand slam tournaments, the United States Amateur at Merion, was almost anticlimactic.

No one doubted for a moment that Jones would win. He captured the qualifying medal. He routed Jess Sweetser, 9 and 8, in the semifinal round, and in the final he defeated Gene Romans 8 and 7. The crowd surged around him so wildly that it took a detachment of United States Marines to get him out safely.

Soon after, he retired from tournament play and made a series of golf motion pictures, the only time he ever made money from the game. Later, he became a vice president of A.G. Spalding & Bros., the sporting goods manufacturer. He became a wealthy lawyer and soft-drink bottler and a business and social leader in Atlanta.

He never played serious tournament golf again. He didn't seem to mind.

"Golf is like eating peanuts," he said. "You can play too much or too little. I've become reconciled to the fact that I'll never play as well as I used to."

A few years later, Jones and the late architect, Alister MacKensie, designed the Augusta National Golf Course in Georgia. In 1934, the Masters tournament was started there and in Jones's lifetime many golf people considered it the most important tournament of all.

Jones played in the first Masters and in

several thereafter, but he was never among the leaders. He always wore his green jacket, signifying club membership, at victory ceremonies, and he served as club president.

He became strong enough to rip a pack of playing cards across the middle, but his health deteriorated. He underwent spinal surgery in 1948 and 1950. He was forced to use one cane, and then two canes, and then a wheelchair, and his weight dropped to less than 100 pounds. He last saw the Masters in 1967.

He was a close friend of Dwight D. Eisenhower, and the President often used his cottage adjacent to the Augusta National course for golfing vacations. During his first term in office, the President painted a 40-by-32 inch oil portrait of Jones at the peak of his game. On the back was printed by hand:

"Bob — from his friend D.D.E., 1953."

In January of 1953, three months after a heart attack, Jones was honored at Golf House, the United States Golf Association headquarters in Manhattan. Augusta National members, including General Eis–

enhower had donated another oil portrait to be hung at Golf House. A highlight of the ceremony was the reading of a letter from the President.

"Those who have been fortunate enough to know him," the letter said, "realize that his fame as a golfer is transcended by his inestimable qualities as a human being… His gift to his friends is the warmth that comes from unselfishness, superb judgement, strength of character, unwavering loyalty to principle."

Bobby Jones listened and cried.

Jones is Mourned at Scottish Links
Royal and Ancient Club Flag is Lowered in Memory

ST. ANDREWS, Scotland, Dec 18 (AP) — The town of St. Andrews and the Royal and Ancient Golf Club, headquarters of the game, mourned the great Bobby Jones today.

Golfers stopped on the Old Course when the news of his death reached them. The flag on the clubhouse was lowered to half staff.

It was on the St. Andrews course that Jones won the British Amateur as part of his grand slam in 1930. Three years earlier he had won the British Open here.

An Honorary Freeman

Later Jones was made an honorary freeman (citizen) of the old town.

The Royal and Ancient Club cabled a message of sympathy to the great golfer's widow.

Keith MacKenzie, secretary of the club, said: "Bobby Jones was an honorary member of this club and his death is a tremendous personal loss to us. We are cabling Mrs. Jones in the name of the captain and members expressing our deepest sorrow."

Mayor Feels His Loss

David Niven, the provost, or mayor, of St. Andrew's said: "What can one say about Bobby Jones? He was a great golfer and the game is poorer for his death. But he was a freeman of St. Andrews, too, and in common with all Scotts, we are saddened by the news."

"He was held in great affection by the citizens of St. Andrews."

Arthur Havers, British Open champion in 1923 and an opponent of Jones in many tournaments, said: "He was a wonderful man and all professional golfers held him in esteem. He was always a possible winner in any event he entered. Because of his build he had an unusual style, but it was certainly effective and he was a beautiful putter."

Havers, now 75 years old, once defected Jones, 2 and 1, in a 36-hole exhibition match.

Jones, with his goose-necked putter, Calimity Jane, after winning the British Open at St. Andrews, Scotland, in 1927.

Alexa Stirling Fraser—a legend

by Eddie MacCabe

A truly glorious figure in golf history, Mrs. Alexa Stirling Fraser, died yesterday morning at the Riverside Hospital in Ottawa after a long illness. She was 79.

A litany of Mrs. Fraser's championships and achievements in golf would fill this page, so we'll touch only some high points.

She played in the United States national championships nine times, winning the title three times, finishing runner-up three times, twice reaching the semi-final round and losing out in the first round one time.

She won the Canadian ladies' championship twice and the Southern U. S. Amateur three times, beginning play in that competition when she was only 13.

She also won the Berthellyn Cup at Philadelphia twice and won the Women's Metropolitan championship of New York twice.

She became a member of the Royal Ottawa Golf Club in 1925 and won the ladies title that year, and then again in '27, '30, '32, '33, '35, '36 and '52, and old timers around the Royal will tell you she could have won it many more times but she chose not to compete.

Mrs. Fraser was an honorary member of the Royal, the only person accorded that honor other than the Governor General, and she was also an honorary life member of the Ottawa Hunt.

First fame in Atlanta

She was born Sept. 5, 1897 in Atlanta, Georgia to Dr. and Mrs. Alex Williamson Stirling. She was frail as a youngster and Dr. Stirling, an eye specialist, moved the family out of town to an English style cottage on a lake, and opposite the 10th tee of the East Lake golf course.

One of her playmates in the area was Bobby Jones who grew into one of the towering legends in sports. She began playing with him and other youngsters on the East Lake course and in her first tournament, against the neighbourhood boys, she won.

The trophy, however, was awarded to Jones because the scorer, Frank Meador figured, "We couldn't have a girl beating us."

Years later, Bobby Jones, who never understood why he got the trophy, wrote:

"I am sure Alexa should have had the cup. Please tell her for me, however, that it is too late now because I consider that the statute of limitations has run against her claim. Please also give her my affectionate regards."

Mrs. Fraser, too, minimized that win over Jones, and said only last year:

"I had an advantage over Bob those days. I was 12 and he was only seven and I have to be honest. It wasn't very long until he was defeating me."

Swing like Jones

It has often been noted that Bobby Jones and Alexa Stirling had remarkably similar golf swings, and she attributed that to their first instruction from a pro named Jimmy Maiden, and later, Stewart Maiden. Mrs. Stirling said:

"Bob and I had similar swings because we copied Stewart Maiden."

It was during World War I that she and Bobby Jones started touring America, playing games for Red Cross benefits, and it was during a game for the Red Cross here in Ottawa that she hit a shot into a sand trap that changed her life.

She was a slim, auburn-haired girl, 5'3'' and about 110 pounds with deep brown eyes. When she went down into that trap, a man in the gallery thought she looked so small, and so fetching, that he contrived to meet her after the match.

That was Dr. W. G. Fraser, originally from Pembroke, and a practising ophthamologist in Ottawa. A year later, in 1925, they were married in Atlanta, enjoyed a small reception set up for her by her golf club, the East Lake Club, and they set sail on the Mauretania for a two-month honeymoon in Europe.

When they returned, they came to Ottawa and golf became a casual recreation as she turned her attention to being a wife and raising a family.

Great iron player

She was a small lady, and while her hands were not large, they were unusually strong, and she was particularly gifted as an iron player, hitting those crisp shots time after time.

She was never a long hitter, although she moved it off the tee comfortably better than 200 yards. But her irons were her strength and of all the shots in golf, she once said:

"My favorite shot is a mashie pitch to the green. There is more satisfaction to me in playing a well hit mashie shot fairly close to the pin than any other part of golf."

While there was a variety of mashie clubs in those days, the mashie was basically the club we now call a five iron.

In those days, too, women played in long skirts, oftenwith long sweaters, belted around the waist, and Mrs. Fraser said once:

"We could do much better in knickerbockers. The skirt is a big handicap in putting, especially on windy days where it may often hide the ball just as you go to hit it."

She was quite a lady . . . quiet when standing over the ball, quiet in her manner whether things were going well or not, gentle and considerate in conversation when walking over the Royal, or sitting on the broad verandah in easy conversation.

And somehow regal

A lady said to me yesterday:

"There was something regal about her, not in a forbidding way at all, but a certain kind of majesty. I often felt, when she looked in a particular direction, I should run and fetch whatever she was looking at."

And that was true. She also wearied, just a little, of golfers coming to her looking for shortcuts, that little tip that would put it all together, like magic.

Once, many years ago, I was standing with her and Ernie Wakelam, and a player came up complaining of his luck and the game and said to her:

"What am I doing wrong? I can't get my drives into the air?"

We had stood watching him flail at the ball with no idea of what he was about, and she smiled and said:

Did you ever think about taking a lesson?"

But she was gracious and pattient with people who came to her for help, and long-time Royal Ottawa member Al Wotherspoon said yesterday she

was always "pleased and willing to assist any member, regardless of calibre . . . she was a remarkable person."

Finals nostalgic run

Although indifferent health, she want back to Atlanta last year with her daughter Sandra (Mrs. Ron Carwardine) at the invitation of the United States Open committee.

The Open was being played at the Atlanta Athletic Club, and a room was being opened in memory of the immortalBobby Jones. In that room was a special showcase to display the memorabilia of the career of Jones' early playmate, Alexa Stirling.

Mrs. Fraser's daughter Sandra knew, of course, of her mother's accomplishments and records, but the magic of her name in Georgia she found an overpowering experience.

"I had really had no idea," she said.

It was a final nostalgic run for the grand lady of golf, back to the scenes of her childhood and her early triumphs. She saw many of her old friends, she was on stage with many celebrated old golfers at a special show at the Atlanta Arts Centre, emceed by Fran Tarkenton. She saw her old home, and her golf club, and even saw again the trophy she won as a girl, the one awarded to Bobby Jones.

She was, unquestionably, a legend in her own time, and she wore it lightly . . . a truly great golfer, and a truly elegant lady.

When Mrs. Fraser returned to Ottawa, her health continued to decline. She had had cobalt treatments, and entered hospital again in mid-February.

She is survived by her daughter Sandra (Mrs. Ron Carwardine of Ottawa), two sons, Glen (a former Canadian ski champion) and Dick, and seven grandsons; and two sisters, Nora Stirling of New York, and Mrs. Janet Davison, of Baldwin, Georgia. She was predeceased by her husband in 1967.

Mrs. Fraser is resting at Hulse and Playfair on McLead street and funeral service will be held in the chapel Monday morning at eleven o'clock. Interment will be in her husband's family plot in Pembroke.

Summer Sunset

© Chet Burgess

ACKNOWLEDGMENTS

I wish to thank the many people who helped create this book: My wife Priscilla for her patience and support; Tom and Ann Cousins for saving the 180 acres that hold all the memories and stories; Rees Jones for his advice and the foreword; Charles and Sylvia Harrison for details of their work with the children of East Lake; Rick Burton and Chad Parker for their leadership and for their comments on the golf course; the staff at East Lake for their photographs; editors Robert F. Kibler, Jane Saral, Chad Parker, Seaborn Jones, Tom Cousins, Charlie and Comer Yates, Bob Crosby, Ralph Kepple, Harry Kennedy, David Cleghorn, Spencer King, Mary and Ken Zeliff, Rie Calcaterra, John Kennedy, John Porter, Bruce Wolf, and Kevin Newell. Special thanks go to John Carlin and Robin Dacus of Fuse Graphics for their time, technical expertise, and patience, and to Mike Hobbs for his professional help, encouragement, and especially for the photograph on the front cover.

My thanks also go to Dave Sansom and Chet Burgess for their photographs and Tim Rawlings for the eighteenth in the snow; St. Andrews University, Cowie Collection, for the photograph of Bobby Jones speaking at St. Andrews; Sid Matthew for his advice, his quick and accurate answers to questions, and for the use of the photographs of Bobby Jones with King George VI at the Walker Cup, of Bobby holding the U.S. Open and U.S. Amateur trophies, and for the sketch of Alexa by Edward Kasper; Neal G. Patton for his photograph of the Atlanta Preservation Center; Alison Hepner for *The Golfer and the Carpenter* by her father, James A. Barclay; Kim Crisp and Shannon Baller of the Georgia State Golf Association for the biographies and photos of East Lake's Hall-of-Fame amateurs and the picture of Charlie Yates from *Golf Georgia*; Debra Nadelhoffer for her painting of the Ryder Cup sixth green; John Companiotte for introducing me to John Carlin; Catherine Lewis for her advice; the Bobby Jones Scholars for their photographs; Gabrielle Dean for her assistance at the Atlanta Preservation Center; Richard Harker for arranging the photograph of the gravesite at Oakland; and to Mary Ellen Imlay for her picture of John in Scotland.

Four archivists made their collections and photographs available and offered valuable advice: Katie Long at Nonami Enterprises, Caroline McGill at East Lake Golf Club, Margaret Almand at the Atlanta Athletic Club, and Meggan Gardner at Golf Canada in Toronto. I'm grateful to each of them. Certain photos of Alexa Stirling are courtesy of the Canadian Golf Hall of Fame and Museum/Golf Canada. I offer my thanks to The Toronto Golf Club for the use of its motto, "Respice Finem;" Jim Fraser and Harry Kennedy in Toronto for their hospitality during my visit; and to Ted Ryan, archivist of the Coca-Cola Company, for the photograph of Bobby and his father having a Coke.

I am indebted to those who contributed their written material and their stories: the family of Charlie Elliott for excerpts from his book, *East Lake Country Club History*; Chuck Palmer, for "Before Tom Stepped In;" Jack Schroder, John Lambert, and John Martin for "The Final Years;" Harry A. McCusker for "One Down with One to Play;" Sandra Carwardine, daughter of Alexa Stirling Fraser, for her memories of her mother and the use of portions of her sister Janet's family history; Charles and Comer Yates, for their editing and their memories of their father; Rachel Barnes for her stories about Tommy; Anne Thomas and John Vardeman and the *Gainesville Times* for her interview; Frazer Durrett, Bob Foreman, Dale Harman, Jack Glenn, Bill Rooker, John Imlay, and Bob Young for their contributions to "Remembering Mr. Jones;" and other friends of Bobby Jones who contributed earlier: Harvey Hill, Fred Russell, Cy Strickler, Eugene Branch, Marion and Ralph Williams, Richard Courts, and Mariana Goldsmith Knox Eager.

APPENDIX

THE FIRST GOLF COURSE AT EAST LAKE[1]

(Today's course is in bold)

Bobby Jones: *The old course was sort of a strange layout as golf courses go because it had only two par-three holes, the first and the third. The rest were short par fours and fives. From other standpoints it was an interesting course. We had names for some of the holes. A couple I recall were the sixteenth that we knew as the Circus Ring, because of its appearance, and the fourteenth where you had to play over the Spectacle Bunker, a double trap which was, of course, shaped like a pair of spectacles, or eyeglasses.*

Charlie Elliott: (Edited to use the present course as his reference). The original first tee lay almost on the site of the present clubhouse. Play was over the **ninth green** to the site of the **back tees for number one**. The second, third, and fourth holes followed the same layout as the current **first, second, and third**. The tee for the fifth was about where the **ninth tee** is now, and it played south to a green near the present **professional tee for number six**. From there play on the sixth was back north to a green located between the **fourth tee and eighth green**.

The old number seven and eight were about the same as the present **fourth and fifth**. The ninth tee was reached by walking seventy-five or eighty yards up from the old eighth green, **today's fifth green**, to the ninth tee. It was opposite a swath that was cut through the woods for the ninth fairway. The drive was across today's **sixth fairway** and woods to a landing area in the **seventh fairway**. Then you played a sharp dogleg to the right. The ninth green was where the **seventh green** is now.

To begin the second nine, you walked across the dam to a tee at the **fifteenth tee**, and you played the tenth up the **fourteenth fairway** to the center of that fairway. The tee of the eleventh was on the edge of the woods toward Glenwood Avenue and played uphill through the woods to a green near the southwest corner of the property. From there, you played the twelfth along Second Avenue to where it cornered with Alston Drive. The twelfth was really the **thirteenth** played in the opposite direction.

The thirteenth was played along Alston Drive to a green in the hollow now occupied by the pond in front of the **eleventh green**. The fourteenth was along the right side of the current **tenth fairway** to a green at the **eighteenth tee**, and the fifteenth ran parallel to and east of the old twelfth back up to a big oak near the **thirteenth green**.

The par five sixteenth [the Circus Ring] ran from that big oak tree back to the **fifteenth green**, which was an island green then with a canal around it. The old seventeenth hole ran from a tee at the current **sixteenth tee** straight up to a green situated between the **upper practice tee and seventeenth fairway**. This is the site of the par three green for the eighth hole of the Donald Ross course. From there you walked down to the eighteenth tee, behind the current **forward tee**, and played your eighteenth on the same land as the **eighteenth** of today (Elliott 1984).

---

1 There have been four golf courses: by Tom Bendelow, 1907/08 – 1913 (Formal opening was in '08, but there was play in '07); Donald Ross, 1915 – 1960; George Cobb — Renovation for the Ryder Cup, 1963 – 1994; and Rees Jones — Renovation, 1996 to present;

And four clubhouses: Building #1, July 4, 1908 – March 22, 1914 (Fire); #2, May 8, 1915 – November 22, 1925 (Fire); #3, August 7, 1926 – 1994; and #4, the Tom Cousins renovation, 1995 to present.

WHAT GOLF MEANS TO ME

Linton C. Hopkins, Sr.[1]

1915

To get a Wednesday afternoon for golf, I have to rush around in the office all morning, doing a whole day's work in half a day. When 12:30 comes, screwed up to about a thousand pounds pressure to the square inch, I gallop downstairs to the lunch counter and swallow a pie and a cup of coffee. Grabbing my car, I beat it for the country club. In a few minutes, I develop a terrible indigestion. On the way, I usually get arrested for speeding. That causes delay, so when I get through arguing with the policeman, I have to hurry faster than ever. At the club, I hurry out of my clothes. I usually tear my unions badly. I hurry out to the first tee. Then I try to calm down. I give myself auto-suggestions. I say,

I will relax. I will not hurry. I am not in a hurry. I'm very quiet and calm now. But inside I know I'm a terrible liar.

Then I start out. And I hittem in the rough. I hittem in the lake. I hittem in the woods. I hittem on top. I hittem on the bottom. I hittem everywhere but in the middle. I lose my balls. I lose my money. I lose my temper. I lose my Higher Nature.

I hole out finally at number eighteen, ineffably weary, disappointed, discouraged, disheartened, disgusted, and dishonored. I cuss the caddie. I tell him it was all his fault. I dress and go home. I eat my supper. I fuss with my wife and carp at the children. Then I kick the dog and go to bed.

Next morning at the office I tell the boys what a glorious afternoon I had.

You ought to have seen that putt I made on sixteen, I say. Then I turn to my calendar and figure out how many days will elapse before another Wednesday arrives.

---

1   Linton C. Hopkins, Sr. (1872–1943) was an Atlanta attorney and mystery writer who was a contemporary of Bobby's father, Robert P. Jones. He was a longtime member of the Atlanta Athletic Club, and he taught his five children (Nina, John, Cabell, Linton and Ellet) to play golf at East Lake back before WWI.

THE ATLANTA JOURNAL   *Sunday Morning, September 17, 1922*

BOB JONES LOWERS HIS OWN RECORD AT EAST LAKE TO 63

Probably Greatest Round of Golf Ever Shot; Nine Birdies Included on Card

by O. B. Keeler

Two years ago, Bob Jones cut the course record at East Lake from 68 — set by himself — to 66, and has been shooting at it ever since. Four times he has equaled it, but he never could bust it.

And then, along in the cool of the evening of a waning September Saturday — yesterday, to be explicit — the patron saint of golf, St. Andrew, past question, took a good look at Bobby, as he started out with his dad and Tess Bradshaw and Abe Adair, and he said, said the good saint:

"Bobby, this is your day!"

And as night drew round about the match, dropping from the sky like a "feather from an eagle in his flight," Bobby stood on the last tee with a par 3 to make for a 63 — and he made it.

A 63, nine under fours. Nine over threes, if you prefer to put it that way. A miracle round. It was Bobby's day.

"I never played an easier round," Bobby confessed afterward. "That usually is the way, though. Your best scores come easily. You can't force them. When you work hard you don't score well. The ball rolls for you — or it doesn't. Dad and Brad and Abe were pretty much worked up, along on the last three holes, but I didn't feel worried at all until I stood on the last tee, and it was getting dark, and I thought for just a moment of all the things that might happen to that shot."

Iron Club - Iron Nerve

Just a moment. Then Bobby drew the trusty old driving iron, no wood for him on that shot. And through the thickening dusk the little white sphere bored its way, upheld by the backspin, climbing, climbing — to drop lightly, just at the right of the green, where Bobby's perfect chip shot, directed by his iron nerves, curled up dead at the cup, dead for a 3, and 63 for the round, probably the greatest round of golf ever shot on as long and hard a course in the history of golf.

It was Bobby's day. St. Andrew was right. And so was Bobby. And I think the good old Saint smiled to himself as he rarely has smiled before, as the youngster with the tousled hair above his steady young face tapped the ball into the last cup and smiled at last upon his work, seeing that it was good.

Here is the card with par:

Par (Out)	443	553	435	–	36		
Jones	324	443	434	–	31		
Par (In)	434	455	443	–	36	–	73
Jones	433	454	333	–	32	–	63

Nine birdies. Nine holes in par. That's all. Not an eagle. Not a buzzard. The mistakes — save the mark — cost him birdies; a few. A missed putt of four feet on No. 3 — after perfect drive and pitch. A bunkered mashie on No. 7, the only trap he was in. A short approach and then a bit too strong a little pitch on No. 14, costing his only 5 of the round. That was the toll.

The Details

Perhaps the best way to commend that wonder round is just to give the detail, and here it is. You may clip this out and paste it in your scrapbook, for it is unlikely that you will see its like again, either in print or on the turf.

No. 1. 400 yards, Par 4 — Drive. Spade mashie to 20 feet from the cup. One putt.

No. 2. 150 Yards, Par 3 — Spade mashie to one yard from the pin. One putt.

No. 3. 320 yards, Par 4 — Drive of 290 yards. Wee pitch with mashie-niblick to four feet from the pin. Missed putt. Took a four.

No. 4. 450 Yards, Par 5 — Long drive that ran into the rough at the edge of the fairway. Iron to 25 feet from the pin. Two putts.

No. 5. 590 Yards, Par 5 — Drive 310 yards. Brassie 260 yards to edge of green. Chip dead. One putt.

No. 6. 175 Yards, Par 3 — Mashie to ten feet from the pin. Missed putt. Took par 3.

No. 7. 380 Yards, Par 4 — Drive.

Mashie to trap at left and in front of green. Niblick out to a yard from the pin. One putt.

No. 8. 230 Yards, Par 3 — Iron off to the right in rough. Niblick to eight feet from cup. One putt.

No. 9. 525 Yards, Par 5 — Fair drive to heavy lie. Brassie short of green. Niblick chip to eight feet from cup. One putt.

Out in 31, a stroke better that his wonderful outward journey in the recent southern championship. Bob took twelve putts on the nine greens, getting down with a single putt on six.

The Second Nine

No. 10. 425 Yards, Par 4 — Drive far up the hill. Mashie to ten feet of the cup. Missed putt, ball hitting cup. Took a 4.

No. 11. 175 Yards, Par 3 — Jigger to twenty feet from pin. Two putts.

No. 12. 390 Yards, Par 4 — Drive. Mashie-niblick to eight feet from cup. One putt.

No. 13. 380 Yards,

Par 4 — Drive 260 yards. Spade mashie to 20 feet from the cup. Two putts.

No. 14. 465 Yards, Par 5 — Drive 300 yards down alley. Mashie short of green, pin in front of green, and a wee pitch failed to stop promptly and rolled fifteen feet past pin. Two putts.

No. 15. 505 Yards, Par 5 — Drive 260 yards. Brassie to edge of green, thirty feet from pin. Two putts.

No. 16. 405 Yards, Par 4 — Drive 260 yards. Mashie-niblick twenty feet past pin. One putt.

No. 17. 400 yards, Par 4 — Drive 250 yards. Mashie 20 feet from pin. One putt.

No. 18. 205 Yards, Par 3 — Driving iron just off green to right. Chip dead. One putt.

Length of course from back tees as played: 6570 yards. Par 36 36 – 72. All putts holed. 12 putts going out; 14 coming in.

Paste It
In Your Book

File this with your records. Paste it on your club bulletin boards. You are not likely to see its like again. The bright Genius of Golf was on the blond brow of Bobby Jones the afternoon of Saturday, September 16, 1922, and the record he set at old East Lake, toughest championship course of the Southland, is likely to endure until our generation has passed away.

"I don't believe I'll ever break it," said Bob simply.

It will be engraved in silver, too.

Eight years ago this month a silver cup was designed to bear the amateur records made at East Lake, the maker of each successive record to hold the cup until the record was broken by another. The first name on it is the name of the late George Adair, a great name in southern golf. On September 8, 1914, Mr. Adair shot a 79, a new amateur record for the course just after it was remodeled in present form.

The next name is that of D. E. Root, 78, July 2, 1915. Then Bob Jones took charge of the cup — and I suspect he will hold it from now on. The subsequent engravings read as follows:

R. T. Jones, Jr. 77, July 7, 1915

R. T. Jones, Jr. 74 July 4, 1916

R. T. Jones Jr. 70 July 18, 1918

R. T. Jones, Jr. 69 July 16, 1919

R. T. Jones, Jr. 68 September 11, 1919

R. T. Jones, Jr. 66 September 13, 1920

MORE HALL OF FAME MEMBERS FROM EAST LAKE

Perry Adair
Inducted 1989

Perry Adair grew up in Atlanta, Ga., playing golf at East Lake with the likes of Bobby Jones. He was an integral part of the "Golden Age of Golf." Adair toured the country as part of the "The Dixie Kids," along with Jones and Alexa Stirling, playing in matches to raise money for the Red Cross during World War I. Adair was the 1914 East Lake Country Club Champion, 1921 and '23 Southern Amateur Champion, and 1922 Georgia Amateur Champion. He was inducted into the Georgia Tech Hall of Fame in 1973.

Stewart Cink
Inducted 2017

Stewart E. Cink of Duluth, Ga., was a standout of the Georgia Tech golf program and is a major champion on the PGA TOUR who has brought honor to the game both as an amateur and professional. Born in Huntsville, Ala., he attended Bradshaw High School in Huntsville. He moved to Atlanta and played golf at Georgia Tech from 1992 to 1995. He was an All-American in 1993, 1994, and 1995, and was an All-Atlantic Coast Conference (SCC) selection those years as well. He was named ACC Player of the Year in 1995 and was on its academic honor roll in 1992 and 1993. He played in 38 team events while at Georgia Tech with a career stroke average of 72.47. He was the recipient of the Fred Haskins Award in 1995, given to the most outstanding collegiate golfer in NCAA Division I, and the Jack Nicklaus Player of the Year award. He was inducted into the Georgia Tech Athletic Hall of Fame in 2005. After a successful collegiate and amateur career, he turned professional in 1995. He is enjoying a professional career that includes six PGA TOUR victories, highlighted most recently by The Open Championship in 2009 at Turnberry Resort in Scotland. He also won the 2008 Travelers Championship, 2004 MCI Heritage, 2004 World Golf Championship-NEC Invitational, 2000 MCI Heritage, and the 1997 Canon Greater Hartford Open. He was named PGA TOUR Rookie of the Year in 1997. In international competition, he was selected to the United States Ryder Cup team five times (2002, 2004, 2006, 2008, 2010) and the President's Cup four times (2000, 2005, 2007, 2009). He founded Cink Charities in 2011, and the Cink It Challenge was developed to raise funds for two Atlanta area charities. He and his wife, Lisa, live in Duluth, Ga., and have two sons — Connor and Reagan.

Thomas G. Cousins
Inducted 2002

Tom Cousins became a golf enthusiast the day his family joined East Lake Golf Club in Atlanta during World War II. After college and a stint in the Air Force, Cousins began Cousins Properties Incorporated with his father in 1958. Today that company is listed on the New York Stock Exchange. Despite his focus on building a great company, Cousins never lost his enthusiasm for the game of golf. He developed the Atlanta area's first golf courses centered in residential communities, including Indian Hills, Hidden Hills, Cross Creek, and Big Canoe. His vision to revitalize his old home club, East Lake, and its surrounding neighborhood serves as a model for other cities and philanthropists to follow. The American Society of Golf Course Architects presented Cousins with the 2004 Donald Ross Award in recognition of his work at East Lake. In addition, he was one of the 25 original founders of the Atlanta Country Club, the site of more than 30 PGA events, a U.S. Women's Amateur, and a U.S. Senior Amateur. In the 1960s, Cousins built The Omni, Atlanta's first world-class arena, and brought major league professional basketball and hockey to Atlanta. He is a member at Augusta National Golf Club, Cypress Point Club, East Lake Golf Club, National Golf Links of America, Peachtree Golf Club, Seminole Golf Club, The Honors Course, and The Royal and Ancient Golf Club. In 2012, he was honored with the Distinguished Service Award from the Metropolitan Golf Writers Association.

Watts Gunn
Inducted 1989

Born in Macon, Ga., on January 11, 1905, Watts Gunn made golfing history in the 1925 U.S. Amateur, setting the world record for international championship golf by winning 15 straight holes in the first round of the 36-hole match. In that tournament, he went to the finals against friend and rival Bobby Jones, marking the only time two players from the same club ever met for the U.S. Amateur crown. At Lanier High School, Gunn captained golf teams that never lost a match. In 1926 and '28, he played on the Walker Cup teams with Jones, defeating the British team both years. He played many benefit tournaments, including several exhibitions with Jones in 1927 and '28. He also won the Georgia Amateur title in 1923 and '27, with a runner-up finish in 1925. Gunn passed away in 1994 at age 89.

O.B. Keeler
Inducted 1996

Oscar Bane "Pop" Keeler was born on June 4, 1882, and spent most of his boyhood in Marietta, Ga. He was one of those wonderful characters of old-time newspapering who have become all too scarce in present-day journalism. He was a veteran Atlanta Journal sports staffer, covering more than 80 major golf tournaments of national and international importance. He won national recognition and fame as a writer and authority on golf. But, most importantly to the Georgia Golf Hall of Fame, Keeler chronicled every tournament stroke ever played by the legendary Bobby Jones. He saw Bobby Jones — just 14 years old — win his first big tournament, the Georgia Amateur in 1916. Soon after, the two became close companions. He traveled 150,000 miles with Jones and is the only man to witness all of Jones's 13 major championship wins — most notably the grand slam victories of 1930. A unique individual, he was one of the best-known and liked of all the newspapermen in the business. Keeler passed away on October 15, 1950, at the age of 68.

Stewart "Kiltie" Maiden
Inducted 2016

Stewart "Kiltie" Maiden was well-known for his teaching and club building and has been recognized for his expertise on the golf swing. Maiden was born in Angus (Carnoustie), Scotland, in 1886. Following his brothers, he came to the United States, specifically to be the golf professional at the East Lake facility, in 1908. He spent nearly 40 years in America, mostly in Georgia, prior to his death in 1948. Among the many golfing legends Maiden taught during his career are the great Bobby Jones, Alexa Stirling, Perry Adair, Watts Gunn, and Charlie Yates, all members of the Georgia State Golf Hall of Fame. Maiden's most-famous pupil, Bobby Jones, once said, "The best luck I ever had in golf was when Stewart Maiden came from Carnoustie, Scotland, to be the professional at East Lake." Though his accomplishments and career in the golf industry began well over 100 years ago, his students and all the individuals he impacted will be forever embedded in Georgia golf history.

George Sargent
Inducted 1995

George Sargent was born in Dorking, England, in 1882, He began his golf career at age 12 at Epsom Downs Golf Club. When he was 17 years old, he signed on with the illustrious English golfer Harry Vardon, who recommended him to Sir Edgar Vincent. Sir Vincent coached Sargent and helped him enter the 1900 British Open at age 19, where he placed fourth. Sargent later traveled to Canada, where he served as a golf professional at Royal Ottawa Golf Club. He placed second in the 1908 Canadian Open, won the 1909 U.S. Open, and won the 1912 Canadian Open. Sargent became a member of the United States PGA at its inception in 1916, and served as its president for five years. His most noted contribution to golf was the introduction of motion pictures to study the golf swing in 1930. Sargent was the head golf professional at Ohio's Scioto Country Club from 1912–24, at Minneapolis' Interlachen Golf Club from 1924–28, and at the Chevy Chase Club from 1928–32. In 1932, Bobby Jones brought him to East Lake Country Club, where he served as head golf professional for 15 years. Sargent died on June 6, 1962. George Sargent's two sons, Harold and Jack, were also accomplished golfers and Georgia Golf Hall of Fame members.

Harold Sargent
Inducted 1989

Harold Sargent was born in Bethesda, Md., on October 16, 1913, and moved to Atlanta in 1932. He was handpicked by Bobby Jones to be head golf professional at the Atlanta Athletic Club's East Lake facility in 1947, just as Jones had chosen his father, George, for the same job in 1932. Sargent served at two Atlanta Athletic Club courses for a total of 32 years, 15 of which he served as his father's assistant. George and Harold Sargent are the only father-son tandem ever to hold the distinction of serving as president of the PGA of America, with the latter holding the office from 1958–60. Harold Sargent's efforts brought the Ryder Cup matches to East Lake for the first time in 1963. As the national chairman of the Professional Golfers Teaching Committee from 1951–57, Sargent inaugurated the PGA's teaching manual. He was named Golf Professional of the Year by the Georgia PGA in 1972. He was also the longest serving member of the rules committee for the Masters Tournament.

Danny Yates
Inducted 1994

Danny Yates was born in Atlanta, Ga., on May 3, 1950. He is the son of P. Dan Yates, Jr., and nephew of Charlie Yates, both Hall of Famers themselves. He won the 1970 Spirit of America and played on the 1971 and '72 Georgia SEC Championship Teams. In 1971, Yates made the cut at the U.S. Open. He has won the Southern Amateur, the 1992 U.S. Mid-Amateur, and pocketed both the Georgia Amateur and Georgia Mid-Amateur titles three times each. He was runner-up in the 1974 North-South and runner-up in the 1988 U.S. Amateur. He was a member of the 1988 U.S. World Amateur team, the 1989 and '93 Walker Cup Teams, and captained the 1999 and 2001 Walker Cup Teams. Because of his amateur accomplishments, he played in the 1989 and '93 Masters Tournaments. Yates served as a director of the GSGA for seven years, as a director for the Atlanta Junior Golf Association for 10 years, and a member of the USGA Junior Golf Committee for 12 years. He currently serves on the USGA Green Section Committee.[1]

P. Dan Yates, Jr.
Inducted 1996

P. Dan Yates, Jr., father of Danny, is a native of Atlanta, Ga., and was born in 1918. He grew up on the golf course at East Lake Country Club, tagging along with his older brother, Charles, and the great Bobby Jones. From 1938–41, Yates was a member of the Georgia Tech golf team, serving as captain for three years. Some of his amateur golf victories include the 1939 Georgia Amateur, the Dogwood Invitational, the Atlanta City Championship, and the Durham, N.C. Invitational. In 1946, he was runner-up in the Georgia Amateur, and in 1941 and '46, he was runner-up in the Southern Golf Association Four-Ball. Yates continues to contribute to the world of golf through association. He served as a director of both the Georgia State Golf Association and Georgia State Golf Foundation. Yates passed away on May 12, 2017.[2]

---

1   In an interview in 1917, Danny said, *I didn't grow up or learn to play at East Lake, but I learned to compete there.*

2   Dan was known as a great putter. When asked if he could say more about that, he explained, *Let's just say I never met a man I would let putt for me.*

THE FRIENDS
OF BOBBY JONES

This is a broad association conceived and created by John Imlay and Emory University to promote the values and legacy of Bobby Jones, the scholarship named for him, the Jones Program in Ethics, and the Jones Fellowships in biomedical engineering with Georgia Tech.

John had been president of the Athletic Club, and he inspired golf clubs in Atlanta to host birthday dinners close to March 17th to honor Bobby and keep his memory alive. John knew that friends of Bobby Jones exist wherever golf is played and thought a yearly dinner would generate interest in his career and his character. At East Lake, the Bobby Jones Legacy Golf Tournament precedes the dinner.

The chairman of Friends is Gene McClure, a member of the Georgia Golf Hall of Fame and the USGA Executive and Rules committees. He is a former president of the Georgia State Golf Association.

BIBLIOGRAPHY

"Alexa Stirling's Game." The *Atlanta Journal Magazine,* July 20, 1919.

Barclay, James A. *Alexa Stirling Fraser, The Golfer and the Carpenter.*
    Manuscript. Toronto: Museum of Golf Canada, 2001.

Beacham, Frank. "ENG (Electronic News Gathering) in the 1970s:
    A Personal Look Back," PLAYOUT, February 3, 2014.

Beckley, Zoe. "Women Now People: Alexa Stirling, Bond Saleswoman,
    Considered Exhibit A." The *New York City Mail,* November 26, 1921.

Darwin, Benard. *Golf Between Two Wars.* London: Chatto & Windus, 1944.

Elliott, Charles. *The History of the Atlanta Athletic Club.*
    Manuscript. Atlanta: Archives of the Atlanta Athletic Club, 1973.

Elliott, Charles. *East Lake Country Club History.* Marietta: Cherokee, 1984.

Fraser, Alexa Williamson. 'The Most Unforgettable Character I've Met."
    Reader's Digest, April 1960.

"Glorious Golfing Girl." *Canadian Golfer* Vol VI, No. 7, November 1920.

"Golf." The *New York Times,* October 4, 1920.

Imlay, John P. *Jungle Rules.* New York: Dutton. Penguin, 1994.

Jones, Robert T., Keeler O. B. *Down the Fairway.*
    New York: Minton, Balch, 1927.

Jones, Robert T. *Golf Is My Game.* New York: Doubleday, 1960.

Jones, Robert T. *Bobby Jones on Golf.* New York: Doubleday, 1966.

Jones, Robert T. *Bobby Jones on the Basic Golf Swing.*
    Afterword by Charlie Yates. New York: Doubleday, 1969.

Keeler, O. B, and Rice, Grantland. *The Bobby Jones Story.*
    Atlanta: Tupper & Love, 1953.

Keeler, O. B. "Bob Jones Lowers His Own Record at East Lake to 63."
    The *Atlanta Journal,* September 17, 1922.

Kurtz, Kent W. "The History of Golf Course Irrigation."
    Hole Notes, May 2003.

Lewis, Catherine M.
    A Host to History The Story of Atlanta Athletic Club. 2016.

Litsky, Frank. "Bobby Jones, Golf Master, Dies; Only Player to Win
    Grand Slam." The *New York Times,* December 19, 1971.

MacCabe, Eddie. "Alexa Stirling Fraser — A Legend." The *Ottawa Journal,*
    April 16, 1977.

Matthew, Sidney L. *Champions of East Lake.* Tallahassee: I.Q. Press, 1999.

McElreath, Walter. *An Autobiography.* Macon: Mercer, 1984.

Penick, Harvey. *Harvey Penick's Little Red Book.*
    New York: Simon & Schuster, 1992.

Pressfield, Steven. *The Legend of Bagger Vance.*
    New York: Perennial. Doubleday, 2000.

Price, Mark. *The Grand Slam.* New York: Hyperion, 2004.

Schmidt, P.J. "Charles Drew, a Legend in Our Time."
    Transfusion 37:234–236, 1997.

Stirling, Alexa Williamson. "An Autobiography."
    Golf Illustrated, March 1917.

Suptic, Spring. "The TV Camera: Past, Present, and Future."
    TV Technology, March 1, 2009.

Wind, Herbert Warren. "One of the Great Opens."
    The New Yorker, July 26, 1976.

Winfrey, Lee. "Golf Channel Tees Off."
    Knight-Ridder/Tribune News Service, January 1995.

INDEX

Bold numbers indicate chapters; italics are photo-pages.

Linton C. Hopkins came to East Lake in 1989 and began writing down stories he heard from Tommy Barnes and Charlie Yates. Four years later, when he told Tom Cousins he wanted to publish the stories with some history of the place, Tom said, *If you write it, I'll sell it.* That book sold out and this is its sequel.

Linton is a retired neurologist, and many of his patients came to see him in wheelchairs. Like Bobby Jones, they inspired him with their nobility of spirit. He lives in Atlanta with Priscilla, his wife of fifty-six years. They have two children and five grandchildren.

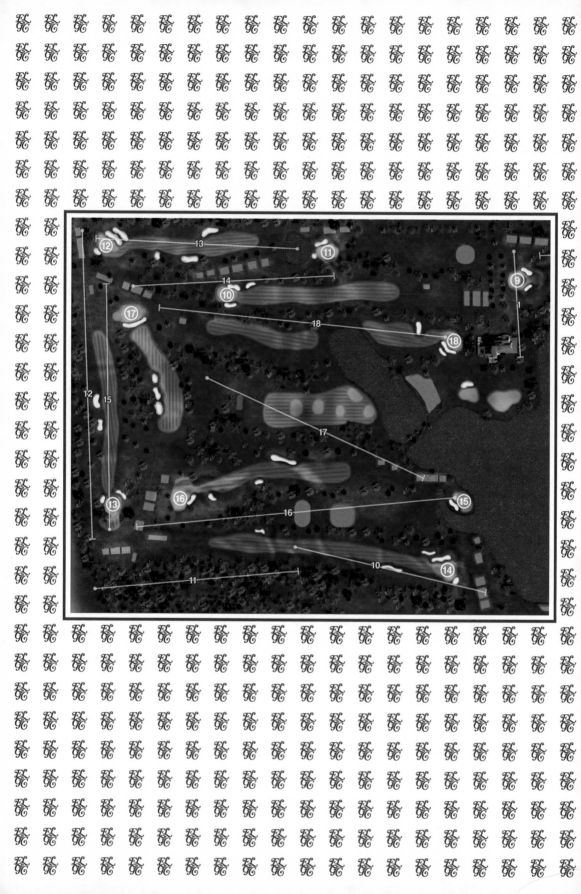